Liberalism and the Culture of Security

The Nineteenth-Century Rhetoric of Reform

KATHERINE HENRY

THE UNIVERSITY OF ALABAMA PRESS
TUSCALOOSA

Copyright © 2011
The University of Alabama Press
Tuscaloosa, Alabama 35487-0380
All rights reserved
Manufactured in the United States of America

Typeface: Adobe Garamond

∞

The paper on which this book is printed meets the minimum requirements of American National Standard for Information Sciences-Permanence of Paper for Printed Library Materials, ANSI Z39.48-1984.

Library of Congress Cataloging-in-Publication Data

Henry, Katherine, 1956–
    Liberalism and the culture of security : the nineteenth-century rhetoric of reform / Katherine Henry.
        p. cm.
    Includes bibliographical references and index.
    ISBN 978-0-8173-1722-5 (cloth : alk. paper) — ISBN 978-0-8173-8510-1 (electronic)
1. American literature—19th century—History and criticism. 2. Politics and literature—United States—History—19th century. 3. Rhetoric—Political aspects—United States. 4. Liberalism in literature. 5. Liberalism—United States—History—19th century. I. Title.
    PS217.P64H46 2011
    810.9′3581—dc22

                                                                        2010025036

Cover: John Sartain, "The Burning of Pennsylvania Hall," 1838. Courtesy of the Library Company of Philadelphia.

for Griffin

The sole end for which mankind are warranted, individually or collectively, in interfering with the liberty of action of any of their number, is self-protection.

—John Stuart Mill

Contents

Preface

In some ways, I think we have to protect our children from society, rather than raise them to fit into society.

—Laura Bush

This book examines a certain pattern of argument and counterargument that is ubiquitous in American political discourse. It is initiated when something is identified as both precious and endangered—our children, for example, or our civil or religious liberties, or the American way of life, or traditional marriage, or privacy, or the environment, or the right to bear arms—and the solution is figured as a shelter or asylum within which it can be protected and defended from the perceived threat. The opponents then counter the argument by claiming that the threat has been manufactured or exaggerated, or by reconceiving the shelter as a hiding place for ignorance or iniquity, as itself potentially injurious to a vulnerable constituency. The terms of this pattern of argument, then, turn out to be remarkably fluid. What in the original argument is figured as the protection of virtue is in the counterargument refigured as secrecy or conspiracy or the preservation of unfair advantage. Likewise, what in the original argument is figured as an unwarranted imposition of power or an invasion of privacy is in the counterargument refigured as salutary openness or oversight. The crucial elements of this rhetorical pattern are familiar to anyone who has listened to a politician defending her or his position on an issue, or watched the evening news, or listened to talk radio, or read a progressive or conservative blog.[1] Its primary components are an active and menacing threat and the precious object it is targeting, a spectacle of injury or imminent injury, and its principal figure is protection—shelters, sanctuaries, refuges, and safeguards. Its secondary components are equally familiar: exposés of unscrupulous actors who feign victimization in order to elicit public sympathy, of lawbreakers or conspirators or "special interests" who hide behind legal protections or "executive privilege," of public officials who claim "national security" in order to prevent the disclosure of embarrassing secrets. Its tone is one of urgency, moral indignation, and outrage.

The following chapters examine a series of nineteenth-century applications of this rhetorical pattern that contest the boundaries of citizenship. I trace the origins of this rhetorical pattern to a dynamic fundamental to eighteenth-century republican political theory: the mutually constitutive opposition of liberty (the precious object) and tyranny (the active and menacing threat). Bernard Bailyn has described it thus: "What gave transcendent importance to the aggressiveness of power was the fact that its natural prey, its necessary victim, was liberty, or law, or right. The public world these writers saw was divided into distinct, contrasting, and innately antagonistic spheres: the sphere of power and the sphere of liberty or right. The one was brutal, ceaselessly active, and heedless; the other was delicate, passive, and sensitive. The one must be resisted, the other defended, and the two must never be confused" (57–58). The crucial point here is that the presence of a persecuted "liberty, or law, or right" is what *gives* "transcendent importance" to power. I will argue that the opposite is equally true: it is the presence of an inherently encroaching power that gives liberty its transcendent importance, and the more "brutally" power exerts itself, the more compelling liberty is. Moreover, Bailyn's language suggests the striking capacity of this formulation to engage the emotions.[2] Liberty is not simply an abstract principle; it is a "delicate, passive, and sensitive" "victim," pursued by a "brutal" and predatory foe. Jason Shaffer has recently examined this drama of liberty and tyranny as it was enacted in American theater of the Revolutionary period, noting not only its tendency to be played out in gendered terms but also the radical instability of the categories. What he describes is not a pair of terms with stable definitions, but a relation with tyranny as "the defining Other of patriotic partisan rhetoric," figures that tend "to blend with one another or to exchange positions, sometimes in surprising ways" (23, 22). Shaffer's analysis suggests that when Bailyn writes "the two must never be confused," we should read it as a normative rather than a descriptive statement, an effort to dispel an underlying anxiety that the spheres of "liberty" and "power" may be more prone to confusion than we wish to believe. Indeed, the readings that follow consider political arguments that are carried out as contests for control over precisely these terms: contests to represent one's own cause as the cause of an aggrieved liberty, and one's opponent's cause as the imposition of an aggressive and invasive power.

Although my primary focus in this book is how this rhetorical pattern gave shape to arguments over citizenship in the nineteenth century, I am also interested in how it is playing out in contemporary public discourse, and I would like to preface my historical readings with a few brief speculations on American political rhetoric at the beginning of the twenty-first century. The most striking quality of this pattern of argument today is its remarkable capacity to accommodate with equal efficacy a broad spectrum of political positions, from the progressive to the traditionally conservative to the reactionary.[3] In August of 2009, for example, the mainstream news media were reporting a striking intensification in the arguments over health insurance reform. At first glance, the cause of offering health insurance coverage to more Americans would seem ideally suited to a rhetoric whose principle figure is protection from injury. Nevertheless, by early August, the conventional wisdom was that momentum had shifted away from the Democrats and their efforts to pass health care reform legislation and, as Katharine Q. Seelye blogged for the *New York Times,* "President Obama's ability to control the debate appeared to be eroding."[4] Opponents of the Democratic health care reform proposals were crowding town-hall-style meetings to taunt and shout down members of Congress, chanting "tyranny" and in some cases hanging their representatives in effigy.[5] Although many of their claims were preposterous if not demonstrably false—that health care reform would turn America into something akin to Nazi Germany or the Soviet Union, or that Barack Obama wanted to establish "death panels" to decide which citizens were worthy of living, or that Obama wasn't a legitimate president because he wasn't really an American citizen—opinion polls showed that substantial numbers of Americans held such beliefs, seemingly impervious to reason.[6] In short, opponents of health care reform had capitalized on a highly charged combination: a deep-seated conviction among the right wing that something precious was under siege—a conviction confirmed not only by the election results of 2008 but also by the widespread images of celebration that surrounded it—and a powerful rhetoric that gave voice to that conviction. Consciously echoing the rhetoric of the American revolutionaries,[7] these self-described "patriots" had refashioned an argument against expanding health insurance into an argument defending the people's liberties against an overreaching and tyrannical government, personified by President Obama. "Control" over the debate, then, hinged not only on an ideal of protection for the vulnerable but also on identifying a tyrant, and President Obama, in this historical moment, proved a more sharply defined object of rage than either the health insurance companies or the still more nebulous threat of illness.

Two summers earlier, in the seventh year of the Bush administration, broad issues of national security were commanding public attention, in particular the existence of a previously secret, warrantless wiretapping program. At the same time, a less prominent issue—whether the federal government should be allowed to collect and share information on the buyers and sellers of firearms—was being debated in strikingly similar language. On PBS's NewsHour the Democratic mayor of Milwaukee, Tom Barrett, claimed that access to the data would aid law enforcement and save lives.[8] Laws permitting information to be collected only when a "specific crime" is suspected are not sufficient, he contended, because investigators need a larger pool of data in order to identify "trend[s]." "We want that data before the homicides occur," he asserted. "It doesn't do me any good to call that mother and say, 'I'm sorry your son was killed.'" Representative Todd Tiahrt of Kansas, a conservative Republican, by contrast, characterized the limits on federal power as themselves essentially protective—safeguarding the "law-abiding" majority of this class of citizens "from unwanted inquisitions," as NewsHour's Judy Woodruff put it in her introduction to the segment. Tiahrt argued, more specifically, that easing the restrictions on the collection and dissemination of information could jeopardize undercover police officers. His legislation, he repeated five times during the segment, would "protect those who protect us." "I'll tell you, Judy," he added, "a lot of people in America get nervous when somebody who's elected says, 'Just give me a little more power and I will make you safe.'" However, when we look at the Bush administration's defense of its warrantless wiretapping program, we can see precisely the same lines of reasoning being applied to precisely the opposite sides. In this instance, what the Bush administration claimed was necessary to disrupt terrorist plots and protect the American people, its progressive opponents claimed was a dangerous expansion of the state's power to spy on its citizens. Both sides in both of these debates claimed the mantle of safeguarding a vulnerable citizenry from a grave threat. For one side, the threat—one that, Mayor Tom Barrett claimed, "may be coming to your community next"—issued from criminals and terrorists; for the other side, the threat issued from government officials who want "just . . . a little more power" and, especially, from an unrestrained capacity to collect and disseminate private information.

This is in no way to minimize the differences between progressive and conservative viewpoints as they have developed in American politics. On the contrary, I would argue that the persistent recourse on both sides to rhetorics of protection often functions to obscure the real differences in their worldviews and their constituencies. In *Moral Politics: How Liberals and Conservatives Think,* George Lakoff offers a persuasive account of the progressive worldview as subscribing to an ideal of the nurturant parent, and the conservative worldview as subscribing to an ideal of the strong father. In each case, according to Lakoff, what is at root a belief about the right kind of family is expanded into a coherent set of beliefs about the role and function of government. Lakoff's account is particularly useful in unpacking the real differences that underlie arguments such as those about health care, or about government surveillance of gun sales or overseas telephone calls—differences, he argues, that cannot be explained simply in terms of defending citizens' rights or opposing the coercive powers of the state. "Without an account of what rights count and what coercive powers of the state are bad," he writes, "the classical theory of liberalism cannot distinguish political liberalism from conservatism" (150). Progressives and conservatives, in other words, are promoting different kinds of rights and opposing different types of state power—agendas that can ultimately be traced, according to Lakoff, to their different ideals of the nurturant parent and the strong father. For progressives, then, the rights that count are the rights of vulnerable individuals to a life in which their basic needs can be met and their talents can be nurtured; for conservatives, it is the father's right to protect and provide for his family, to exert the necessary authority, and to impose the necessary discipline. Conversely, "good" state power is, in each case, power that protects this particular set of rights, while "bad" state power is power that injures or impedes it. Thus we can have progressives arguing that state surveillance of gun purchases is necessary to protect potential victims of gun violence, while conservatives see it as an intrusion on the father's right to protect his family; conservatives arguing that state surveillance of telephone communications is necessary to protect potential victims of terrorism, while progressives see it as a violation of the right to privacy. "What is one man's constraint on free movement," Lakoff observes, "is another man's protection against encroachment" (87).

Nevertheless, what remains common to both progressives and conservatives today is the overwhelming sense that they are righteously defending a "right" or "liberty" that is under siege. That sense has a history, and it is my hope that this book will offer some insight into a particular chapter of that history. As Lakoff argues, "part of our conceptual systems, whether we are liberals, conservatives, or neither, is a common metaphorical conception of the Nation as Family, with the government, or head of state representing the government, seen as an older male authority figure, typically a father" (153). It is that shared paternalistic metaphor, I will argue, that generates this rhetorical pattern by establishing the expectation that power should protect. In *Common Sense,* Thomas Paine famously turned the British propaganda of "the . . . *parent* or *mother country*"—a phrase "jesuitically adopted by the king and his parasites"—against the crown by accepting its premises and then portraying Britain as having violated its parental duty to protect its children, adding that "even brutes do not devour their young" (88). If paternalism is an ideology that masks power by imagining it as protection, then, it is also peculiarly vulnerable to criticism when it exerts force, as ultimately it must. As Richard Sennett has observed, "the way the paternalistic metaphor is constructed invites negation" (66). I would suggest, moreover, that we can better understand the peculiarly intense emotional content of this rhetorical pattern when we see our outrage at violations of rights and liberties rooted in our emotional investment in the figure of the child of abusive parents. Finally, I see the same rhetorical strategies that in the antebellum period constituted the creative impetus for progressive political reform today contributing to what many observers see as the decline in civility and the increasing polarization of public discourse.[9] To that conversation, I hope this book will contribute a way of looking critically at the conviction that we are defending something that is under siege. To those who see themselves as working to protect children from Internet predators, or the uninsured from facing bankruptcy because of an illness, or the homeland from "Islamic extremism," or our civil liberties from an arrogant and overreaching executive, the idea that they are defending something that is under siege seems like a self-evident matter of fact. But here I would agree with George Lakoff: "it is the commonsensical quality of political discourse that makes it imperative that we study it" (4).

Acknowledgments

This book began more than a decade ago, and although it has evolved considerably since then, I am deeply indebted to Michael Warner, Myra Jehlen, and Bill Galperin for their guidance and example, for challenging me to read and write with precision, and for fostering in me habits of thought that continue to serve me well. Their influence is evident throughout this book, and it is my privilege to have worked with scholars of such stature and consequence. I have also been fortunate over the years to have received guidance, advice, and encouragement in various forms from many mentors, colleagues, and friends, including Ruth Anolik, Katey Borland, Jared Gardner, Josh Lukin, Shannon Miller, Don Mull, Dan O'Hara, Susan O'Hara, and Sue Wells, and from writing groups at Haverford College, Ohio State University, and my current one composed of scholars of early and antebellum American literature in the Philadelphia area. Both Ohio State University and Temple University supported this project with research leaves, enabling me to focus on writing and revising to an extent that otherwise would not have been possible. The staff at The University of Alabama Press has been immensely helpful in moving my manuscript toward publication, and the process of peer review, thanks to the careful reading and astute criticism of the two anonymous readers, prompted me to rethink and tighten my central argument and has made this a significantly stronger book. I am profoundly grateful to Kara Clevinger for her invaluable assistance in preparing my manuscript to go to press. An earlier version of chapter 2 was published in *American Quarterly* as "Angelina Grimké's Rhetoric of Exposure." Finally, this book is dedicated to Griffin, to whom I am indebted more than I can say. But the rest of my family, too, is an ongoing source of energy, wonder, and inspiration: to my late parents, Ed and Peg Caruthers, Brick, Jeannie, Rhonda, Steve, Rebecca, Gabriella, Miranda, Leroy and Amoy, this project would have been neither possible nor fulfilling without your presence in my life.

Liberalism and the Culture of Security

Introduction

The Rhetoric of Protection

The point . . . is that violence itself is incapable of speech, and not merely that speech is helpless when confronted with violence.

—Hannah Arendt, *On Revolution*

I tell you that which you yourselves do know,
Show you sweet Caesar's wounds, poor, poor, dumb mouths,
And bid them speak for me.

—Shakespeare, *Julius Caesar*

There is a rich body of scholarship that examines the mechanisms by which those constituencies identified by race and/or gender have been excluded from full citizenship and relegated to the private realm. In the tradition of classical republicanism, a citizen would above all have been independent and self-sufficient, able to meet his own and his household's needs without relying on outside help. That self-sufficiency would have made him capable of civic virtue—capable, that is, of transcending his own self-interest or the interests of a patron, and participating in rational deliberation for the common good.[1] The legitimacy of civic exchange, moreover, stemmed from its negative relation to persons, its construction of an abstract region in which ideas could compete and clash while persons remained protected. In her explication of Aristotelian political theory, Hannah Arendt has argued that the crucial difference between polis and household is that the former was ruled by persuasion while the latter was ruled by violence, and being subject to violence signified bondage to one's body and disqualified one from entrance into the civic realm.[2] Michael Warner has explained how eighteenth-century print culture, in particular, enabled and promoted fictions of self-abstraction and disembodiment.[3] In antebellum America, both by law and by custom, women and nonwhites would have been largely prohibited from attaining this version of citizenship. Legally compelled into various forms of dependency on white men, and identified by their physicality and their bodily characteristics in literature as various as medical and scientific treatises, artistic and dramatic representations, and historical accounts, women and nonwhites constituted the unfree "other" against which the white, male citizenry was defined.[4]

Given this context, by what logic did nineteenth-century abolitionists and women's rights activists make the case for a more inclusive body politic? Much of the scholarship to date has focused on their challenges to the legal and social apparatuses that rendered women and nonwhites unfit for citizenship, and to the insidious ways in which racial and gender difference informed the structure of American civic life.[5] This book focuses instead on gradually changing assumptions about the nature of citizenship and civic liberty. I will argue that citizenship was coming to be understood less as mastery, and more as a zone of protection, with the state functioning paternalistically as the protector of its citizens. Concurrently, liberty was more and more commonly being figured negatively, as freedom *from* tyranny, as a precious and endangered article that had to be protected from the powers that were always threatening to encroach. Implicit in these changes in emphasis was a theory of good and bad government: good government was protective of its citizens' liberties, acknowledging limits to the extent of its authority, while bad government was intrusive and injurious. Nineteenth-century reformers embraced these structures of thought and applied them to the circumstances of women and slaves, arguing that women and slaves were the victims of tyranny and therefore in need of the protections of citizenship. Employing a pattern of argument that I call the "rhetoric of protection," they charged the system that established white men's rule with injuring the very subjects it was supposed to protect. In other words, instead of asking how women and slaves were challenging the legal and social mechanisms of civic exclusion, I will be asking how the civic sphere was coming to be understood in ways that could accommodate women and slaves.[6]

Clearly, such arguments could not have been made unless household rule could be seen as analogous to state government. I will address this problematic analogy specifically later in this introduction. For now, I wish to make a few general observations about paternalism, which I will define broadly as an ideology that legitimizes power by imagining it as protection from injury and violation, and that obscures the mechanisms by which subjects are confined and controlled by writing them into a narrative that can range from benign custody to fatherly affection. Much of the critical scholarship on paternalism has focused on its necessary tendency to infantilize its subjects and compromise their autonomy.[7] But modern paternalistic authority is also necessarily figured as limited: it cannot be seen to be abusive and, as expectations regarding the nature of parenting change, so do the limits of paternalistic power. Its mechanisms of control—its inevitable reliance on the use or threat of force—cannot be seen as having crossed a certain threshold. And because its legitimacy stems from its being seen as protecting and nurturing its subjects, such authority risks being denounced as illegitimate when its reliance on force is exposed. It is this loophole that rhetorics of protection exploit. In examples from *Common Sense* to the antislavery fiction of Harriet Beecher Stowe, we can see the outrage that is generated when an authority that claims to be paternalistic is exposed as abusive. However, it is also important to note that such strategies are thoroughly invested in the foundational assumptions of paternalism—namely, that power can and should be protective. They capitalize on paternalism's own internal contradictions and are therefore incapable of mounting a comprehensive critique of paternalism as an ideology. Many of the antislavery and women's rights arguments that I examine in this book, then, are not incompatible with conventional and oppressive assumptions about gender and racial difference; indeed, at times they embrace such assumptions.

It is the gradually increasing emphasis on citizenship as a zone of protection from tyranny—not a challenge to the structures of thought that marked women and slaves as unfit for citizenship in the classical republican sense—that underwrites the rhetorical strategies I consider in the following chapters. That shift in emphasis generates a deceptively simple logic: to be *in need of* protection is to be deserving of citizenship. Such logic can at times be explicit. In *Woman in the Nineteenth Century,* after describing a wife's legal subjection to her tyrannical husband, Margaret Fuller concluded: "men must soon see that, on their own ground, that woman is the weaker party, she ought to have legal protection, which would make such oppression impossible" (258). Twenty-four years later, John Stuart Mill would make virtually the same argument in *The Subjection of Women:* "even if every woman were a wife, and if every wife ought to be a slave, all the more would these slaves stand in need of legal protection" (*On Liberty and Other Writings* 169). Such arguments are built, as Fuller says, "on [men's] own ground," accepting as their premise woman's vulnerability to injury, and leaving aside the question of whether that vulnerability is a matter of law, custom, or nature. Claims of injury or vulnerability to injury are therefore at the very heart of the rhetoric of protection—constituting not only their logical ground but also their emotional appeal—as we can see when the women of Seneca Falls depicted "the history of mankind [as] a history of repeated in-

juries and usurpations on the part of man toward woman," or when the antislavery orator Theodore Dwight Weld "kindle[d]" the hearts of his auditors
"into an indignant flame as he lifted before them the bleeding victim of oppression."[8] Bypassing the classical reasoning that women and slaves should be excluded from citizenship because they lacked the necessary autonomy to make
independent decisions, this new logic appealed directly to the sense that vulnerable creatures should not be injured, that the protection of selves is a fundamental value.[9] And so, in an ironic twist, their opponents' paternalistic arguments often ended up playing right into their hands: the frequent reminders of
the dependency and vulnerability of women and slaves, their reliance on white
men for whatever security they enjoyed—reminders intended to justify and reinforce their exclusion from citizenship—paradoxically became the very basis
of their claims to public recognition.

At issue here are clusters of ideas that scholars have frequently categorized as
"liberal" or "republican." The influence of classical republicanism on eighteenth-
century political thought and, in particular, on the leaders of the American
Revolution, has been well documented.[10] However, the extent to which liberalism and republicanism constitute distinct and competing political philosophies
can be overstated, as can the historical narrative in which liberalism replaces republicanism as the dominant American political philosophy.[11] In *Cato's Tears
and the Making of Anglo-American Emotion,* for example, Julie Ellison considers a group of eighteenth-century plays about classical Rome she calls "Republican tragedy," tracing "the oppositional allure of sensibility performed in liberty's name"—an approach, as she points out, that "cuts across or even displaces
these more familiar analytical frameworks [of liberalism and republicanism]"
(74, 18). The civic ideal presented in the dramas, Ellison argues, is not simply
the classical one of self-mastery and self-sacrifice; rather, it is a mutually generating dynamic of stoicism and sensibility, stoicism that is both proven and belied by the hero's confrontation with the suffering of his vulnerable dependents.
Classical republican rhetoric and stories of republican Rome were repeatedly
used to construct models of civic participation that have more often been associated with liberalism. Similarly, eighteenth-century republican accounts of
liberty often rely on tropes that are characteristic not of positive, but of negative liberty—the version of liberty that is central to a major branch of liberal
theory. Bernard Bailyn's description of liberty in eighteenth-century republican
theory, for example, is strikingly similar to Isaiah Berlin's description of negative
liberty in that both are imagined as having to be defended against an inherently
invasive power. "The image most commonly used," Bailyn explains, "was that
of the act of trespassing"—an image reiterated in Berlin's description of nega-

tive liberty as an "area [reserved] for private life over which neither the State nor any other authority must be allowed to trespass" (Bailyn 56; Berlin 198).[12] Such figures imagine liberty as private property, but they place the emphasis on the insecurity—not the security—of its boundaries.

It is this tendency of the liberal imagination to produce *both* fantasies of security and fantasies of insecurity that underlies and enables the arguments examined in this book. To figure liberty negatively is to imagine it as always in danger of being infringed, as subject to an aggressive, invasive power or tyranny that is in need of restraint. Together, the ideal of protection and the threat of injury constitute a dynamic field within which negative liberty comes into being; negative liberty is less a fixed state than the protagonist in a drama of protection, a father defending his home from invasion, or a fugitive in search of asylum. In *Race, Slavery, and Liberalism in Nineteenth-Century American Literature,* Arthur Riss frames the antebellum debate over the limits of citizenship in the context of a contest over the definition of "personhood," which he understands as "the term that we attach to whomever we designate as deserving liberal rights and protections" (30). Countering what he deems a widespread assumption that emancipatory arguments for the extension of citizenship are grounded in the liberal concept of the rights-bearing "person" as a disembodied abstraction, Riss argues that an essentialist version of "personhood" was also commonly advanced and—as in the case of Harriet Beecher Stowe—was equally capable of sustaining an antislavery politics. Like Riss, I wish to trace an argument that grounds entitlement to citizenship not in a capacity for self-abstraction, but in embodiment and vulnerability to injury. I differ from Riss, however, in that I see these versions of civic entitlement not as competing models with independent genealogies, but as a dynamic and mutually constitutive opposition that is produced by the liberal imagination. It is the movement between these two ideals, I contend—the vulnerable subject's fantasy of security, for example, or the scandal of abuse that is carried out in the name of protection, or the protected citizen's fantasies of sympathetic identification and rescue—that generates the arguments examined in the following chapters.

Because it inhabits the dynamic space between protected abstraction and embodied vulnerability, sentimentalism has performed much of the work of such arguments. As a literary strategy that turns on the tension between the irretrievable abstraction of language and the promise of sympathetic identification, between the reader's helpless separation from the suffering to which his attention is drawn and the fantasy that his heart, too, has been stung by the ordeal, the sentimental response can produce problematic structures of civic engagement.[13] According to Lauren Berlant, nineteenth-century "national sentimentality . . . involved replacing citizenship's original status as a property- or identity-based condition of political legitimacy with a notion of citizenship as a private and personal formation based on subjective relations of identification and similarity," and was "a terribly flawed vehicle for inducing a more racially and economically equitable mass democracy" (*Queen of America* 264–65 n. 22).[14] Although the earlier model of citizenship explicitly excluded certain subjects on the basis of property and identity, "national sentimentality," Berlant argues, produced only an illusion of inclusiveness, a fantasy of "public intimacy" that by the late twentieth century had been enlisted into the service of conservative and reactionary political agendas. The readings in this book show strategies of sentimentalism being deployed to a variety of political ends: proslavery and antislavery, in favor of women's civic participation and in favor of their relegation to a privatized sphere of domesticity, in defense of Jim Crow and in opposition to racial segregation, functioning both to give those areas of life deemed "private" a public face and to reinscribe them as irretrievably private. In these readings, sentimentalism appears as a strategy for building a sympathetic constituency by aligning one's own cause with that of a vulnerable liberty in search of protection, and depicting one's opponents' cause as a form of tyranny that is in need of restraint; at issue is not whether sentimentalism is inherently progressive or conservative, but which side successfully controls the terms of the discussion. I disagree, then, with Berlant's characterization of the citizenship produced by sentimentalism as necessarily "a private and personal formation based on subjective relations of identification and similarity." Rather, I argue that sentimentalism in the nineteenth century is as invested in promoting fantasies of self-abstraction and civic protection as it is in "turn[ing] the nation into a privatized state of feeling," to use Berlant's words; it is as capable of denying the possibility of sympathetic identification as it is of advocating it (*Queen of America* 11).[15] I would argue that it doesn't "replace" the property- and identity-based model of citizenship so much as it reimagines it as a safe and protected space—precisely the sort of refuge to which the vulnerable aspire. At the same time, the sentimental imagination fantasizes those spots of safety as themselves potentially vulnerable, the forces of tyranny always poised to trespass across their protective boundaries.

   A well-known moment from Harriet Jacobs's *Incidents in the Life of a Slave Girl* can serve as an illustration. Acknowledging her out-of-wedlock pregnancy, Jacobs directly addresses her readers whose "homes are protected by law": "O virtuous reader! You never knew what it is to be a slave; to be entirely unprotected by law or custom; to have the laws reduce you to the condition of a chattel, entirely subject to the will of another" (384, 386). Although her overall aim is to enlist the sympathy of her readers, here Jacobs asserts the limits of sympathetic identification.[16] However, what might at first appear to interrupt the cultivation of sympathy actually functions, paradoxically, to heighten it: sympathetic identification is best understood not as a single event, but as an epistemological process wherein the reader is conscious of both sameness and difference, both shared experience and experience that cannot be shared because it cannot be abstracted into language.[17] Moreover, Jacobs defines the key difference between slave women and free women specifically in terms of personal and domestic security, implying that their protected privacy stands as an impediment to a certain kind of knowledge. What her "virtuous readers" cannot know is the slave's experience of profound personal and legal vulnerability and subjection to tyranny. Just as the process of sympathetic identification depends, paradoxically, on limits to the extent of sympathy, Jacobs represents her knowledge as to some extent inadmissible to the public sphere of private persons. Refiguring her exclusion from that public sphere as access to another kind of knowledge, then, Jacobs posits what can be seen as parallel and mutually constitutive public spheres that function according to opposing sets of rules. On the one hand is the conventional liberal public sphere, where persons with secure private lives engage in rational exchange that is legitimate by virtue of its abstraction. On the other hand is a kind of shadow public sphere, where knowledge is imagined as bodily experience, and self-protection appears as a barrier to sympathetic identification, a prison that one's own humanity is urging one to escape. The qualities that exclude someone from the former are precisely those that qualify someone for the latter. Both of these ideal public spheres arise from the liberal imagination, and the liberal discourse that is the subject of the following chapters thrives on the tension between them—between the ideal of protection and the spectacle of injury, between the abstraction of language and the desire for sympathetic identification, between the fantasy of security in the face of our tragic vulnerability and the fantasy of shared pain in the face of our tragic seclusion.

Negative Liberty

Negative liberty has conventionally been understood to signify a region of life that is free from the interference of authority. As rhetoric, however, negative liberty comes into being under the threat of interference, and the more severe the threat, the more rhetorically compelling it is.[18] The readings that follow, then, challenge certain assumptions commonly made about the rights-bearing subject of American liberalism and the nature of negative liberty. Jedediah Purdy's recent intellectual history of the significance of freedom in the American liberal tradition can serve as an example of one kind of conventional narrative on which this book offers a critical perspective. What Purdy calls "the American sensation of freedom," he claims, "began in the deep belief that freedom meant the opposite of slavery and was no mere convenience but the basis of identity and honor" (19–20). Drawing on Edmund Burke's largely sympathetic account of the colonial rebels, Purdy describes freedom as "being the one whose will commanded, not the one who cowered before a willful commander" (9). "Political freedom . . . meant being immune to arbitrary power and answering to one's own law" (11). But a close reading of Purdy's own rhetoric suggests that the freedom he describes is not "immunity" to arbitrary power so much as resistance to arbitrary power; not "the opposite of slavery," but rather in defiance of an always present threat of enslavement. Frederick Douglass occupies such a crucial position in Purdy's account, I would suggest, because Douglass's narrative dramatizes for him the establishment of freedom through resistance to tyranny: "in defiance," Purdy writes, "a slave's dignity ceases being the master's plaything and becomes the boundary where the master's abuse must stop" (40). To imagine Douglass's freedom as the drawing and defending of a "boundary" is to define freedom negatively: the "boundary" in Purdy's account of Douglass resembles what Isaiah Berlin called the "frontier . . . between the area of private life and that of public authority" (196).[19] But it is not a neutral boundary. It is a boundary that establishes a highly charged moral distinction, deeming what is on one side worthy of protection—Purdy variously refers to it as "identity," "honor," and "personal dignity," and Berlin goes so far as to call it "sacred"— and what is on the other side invasive, abusive, and in need of aggressive restrictions and limitations. It is this implicit moral judgment, I would argue, that imbues "the language of freedom" with what Purdy calls its "heart and authority" (17). And by figuring American freedom as an ongoing project "made up of millions of small declarations of independence from hierarchy, constraint, and fear," the protective boundary not yet conclusively fixed by the laws of the land, Purdy effectively guarantees the forces of tyranny an ongoing presence in American life (155).[20]

What makes the rights-bearing liberal subject of Purdy's narrative compelling is not its autonomy and "independence," but its coexistence with tyranny and its heroic resistance to an ongoing threat of violation. However, I want to be clear that I am not engaging in the charge that is often made by libertarian conservatives that the progressive political agenda indulges in fantasies of victimization as a rationale for expanding a paternalistic state: such arguments are at least as driven by "intimations of domination or dependence," to use Purdy's apt phrase, as their opponents' are (20). Alan Charles Kors and Harvey A. Silverglate's 1998 book *The Shadow University,* for example, aims to expose a repressive and abusive apparatus that is being implemented by the American system of higher education to enforce certain codes of speech and conduct, by narrating the stories of those who have attempted to defy the repressive apparatus, and have suffered injury as a consequence. Citing the usurpation of "the university in loco parentis" by "self-appointed progressives," the authors identify what they call "an emerging tyranny over all aspects of student life—a tyranny that is far more dangerous than the relatively innocuous parietal rules of ages past. It is a tyranny that seeks to assert absolute control over the souls, the consciences, and the individuality of our students—in short, a tyranny over the essence of liberty itself" (4). Such rhetoric frames the argument as a contest over which side has the more valid claim of injury, the victims of speech codes or the victims of hate speech, and transforms speech codes from protective things into injurious things. It endeavors to control the terms *liberty* and *tyranny* so as to favor a particular political aim, and then treats those terms as uncontested and universal. It generates outrage by depicting a paternalistic authority that—like abusive parents—injures the dependents it is charged with protecting. Libertarians like Kors and Silverglate, in short, engage in the rhetoric of protection rather than critically examining it.

One of Charles Taylor's concerns in his essay "What's Wrong with Negative Liberty" is the location of the normative boundary between liberty and tyranny. Although Taylor challenges the libertarian argument that the boundary between liberty and tyranny is best fixed at what he calls the "Maginot Line" between the subject and any authority external to the subject, he is committed to the larger project of distinguishing what is worthy of protection from the forces that are, as he says, "obstacles" to self-realization. His central point is that these obstacles can be internal to the subject as well as external; nevertheless, he relies on the basic liberal model of selfhood I have been describing, of a true self that is thwarted or "fettered" in its free development by forces that can and should be identified and neutralized—forces that can usefully be called "tyranny." I read his essay not as a challenge to the project of boundary drawing itself, but as an effort to redraw that normative boundary along more nuanced lines. First Taylor identifies certain desires or fears that originate within oneself, but could be relinquished, as he says, "without any loss whatsoever to what I am" (222). He describes such drives or fears as "chain[s]" and "fetters," as motivations that we feel are "not truly ours" because they are "mistaken" or "erroneous" or "not . . . genuine," motivations that "distort our perspective on everything" (224–25). And then he admits the possibility that such false motivations could exist without being acknowledged as such by the subject: "there is such a thing as getting it wrong," Taylor writes, "and the very distinctions of significance depend on this fact" (228). What emerges from Taylor's essay is the idea of a "genuine" self that can be tyrannized by inhibitions or drives that are internal to the subject but "not truly ours"; the distinction may not be the "Maginot Line" between the self and forces external to the self, but it is still a defensive boundary between a vulnerable liberty and an aggressive tyranny, between a true self that must, as Taylor says, be "safe-guarded," and forces that actively inhibit its free development.[21]

The liberal individual has often been understood to be autonomous. In his recent account of the various strands that make up contemporary liberal theory, for example, Paul Kelly explains: "The civil and political rights at the heart of liberal egalitarianism . . . constitute protected spheres that place the individual beyond the reach of the coercive claims of the state or society. . . . [They] provide individuals with a morally protected sphere, and it is this that is seen to involve the idea of autonomy" (10).[22] However, inasmuch as the liberal individual is dependent upon the defensive boundaries that protect it from tyranny, and inasmuch as the presence of tyranny is what imbues the liberal individual with its peculiar character, it is not truly autonomous. I would argue, on the contrary, that "autonomy" can be better understood as representing the liberal fantasy of security as a fixed state or condition—a fantasy that coexists with the apparently opposite fantasy of vulnerability and insecurity. Jürgen Habermas's classic account of the liberal public sphere demonstrates precisely such a conflict. According to Habermas, the economic context of an emerging bourgeoisie in a state that enforced primarily mercantilist policies was crucial to the rise of the liberal public sphere: "the relationship between the authorities and the subjects thereby assumed the peculiar ambivalence of public regulation and private initiative" (24). Habermas explains that it was the public's "awareness of itself as [the state's] opponent" that prompted its critical orientation (23). But a relationship of "public regulation and private initiative" is not simply oppositional; it describes a specific kind of opposition in which "private initiative"—a creative energy that exists primarily as potential achievement—is being not nurtured and cultivated, but confined, thwarted, inhibited. Like the opposition of liberty and tyranny, it situates private initiative in a specifically defensive posture, threatened with being tied up and stifled by bureaucratic regulation. The "target" of this "developing critical sphere," Habermas continues, was "not the notorious dress codes but taxes and duties and, generally, official interventions into the privatized household" (24). It is, in other words, the threat of the privatized household's violation that provokes the "critical sphere" into being.

Habermas points out that constitutional guarantees of rights were crucial to establishing the structures, instruments, and institutions of the bourgeois public sphere, as well as "the foundation of private autonomy (family and property)" (83). The "inviolability of letters," for example, guaranteed that private people could function as "human beings" by engaging in individual communication (83). But such reasoning figures "private autonomy" as always already at risk of violation, and imagines a potentially violating power as an ongoing presence. Moreover, Habermas later relies on the concept of private autonomy to distinguish the bourgeois individual from the mass subject of the social-welfare state. Reiterating his earlier point, he identifies "the catalogues of basic rights [as] the very image of the liberal model of the bourgeois public sphere. They guaranteed society as a sphere of private autonomy" (222). They "protected from state interference and encroachment those areas that in principle were the preserve of private people acting in accord with the general rules of the legal system" (223). The guarantees of the social-welfare state, by contrast, often entail state intrusion into the area of private autonomy that had previously been protected, causing it, Habermas argues, to "lose the character of an area in principle protected from interference" (228). The new social rights can no longer be secured "by defensive and exemptive measures" alone, as could the basic rights of the liberal model; as a result, "private autonomy is then only possible as something derivative" (229). It could be argued, however, that this private autonomy was diminished in the cause of expanding—not eroding—civic protections. The "private autonomy" that was protected in the eighteenth century, after all, did not extend to women or slaves, and to recognize women and slaves as having an "autonomy" deserving of constitutional and legal protection was necessarily to interfere in the "private autonomy" of husbands, fathers, and masters.[23] And the expansion of social rights and governmental regulations in the welfare state are themselves the product of a rhetoric of protection: they are measures to protect children, the poor, public health, the environment, and so on. Habermas contends that there is a difference between protecting private persons from state intrusion and enlarging state authority to include the protection of private persons from such risks as hunger and disease. But I see it as a difference in degree only, not in kind. Liberalism has always promoted the protection of persons from more than just state intrusion, just as the liberal state has always been to some degree the instrument of protection, even against itself.

Habermas's language reveals the extent to which the story he tells unfolds as a drama of protection and encroachment. Private persons become a critical public once they perceive their private lives to be in an adversarial relation to an intrusive state authority. Liberal protections are established to keep state authority at bay, but the eventual outcome is the erosion of private autonomy and the expansion of an intrusive state authority. In other words, a protected private life and an encroaching state power turn out to be mutually constitutive; a protected private life *is* an endangered private life. Like negative liberty, the privacy that Habermas identifies as prerequisite to entering the public sphere comes into being when it is threatened with violation and therefore in need of defense. And that defense—the protection from and redress of injury—becomes a primary objective of liberal public exchange.[24]

Skepticism about the extent to which state guarantees of individual rights actually serve the cause of expanding popular liberty has come from a variety of critical perspectives. Opposing George Mason's proposal to add a bill of rights to the U.S. Constitution, for example, Alexander Hamilton explained in *The Federalist* No. 84 that "bills of rights are, in their origin, . . . reservations of rights not surrendered to the prince." But when a constitution is "professedly founded upon the power of the people, . . . the people surrender nothing; and as they retain everything they have no need of particular reservations" (Madison, Hamilton, and Jay 475). Moreover, Hamilton continued, bills of rights are not simply superfluous in a republic; they are actually "dangerous." Declaring, for example, that the liberty of the press shall not be restrained assumes the prior existence of a restraining power, and thus has the paradoxical consequence of expanding precisely that federal authority it purports to restrict.[25] Hannah Arendt's illuminating reading of these debates over the U.S. Bill of Rights tracks a shift in emphasis from positive to negative conceptions of liberty, which she saw as symptomatic of a broader cultural shift, characteristic of modernity (*On Revolution* 132). Writing during the Cold War, when positive liberty was linked by some political theorists to totalitarianism, Arendt defended the tradition she chose to call "public freedom," tracing it back to classical republicanism.[26] However, if in the passage of the first ten amendments the U.S. Constitution veered "from public freedom to civil liberty, or from a share in public affairs for the sake of public happiness to a guarantee that the pursuit of private happiness would be protected and furthered by public power," Arendt saw in the events of the French Revolution a decade later a much more drastic and pernicious change (*On Revolution* 132). With Robespierre's statement that "under constitutional rule it is almost enough to protect the individuals against the abuses of public power," she claims, "power is still public and in the hands of the government, but the individual has become powerless and must be protected against it. Freedom, on the other hand, has shifted places; it resides no longer in the public realm but in the private life of the citizens and so must be defended against the public realm and its power" (134). Arendt's account makes two crucial links. First, she argues that to secure individual rights and liberties by constitutional decree is not to empower individuals by protecting them, but rather to identify them as "powerless" by assuming them to be in need of protection. Like Hamilton, she points out that the argument for protection "against the abuses of public power" depends upon the prior existence of a potentially abusive public power. And second, she associates this diminished "share in public affairs" with the revaluation of privacy and, in particular, the belief that "freedom" is exercised in our private rather than our public lives.[27] To situate freedom in the private realm is to imagine it in opposition to public power rather than as the exercise of public power.

Wendy Brown's recent critique of liberalism in certain key respects continues Arendt's line of reasoning. Like Arendt, Brown draws a direct relation between state protection of rights and liberties and the supposition of a violating power, describing "rights" as "a paradoxical form of power insofar as they signify something like the permanent presence of an endangering power or violation" (12). "The first imaginings of freedom," she contends, "are always constrained by and potentially even require the very structures of oppression that freedom emerges to oppose" (7). Hence the liberal narrative in which institutions are established so as to secure freedom for increasing numbers of subjects against a historical threat (such as the "arbitrary sovereign") must also, as she writes, "recuperate [the historical threat] as a form of political anxiety" (8). Moreover, Brown extends her critique more broadly to the liberal ideal of the autonomous individual. Following Michel Foucault, she argues that it is liberal subjects' individuation that makes them peculiarly susceptible to modern disciplinary mechanisms: their "false autonomy," she writes, "is also their vulnerability" (19). And by establishing the expectation of self-reliance and autonomy—an expectation that cannot be met—liberalism effectively sets all its subjects up for failure. She asserts, "it is their situatedness within power, and their production by power, and liberal discourse's denial of this situatedness and production that cast the liberal subject into failure" (67). More so than Arendt, however, Brown is interested in the strategies for challenging historically discriminatory and exclusionary practices to which these structures of liberal subjectivity have given rise. Drawing on Nietzsche's analysis of the politics of *ressentiment,* she argues that the strategy of seeking legal redress for injury is problematic in its dependence on "the injury-identity connection it denounces," its legitimation of "law and the state as appropriate protectors against injury," and its ultimate aim of revenge rather than empowerment (21, 27). "In its attempt to displace its suffering," writes Brown, "identity structured by *ressentiment* at the same time becomes invested in its own subjection" (70).

The readings that follow raise similar questions about the liberal project of protecting liberty from the encroachments of power and the claims of injury that are generated by such modes of structuring civic space. However, my readings diverge from Brown's analysis in one crucial respect. Just as they challenge the tendency of some liberal theorists to fantasize protection as a stable condition—a fantasy that we can see represented in the concept of autonomy—they also challenge Brown's tendency to figure injury as a fixed or self-perpetuating condition. According to Brown, "politicized identity . . . enunciates itself, makes claims for itself, only by entrenching, restating, dramatizing, and inscribing its pain in politics; it can hold out no future—for itself or others—that triumphs over this pain" (74). But the nineteenth-century versions of "politicized identity" examined in this book were effective because they did hold out a future of protected citizenship. The Declaration of Independence, which functioned as a prototype for many antislavery and women's rights "declarations," dramatized the colonists' injuries and inscribed their pain in politics, but drew on the dynamic tension between the tyranny of George III and an imagined—indeed, "declared"—independence. Similarly, Stowe's George Harris and Douglass's Madison Washington achieve such profound eloquence not by entrenching their enslavement, but by bringing it into an untenable coexistence with what the texts figure as their dignity and their worthiness of civic protection. I do not wish to argue that injury cannot become fixed as a marker of identity; only that it is not a necessary or inevitable outcome of engaging in the rhetoric of protection. Neither do I wish to suggest that the rhetoric of protection is free of contradiction and not bound by liberal assumptions about civic participation and the nature of power; only that there was, at least in the nineteenth century, a greater potential for emancipatory movements within these problematic structures of liberalism than Brown acknowledges. Finally, by examining politicized subjectivities, like protected abstraction or embodied vulnerability, as strategic rhetorical positions, we can see their fluidity both in the claim to represent a vulnerable liberty in search of protection and in the drive to portray one's opponent's position as a tyrannical force in need of constraint. Indeed, we can see the effort to fix a subject in a particular position as itself a strategy to gain control of the terms of the debate.

The Politics of Privacy

Particularly since Foucault, we have had a healthy skepticism of liberal privacy. In his essay "Public and Private," Michael Warner summarizes the broad contours of that skepticism thus:

Feminists such as Pateman and MacKinnon, for example, point out that the liberal protection of the private from public interference simply blocked from view those kinds of domination that structure private life through the institutions of the family, the household, gender, and sexuality. Arendt tried to show how many of the strongest conceptions of humanity had been lost or forgotten when freedom was identified with the protection of private life rather than with the give-and-take of public activity. Habermas showed that modern society is fundamentally structured by a public sphere, including the critical consciousness of private people, but that these public ideals and norms are betrayed by modern social organization. And Michel Foucault rendered a strong challenge to the liberal tradition almost without using the terms "public" and "private" by showing in great detail how its key terms and immanent values—public, state, private, freedom, autonomy—fail to account for power relations. (*Publics and Counterpublics* 43–44)

With the exception of Habermas, such critiques have largely been aimed at exposing the powerful cluster of ideas surrounding liberal privacy—that it represents a precious region of life worthy of state protection, for example, or that the state can simultaneously represent the invasive threat and be the instrument of protection, or that the very act of protection is somehow benign—as ideological constructs that reinforce systems of domination by passing them off as necessary to individual freedom. Constructed as a region off limits to power, liberal privacy is actually the site of power's most effective mechanisms of control. Lauren Berlant has extended such inquiries into how the fiction of a protected privacy operates in the service of repressive power, arguing that it not only masks power's permeation of private life, but also has transformed U.S. political discourse into what she calls a "world of public intimacy," and made "citizenship into a category of feeling irrelevant to practices of hegemony or sociality in everyday life" (*Queen of America* 1, 11). For Berlant, it is privacy's remarkable capacity to portray itself as apolitical—even as it saturates public life—that has enabled its fictions to infiltrate political discourse and damage the public's capacity for critical exchange.

This book is also interested in the notion that there is a certain hypocrisy at the heart of liberal privacy.[28] However, the readings that follow demonstrate that liberal privacy's capacity to generate fictions that deny its actual effects can support a progressive politics just as easily as it can function in the ways that Berlant and others identify. The key to appropriating for the antislavery, abolitionist, and women's rights agendas the structure of argument in which a vulnerable liberty must be defended against the forces of tyranny, I have suggested, is the problematic analogy of state government to family government—an analogy that I wish to examine as an exemplary instance of liberal privacy's capacity for denial. Locke explicitly refutes the analogy in his *Two Treatises of Government*, declaring "that the power of a magistrate over a subject, may be distinguished from that of a father over his children, a master over his servant, a husband over his wife, and a lord over his slave" (115).[29] And yet this liberal tendency simultaneously to isolate the domestic from the political and to imbue the domestic with original political significance coexists with a seemingly perverse insistence on seeing family and state as analogous. Locke repeatedly uses the language of government to describe familial relations: the "government" of children, he claims, is "more their protection than restraint; and they could nowhere find a greater security to their peace, liberties, and fortunes, than in the rule of a father" (152). Despite his insistence that the family and the state operate according to entirely different sets of rules, here he suggests that fathers ideally perform the same function as states—that is, securing the peace, liberties, and fortunes of their subjects. Similarly, we see political rhetoric that routinely draws upon a rich constellation of familial imagery and concepts—what Jay Fliegelman has identified as the "quintessential motif" of American Revolutionary rhetoric (*Prodigals and Pilgrims* 3). Such rhetoric not only suggests that the body of knowledge that seeks to understand familial organization and child-rearing techniques is somehow applicable to the political realm, but also posits a set of morally charged norms common to both regions of life.

The common norm that is of particular concern to this book is the conviction that good government is limited government, that it exists to serve its subjects' well-being, and should be held to account if it can be shown to have injured them. What constitutes well-being and what constitutes injury can be debated, and the categories clearly have changed over time, but the normative force of any injury claim depends upon something being seen as vulnerable and precious. In the case against the political tyranny of George III, for example, it was the colonists' rights and liberties that were the "object[s] of unjust encroachment" and "victim[s] to arbitrary power," subjected to a "rapid and bold succession of injuries," as Thomas Jefferson wrote in *A Summary View of the Rights of British America* (*Writings* 108, 110). But such arguments could not be applied to the domestic realm until the domestic realm came to be seen as harboring a precious and vulnerable region of life; otherwise, it could not be depicted as damaged by the abusive power of a tyrant. It is therefore what Arendt identifies as "the enormous enrichment of the private sphere" and the growing belief in the sanctity of privacy—developments Arendt views with deep skepticism—that made the concept of "tyranny" applicable to domestic and familial relationships (*Human Condition* 38). It is the idea that the family should be separated off from the outside world and protected from intrusion by inviolable barriers, constituting a refuge for precisely those communal and altruistic values that have no place in politics or commercial society—the belief that private life is sacrosanct and worthy of government protection—that paradoxically underwrites this analogy of family government to state government.

In *The Secret History of Domesticity,* Michael McKeon offers a historical account of the early modern public sphere and its implications for the problematic interrelation of family and state. The public sphere emerging in seventeenth-century England, McKeon argues, was engaged in the epistemological project of making the "tacit" distinctions of traditional society "explicit" by separating out certain concepts that then rendered the traditional distinctions available to critique. The separation of public from private, in McKeon's analysis, is both exemplary and peculiarly fraught. On the one hand, we can see that something like Locke's critique of Filmer's patriarchalism is explicitly grounded in the separation of political relations from familial relations, as well as the separation of state from civil society. On the other hand, literature focusing on domestic relations evinces a persistent recourse to the language of statecraft, "as though," McKeon writes, "the state, quarantined off from civil society, returns from within to control the terms by which society's most private institutions are organized" (15). McKeon attributes this apparent contradiction to the dual functions of privacy as a category in modernity: the project of making the tacit explicit is mirrored in the project of making the private (or hidden) public—the central concern of what he calls the "secret history." And so the private is at once a critical category and the site of precritical, tacit distinctions that must be separated out before they can be subjected to critical analysis. The "privacy" that emerges from McKeon's study, then, is not a static region of life, but rather a dynamic process in which the public is separated out from the private, and the private is progressively subdivided along the same axis into ever-greater privacies.

This is not to say that there isn't also a tendency to fantasize privacy as a fixed state, protected from public exposure and intrusion. But McKeon's analysis significantly revises the argument that liberal privacy necessarily serves repressive power by promoting a fiction of security—a fiction, that is, of a region of individual liberty that is both apolitical and immune from an invasive power. While it doesn't preclude such an argument, it also opens up the possibility that the public-private divide could serve as a tool of critical analysis, and that liberal privacy generates fictions of vulnerability as intensely and prolifically as it gen-

erates fictions of protection. Elizabeth Maddock Dillon reaches a similar conclusion in her recent study of the "literary public sphere" in the seventeenth,
eighteenth, and early nineteenth centuries in America, and its role in producing and reproducing liberal subjectivity.[30] Extending Habermas's distinction
between what he calls the "literary" and "political" public spheres, Dillon argues that the political public sphere's structure of private persons emerging into
a rational-critical public is complemented in the literary public sphere's task of
representing the intimate sphere as the site of, among other things, free choice,
love, and nurturing. "What is exposed in the literary public sphere," she explains, "is subjectivity as interiority and affect, not rationality" (31). According
to Dillon, these two projects are thoroughly implicated in each other, forming
what she calls "a recursive loop": the liberal public sphere requires a pre-political
sphere of privacy from which its participants can emerge, and bourgeois privacy
must be produced publicly and continually reinscribed as pre-political (35). The
dynamic and mutually constitutive public-private divide in Dillon's account,
as in McKeon's, does not function simply to exclude those subjects marked as
private from public participation, or to condemn such subjects once and for all
to silence and subordination. As Dillon explains, women are "tether[ed] . . . to
a private sphere identity . . . by way of publicity, exchange, and desire rather
than by way of biology, linear narrative, and liberal self-possession" (47–48).
Their "voice" is not that of the traditional liberal subject—legitimate by virtue of its abstraction from the personal and its consequent capacity for rational
deliberation—but rather the voice of "liberal subjectification," as Dillon puts
it, the liberal subject's necessary counterpart (48).[31]

Another of liberalism's key fictions that Dillon examines is what she identifies
as its "temporality"—its recourse to teleological narratives of origin and progress. Such narratives, Dillon argues, are "resources deployed in liberal thought
to resolve . . . a fundamental antinomy": the "antinomy between the embodied,
constrained nature of subjectivity and the idea of the subject as free and autonomous" (19). We can see the idea that the liberal subject emerges into public from
a pre-political sphere of privacy, for example, as a fiction that works to deny
both the subject's vulnerability to power and the need for privacy to be publicly
produced and reproduced. To understand the constitution of the public sphere
as an ongoing process rather than a single, originary event is to see the liberal
subject's autonomy as something that must continually be established anew, as
something, in short, that must constantly be defended. But it is also to understand the private sphere's public significance as a peculiarly fraught nexus of
transgression, retreat, and denial. If configurations like "exposure" and "confession" offer a way of imagining the publication of private matters and are par-

ticularly effective at attracting public attention, they also feed on the fantasy of an untouchable privacy and, as Foucault reminds us, construct the subject as vulnerable to various mechanisms of discipline and surveillance. If the structure of the literary public sphere places women in a prominent position because of their association with private subjectivity, it also opens them up to such charges as hypocrisy and immodesty—charges that arise not from what they say or do, but from the very fact of their presence. Privacy's conflicted public significance generates values that are rhetorically compelling but also apolitical and unavailable to critique—indeed, rhetorically compelling because they present themselves as unavailable to critique. The privacy that arises from Dillon's analysis can be seen as generating a rich and varied array of public configurations that can and have served a variety of political agendas.[32]

Karen Sánchez-Eppler's *Dependent States* investigates the cultural significance of children and childhood and illuminates a crucial area in which domestic privacy intervenes in nineteenth-century American public life. That "the political potency of the figure of the child derives from vulnerability and preciousness," Sánchez-Eppler argues, prompts us to reevaluate "conceptions of autonomy, power, and agency as goals of political inclusion" (xxiv–xxv). The book ends with a fascinating close reading of several images of children with American flags, highlighting this uneasy coexistence of dependency and independence, parental authority and state authority. On the one hand, one daguerreotype of a peacefully sleeping child clearly coded as middle class, according to Sánchez-Eppler, "proposes a sort of symmetry between [family and nation] as sites of responsibility, care, and trust"; an image in an 1879 children's book "teach[es] its young readers to claim independence through a reliance upon [the father's] supervisory protection" (221, 224). On the other hand, several Civil War–era images of white-looking children identified as slaves evoke the slaves' profound insecurity and exploitation and call attention to the nation's failure to protect its children. One such photograph of three slave children wrapped in American flags is captioned "Our Protection," "vividly present[ing]," as Sánchez-Eppler puts it, "the future of such children as the responsibility and promise of the nation" (231). What all of the images have in common is that they identify parental values with civic values; they locate an emotionally charged nexus of innocence, vulnerability, and the urge to protect at the very heart of the national narrative.

Viewed in light of Dillon's account of the dynamic interplay of public and private, however, these images can also demonstrate the function of privacy in the constitution of the civic sphere and show how that dynamic can be appropriated to a particular political end. At their most basic, they demonstrate the deep reciprocity of protection and vulnerability—the image of the sleeping child is a scene of protection that at the same time evokes the child's vulnerability, while the image of the slave children depicts their scandalous vulnerability but achieves its impact because of the normative value of protection. To the extent that liberal citizenship entails a denial of vulnerability, defining itself as the emergence from a vulnerable privacy into a public realm that is free by virtue of its disembodied abstraction, these images of children would seem to constitute the reverse. But Dillon's analysis suggests that such images do not undo liberal citizenship, but rather complement it by representing the vulnerable privacy from which the citizen must emerge. Furthermore, because the movement between vulnerable privacy and abstract public participation is circular rather than linear, an image like "Our Protection" can take on civic significance, expanding the parental impulse to protect an innocent child into a morally charged patriotic obligation. As Union propaganda, then, "Our Protection" takes advantage of liberalism's need to construct the domestic as always public and political, but simultaneously deny that it is so: it can convincingly portray the treatment of slaves as a matter of legitimate public concern while at the same time capitalizing on the shared value that our children should be protected from abuse, a value that is presented as beyond debate because it is so irretrievably private. Of course, the proslavery argument took advantage of the same configuration, only rearranging its elements. For supporters of slavery, the scandal was not the treatment of slaves, but the exposure of Southerners' private, domestic affairs to public oversight—an exposure that was frequently imagined as a violation—and the shameful and immodest behavior of abolitionists, especially female ones. And their own version of the vulnerable and endangered thing, abandoned by the nation and in need of rescue, would emerge fully developed by the end of the century in the Myth of the Old South.

Each of the four chapters that follow examines a particular nineteenth-century contest for control over the terms of the dynamic configuration that structures liberal civic space—liberty, tyranny, protection, injury, rescue, exposure, security. Chapter 1 focuses primarily on arguments over slavery in the 1850s that invoke the Declaration of Independence; chapter 2 examines Angelina Grimké's brief but intense antislavery speaking career in the 1830s; chapter 3 turns to arguments over racial segregation and African American citizenship in the 1880s and 1890s, focusing especially on Frances E. W. Harper's 1892 novel *Iola Leroy;* and chapter 4 examines the contest between Olive Chancellor and Basil Ransom for control over the voice of the eloquent girl, Verena Tarrant, in Henry James's 1886 novel *The Bostonians.* The readings are not arranged in precise chronological order in part because they do not track a particular historical development over time. Each chapter can more productively be read as a cross-section of history, a "moment" in which the terms can be seen in especially productive tension. Nevertheless, the central historical events here are the Civil War and Emancipation, which clearly changed the way arguments about civic inclusion and exclusion could be advanced.[33] The most significant rhetorical development, I would suggest, was the potent lexicon surrounding the idea of the "Lost Cause" and the related metaphor of the South as a violated white woman. Although, as I will show, such imagery was not entirely absent from antebellum defenses of the South, the contests I examine in the second half of this book are tonally quite different from those in the first half. Harper's reform rhetoric, for example, does not unequivocally embrace the ideal of self-protection as the primary civic value, taking a more nuanced approach and complementing her own positive vision of reform with a critique of the segregationist claim to be protecting the vulnerable. The epilogue that brings the book to an end considers an 1896 lecture by William James that asks where such a critique of self-protection might be grounded, if not in a masculine ideal of heroism, or a Ransom-like rant against "feminization," or a romanticization of hardship. Ultimately, though, James takes recourse in asserting an inviolable interiority that is both tragic and fortunate, resembling the familiar liberal faith in autonomy, and illustrating just how tenacious a hold these structures of liberal civics continue to have at the end of the nineteenth century.

The two antebellum chapters are concerned with how the dynamics of protection and injury generated by the liberal conception of civic space came to be applied to the progressive agendas of abolitionism and the women's rights movements. Chapter 1 examines the dramatic and mutually constitutive opposition of liberty and tyranny as it was fashioned in the Declaration of Independence, and then appropriated by abolitionists. I read the Declaration, not in the conventional way, as a statement of principle, but rather for the way in which it reenacts the drama of an aggrieved liberty in search of civic protection, and conceives its constituency as under the sway of a tyrannical father figure. The Declaration became such a touchstone for the antislavery movement, I argue, less for declaring independence or proclaiming liberty than for so vividly representing a state of dependency and intolerable subjugation. The chapter then examines in detail several explicit references to the Declaration of Independence in antislavery and abolitionist fiction, nonfiction, and oratory, including Wendell Phillips's prefatory letter to Frederick Douglass's 1845 *Narrative,* Harriet Beecher Stowe's *Uncle Tom's Cabin* and *Dred,* and speeches by Horace Mann and Frederick Douglass. I discuss two potentially problematic tendencies in these appropriations: the possibility that the slave can become rhetorically fixed in a position of embodied vulnerability, and the tendency of these declarations to imagine no outcome other than violence. Douglass's "Fourth of July" speech, I argue, avoids both of these potential problems by its delicate management of the tension between protected abstraction and embodied vulnerability and its skillful movement among various subject positions.

Chapter 2 is concerned with changing assumptions about the nature of eloquence, which tended to elevate an ideal of sincerity and transparency over a more classical conception of oratory. Sincerity was often conceived as entailing the exposure of a vulnerable self to potential injury, and audiences were thought to be affected by a speech to the extent that their comfortable distance from it was penetrated and they were made to feel. Like liberty, eloquence rehearsed the dynamic crucial to rhetorics of protection—the mutually inciting partnership between spectacles of injury and the commitment to protection. Analyzing the abolitionist rhetoric of Angelina Grimké, a daughter of slaveholders who became a popular speaker for the American Anti-Slavery Society, this chapter examines how Grimké—criticized for "yield[ing] the power which God has given her for protection" by "assum[ing] the place and tone of man as a public reformer"—capitalized on her status as an unprotected woman on the lecture circuit, turning her exposure and vulnerability to her rhetorical advantage (Ceplair 211). Among the Americans critical of Grimké's decision to speak on the abolitionist lecture circuit was Catharine Beecher, whose *Essay on Slavery and Abolitionism* charged her with breaching the protective boundary between private and public and therefore risking social collapse. Grimké's response figured those areas of life Beecher deemed "private"—specifically, the feminine and the domestic—as already in some sense public. Moreover, she depicted public exposure as a salutary remedy for the corruption of the domestic sphere under slavery, positioning herself as the true defender of the values of domesticity. Nevertheless, there is evidence to suggest that after her marriage Grimké felt the need to prove that public speaking hadn't ruined her as a wife and mother, and abruptly retired from the lecture platform for some three decades. As much as the dynamic configuration of liberal privacy could be made to sustain a progressive politics, it also carried the potential to reinscribe a restrictive, privatized domesticity.

Bookending the Civil War are two crucial applications of the rhetoric of protection: South Carolina's declaration of secession, modeled explicitly on the Declaration of Independence and claiming that president-elect Lincoln's inauguration would deprive them of their "power of . . . self-protection," and the equal protection clause of the Fourteenth Amendment to the Constitution. The former reappropriated Jefferson's Declaration for the proslavery cause, depicting Southern slave owners as the victims rather than the perpetrators of tyranny, victims of an invasive and authoritarian federal government. The latter ostensibly granted the freedmen the civic protections they had sought, denying them the rhetorical position of extreme legal exposure the antislavery movement had used so effectively. Chapter 3 considers how these new historical conditions affected the debate over racial segregation and Negro citizenship. I begin by examining an exchange published in *Century Illustrated Magazine* between George W. Cable and Henry W. Grady debating the legal segregation of the races. The moderate Southerner Cable argues that it is inconsistent to claim that whites need laws to protect them from coming into contact with blacks and at the same time claim to believe in white supremacy. Although he doesn't answer the charge directly, Grady resorts to a highly charged language that confuses white racial supremacy with feminine vulnerability, demonstrating how deeply the Jim Crow regime's logic depended upon the figure of the vulnerable white woman. The title character of Frances E. W. Harper's *Iola Leroy* has been read as a black heroine who lives up to white standards of feminine beauty, refinement, and virtue. I argue, on the contrary, that Iola's decision not to pass is figured as a rejection of a secure and privatized white domesticity and proposes a different model of civic involvement based on a radical reformation of the relation between the personal and the civic. Instead of engaging in a contest over which race is in greater need of legal protection, Harper's fictional account of Negro citizenship during and after Reconstruction reconfigures the terms of the liberal civic sphere so as to question the white principle of self-protection.

If the first two chapters demonstrate the potential uses for a progressive politics in exploiting the contradictions that arise from the liberal commitment to protected privacy, then, chapter 3 demonstrates that those same internal contradictions can be made to serve a reactionary politics but can also open up a line of critique on conservative and reactionary agendas. In chapter 4, I read Henry James's novel *The Bostonians* as narrating this struggle for control over the dynamic configuration at the heart of liberal civics: Verena Tarrant, I propose, can be read as a figure for liberal privacy, the vulnerable thing with a powerful hold on audiences, over whose service the popular press, the women's rights movement, and reactionary Southern conservatism compete. Verena's appeal for the rights of women turns the paternalistic assumption that women should be protected from the tyranny of men against the patriarchy. But James's narrator is clearly interested in more than just the substance of Verena's appeal, tracking the wide variety of fantasies and scandals she represents for her admirers. Many of those fantasies and scandals—the scandal of an innocent girl in the vulgar hands of the mechanisms of popular publicity and the fantasy of rescue, erotic fantasies and fantasies of domination and conquest, the scandalous fact of Verena's parents—are shared by Ransom and Olive, despite their sharply opposing political convictions and their increasingly bitter rivalry over her affections. What emerges from James's novel is a powerfully evocative matrix of attraction, loathing, indignation, and fierce allegiances, which has no political content of its own but nevertheless is at the core of our national civic discourse. It appears as a kind of medium through which political differences over the appropriate role of women or the proper place of the South in post–Civil War America are experienced and within which they are lived, and at least in James's vision would seem to allow little possibility for reconciliation.

If Henry James presents a rather bleak outlook on the prospects for civility in American political discourse, however, William James's "What Makes a Life Significant" strikes a more optimistic note. He begins by describing the educational summer resort of Chautauqua as a triumph of civility, but then questions whether such a triumph is really to be desired. In the epilogue I read James's musings as an acknowledgment of the truth that liberalism consistently denies: the liberal subject thrives on, and indeed requires, the ongoing presence of tyranny. For James, the problem with Chautauqua is not in the civilized values themselves, but in the loss of the dramatic and dynamic structure within which they battle against injustice; his critique is not an exposure of liberalism's weakness, but rather a sign of its continued power over the American imagination at the end of the nineteenth century.

1

Declarations of Independence, Claims of Injury

He has plundered our seas, ravaged our coasts, burnt our towns, and destroyed the lives of our people.

—The Declaration of Independence

Every Independence Day from 1854 to 1865 many of the most prominent abolitionists in the United States gathered in Framingham, Massachusetts, for an annual rally against slavery: a publicity poster for one such meeting called upon the "Friends of Freedom" to "consecrate the day to the cause of Impartial and Universal Liberty."[1] That these abolitionists would associate their cause with the American Revolution is not surprising: antislavery and women's rights activists in the nineteenth century routinely invoked the Declaration of Independence and the history of the nation's founding in their efforts to focus public attention on the plight of the disenfranchised.[2] Indeed, a reverent attachment to Jefferson's Declaration was one of the few things that crossed the otherwise contentious divisions among the various antislavery camps. Prior even to citing scripture, William Lloyd Garrison began his 1854 speech "No Compromise with Slavery" as he often did, by affirming his belief in the Declaration's claim that "all men are created equal; that they are endowed by their Creator with certain inalienable rights; that among these are life, liberty, and the pursuit of happiness." "Hence," he declared, "I am an Abolitionist. Hence, I cannot but regard oppression in every form—and most of all, that which turns a man into a thing—with indignation and abhorrence" (Lowance 126). Similarly, in an 1854 speech opposing the Kansas-Nebraska Bill, Frederick Douglass argued that the principle of popular sovereignty was incompatible with any legislation permitting slavery, asserting that "the only intelligible principle on which popular sovereignty is founded, is found in the Declaration of American Independence, there and in these words: We hold these truths to be self-evident, that all men are created equal and are endowed by their Creator with the right of life, liberty, and the pursuit of happiness" (Foner 309).[3] And John Brown reaffirmed his own life-long commitment to those principles when he convened the 1858 Chatham, Ontario, convention—an effort to enlist support for his planned raid on Harpers Ferry—by pronouncing slavery "in utter disregard and violation of those eternal and self-evident truths set forth in our Declaration of Independence" (qtd. in Du Bois, *John Brown* 239).

The notion that the Declaration's assertion of equality and inalienable human rights is incompatible with slavery—and that the abolitionist movement cited the Declaration primarily so as to remind America of those founding principles—is now widely assumed, and entails a particular reading of the Declaration's significance.[4] Pauline Maier's *American Scripture* offers the definitive account of that reading. Sometime after the conclusion of the War of 1812, Maier claims, the focus began to shift from the Declaration's practical purpose of asserting and justifying the colonies' break from Britain to its assertion of principles, emphasizing its second paragraph often to the exclusion of the rest of the Declaration, and seeing it as "a moral standard by which the day-to-day policies and practices of the nation could be judged" (154). Abraham Lincoln gave eloquent expression to this revisionist version in the Gettysburg Address and elsewhere: he "saw the Declaration of Independence's statements on equality and rights as setting a standard for the future," Maier argues, "one that demanded the gradual extinction of conflicting practices as that became possible" (205). Foremost among those "conflicting practices" was slavery, and Maier suggests that it was this new emphasis on the Declaration as a guiding statement of principle—what she calls its "sacralization"—that lay behind its appropriation by abolitionists (197). The Declaration's "elevat[ion] into something akin to a holy writ," she contends, "made it a prize worth capturing on behalf of one cause after another" (154).[5]

In this chapter, I will be advancing a different explanation of why the Declaration of Independence was so widely embraced and frequently appropriated by antebellum reformers. My primary focus will be neither on the Declaration's assertion of independent statehood nor on its positive assertion of the principles of liberty and equality, but rather on its situating of those principles in a defensive and dramatic struggle against tyranny, a struggle that it elevates to epic proportions. In terms of the document itself, I wish to shift the focus from the several opening and closing paragraphs to the "long train of abuses and usurpations" perpetrated against the colonists by George III (Jefferson 19). Those abuses transform freedom and equality from abstract, isolated principles into precious articles that the colonists are in imminent danger of losing to the aggressive tyranny of the British king and, in some cases, have already lost. Moreover, just as Garrison's commitment to the ideals of the Declaration attains its rhetorical weight and urgency in the context of slavery—in the presence, that is, of an institutionalized force that is devoted to their elimination—so it is in the context of King George's tyranny that the principles of freedom and equality asserted in the Declaration gain their moral force and earn the audience's devotion. The key to the Declaration's remarkable second life as a prototype for antislavery and women's rights declarations, I will argue, is that it enacts a drama of *dis*enfranchisement—a drama in which liberty is threatened by tyranny and the colonists' participation in civic life is threatened by the aggressive actions of King George. In short, the Declaration offers a blueprint for making a compelling claim to public attention and action on behalf of a constituency that has been disenfranchised by a tyrant.

That liberty is always at risk from the encroachment of power is an idea fundamental to eighteenth-century republican political theory: Bernard Bailyn has observed that the founders seemed to "dwell . . . on it endlessly, almost compulsively" (56). Moreover, it was not unusual for them to write about liberty's vulnerability to power in highly charged terms, as a thing "skulking about in corners . . . hunted and persecuted in all countries by cruel power," to quote John Adams (qtd. in Bailyn 59).[5] "Freedom hath been hunted round the globe," exclaimed Thomas Paine in *Common Sense*. "O! receive the fugitive, and prepare in time an asylum for mankind" (99). Such figures aim to engage the emotions in a specific way, imagining liberty as a victimized creature, alone and in desperate need of a protector. Gordon S. Wood has reconstructed a similar narrative of American liberty from sermons that were printed in 1774 and 1775, in which the clergymen envisioned the project of colonization as liberty's search for a sanctuary: "In the seventeenth century [the settlers] had carried 'the spirit of liberty' from England to the wilderness 'at a time when it was in its greatest purity and perfection'; and in the New World it had flourished. No wonder, then, that 'there seldom ever was a nation . . . more violently assaulted than we have been.' [. . . As a result] liberty was fleeing the Old World entirely and 'seeking an asylum westward'" (*Creation* 42–43). To imagine liberty as a pure and perfect thing, fleeing the violent assaults of a cruel master, and seeking a new home in a place where it can be protected, is to figure it as the touching protagonist of a drama, a Clarissa Harlowe or a Dickensian orphan. It is to promote in the listening or reading audience a certain specific quality of attachment, not simply to a positive good, but to something precious that is in danger of violation. We can, moreover, see this drama of the unprotected wanderer, fleeing tyranny and in search of asylum, as underwriting a wide variety of political appeals, from Thomas Paine's image of the colonies as children of abusive parents to the fugitive slave narrative.[6]

Such configurations are significant because of their crucial implications for the classical republican conception of citizenship. Adams's figure of a "hunted and persecuted" liberty, and the clergymen's dramatic account of liberty "assaulted" and "seeking an asylum" in America, personify the abstract principle of liberty. But the Declaration of Independence takes the figurative struggle of liberty against tyranny and literalizes it as the colonists' conflict with the British monarchy. In other words, what the former imagines metaphorically as human drama—thereby encouraging audiences to identify with the plight of an abstract principle—the latter constructs as an actual constituency. That constituency, under siege and compelling by virtue of its injuries, having been "declare[ed]" by George III "out of his protection," it could be argued, does not constitute a citizenry in the classical sense (Jefferson 21). Indeed, one after another, the injuries and usurpations itemized in the Declaration define its constituency by their exclusion from citizenship as it was classically defined. In Aristotle's seminal account, a citizen is marked by his participation in the affairs of state; in the Declaration, George III is charged with preventing the colonial governing bodies from legislating and, in some cases, assembling at all—preventing the colonists from participating in their civic affairs. Aristotle emphasizes the crucial quality of virtue, which he argues is limited "to those who are in fact relieved of necessary tasks," those who can "occupy [themselves] as virtue demands" because they have already satisfied their basic needs of food, shelter and security (184).[7] Jefferson himself stresses the quality of self-sufficiency in his figure of the independent yeoman farmer, not beholden to anyone for his safety and his livelihood, and therefore not vulnerable to manipulation. As he writes in *Notes on the State of Virginia*, "dependence begets subservience and venality, suffocates the germ of virtue, and prepares fit tools for the designs of ambition" (*Writings* 290–91). But the Declaration of Independence charges George III with undermining the colonists' self-sufficiency and eroding their security—in effect, with consolidating his control over them by making them more and more dependent on him. Aristotle distinguishes the kind of rule appropriate in households from the kind of rule appropriate for the state, defining tyranny as "a monarchy which is exercised like a mastership over the association which is the state" (191). The Declaration depicts George III as just such a tyrant—one who has denied his colonial subjects' citizenship and ruled over them as the master of a household rules over his wife, children, and slaves.

I do not wish to suggest that Jefferson in any way equated his situation with that of his slaves, or imagined the Declaration of Independence as potentially an antislavery or women's rights document; for him the difference was that, unlike women or slaves, he was deserving of full citizenship, that George III had unjustly deprived him of something to which he was entitled. But the Declaration nevertheless gives voice to a constituency that is ruled by a master—a constituency that is prevented from establishing laws for its own protection, that is subjected to violence without legal remedy, that is forced into a state of dependency, that is, in short, in the position of women and slaves. Moreover, its exclusion from full citizenship does not mean that it is excluded from civic deliberation; on the contrary, the Declaration's constituency stakes its claim to public attention on its having been denied full citizenship. The Aristotelian analogy of tyranny to mastery offers one version of the state as a kind of household, subjects as akin to women and slaves. But when paternal authority comes to be seen as ideally protective, tyranny comes to be analogous to a dysfunctional household. This is a crucial change: whereas for Aristotle the problem is in administering the state with techniques that are justified in the household, the analogy of tyrant to *bad* father assumes that the complaints of citizens and those of household dependents are not only analogous, but equally valid. Both groups are figured as the victims of a failed paternalism, dependents whose father-master has turned from protector into brutal tyrant, and who have nowhere to turn for safety. Samuel Richardson's Clarissa can be seen as a prototype, affording some insight into exactly how compelling these figures can be. But drawing on the same set of assumptions and emotions are the American colonists of the Declaration of Independence, who, like Clarissa, "petition . . . for redress in the most humble terms," their "repeated petitions . . . answered only by repeated injuries" (Jefferson, *Writings* 22).[8]

The Declaration's characterization of its constituency as the victims of tyranny—its shift of the focus from liberty's positive definition to its persecution by George III—is what underwrites its formal appropriation by abolitionists and women's rights activists. Such documents as the 1848 Declaration of Sentiments and the Declaration of Wrongs and Rights, adopted by an 1864 national convention of black leaders in Syracuse, New York, consciously echo the Declaration of Independence in their cultivation of outrage over the continued violation of human rights and denial of human equality.[9] Assuming not only the tone but also the actual language of the Declaration, the women of Seneca Falls depicted "the history of mankind [as] a history of repeated injuries and usurpations on the part of man toward woman, having in direct object the establishment of an absolute tyranny over her" (Rossi 416).[10] Similarly, the National Convention of Colored Men reconceived British tyranny as white tyranny, often substituting for the figurative injuries sustained at the hands of King

George the literal injuries of slavery. The ravishing of "our coasts" in the Declaration of Independence, for example, became in the Declaration of Wrongs and Rights "our daughters ravished, our wives violated, and our firesides desolated."[11] What is remarkable about these declarations is their explicit use of "tyranny" to describe the rule of white men over women and slaves. From a classical republican perspective, it makes no sense to use the word "tyranny" to describe rule within a household. Force is not only justified but necessary to establish mastery over one's household dependents; it is wrong only when it is taken out of the private realm and applied to citizens in the polis. But the Declaration of Independence, by emphasizing the colonists' injuries over their positive qualifications for republican citizenship—and, indeed, basing its public appeal on the severity of those injuries—offered a model that was open to just such appropriation. It opened up the possibility that a vulnerable and tyrannized constituency could see itself as having a powerful public claim.[12]

The Voice of the Fugitive and the Rhetoric of Abolition

Both the rhetorical appropriation of the Declaration and its consequences can be further clarified by examining a few particular examples in some detail, and I would like to start by considering the role that antislavery leaders envisioned for Frederick Douglass on the abolitionist lecture circuit, and the public persona they endeavored to fashion for him. Jared Gardner has pointed out the peculiar predicament that Douglass faced as both a slave and an author. By Douglass's own account, his 1845 *Narrative of the Life of Frederick Douglass, an American Slave: Written by Himself* was published largely in response to the widespread belief that he was an impostor, that no slave could be as polished and articulate an orator as Douglass. But telling his story publicly in a way that could be verified—identifying himself, in other words, as a particular slave—consequently advertised his whereabouts to his owner and exposed him to capture under the fugitive slave laws. And so he found himself in a kind of "catch-22": "for Douglass," Gardner writes, "to be anonymous was to not be heard, and therefore implicitly to perpetuate the system of slavery that he had vowed to defeat. On the other hand, to be recognized as the author of his text was to risk, as Douglass indeed did, a return to the slavery that he had only recently escaped" (160).[13] It is precisely this predicament that the abolitionist Wendell Phillips chose to emphasize in his prefatory letter to Douglass's *Narrative,* and I would like to examine both the bearing of Phillips's representation and the use to which he puts it. Phillips represents Douglass's predicament as an exclusion—specifically, an exclusion from the protections of citizenship. But the effect of that exclusion is not to incapacitate Douglass for public participation, but rather to charge his voice with an urgency that is foreign to the discourse of citizens.[14]

Here, then, is Phillips, writing to Douglass:

> After all, I shall read your book with trembling for you. Some years ago, when you were beginning to tell me your real name and birthplace, you may remember I stopped you, and preferred to remain ignorant of all. With the exception of a vague description, so I continued, till the other day, when you read me your memoirs. I hardly knew, at the time, whether to thank you or not for the sight of them, when I reflected that it was still dangerous, in Massachusetts, for honest men to tell their names! They say the fathers, in 1776, signed the Declaration of Independence with the halter about their necks. You, too, publish your declaration of freedom with danger compassing you around. In all the broad lands which the Constitution of the United States overshadows, there is no single spot,—however narrow or desolate,—where a fugitive slave can say, "I am safe." The whole armory of Northern Law has no shield for you. I am free to say that, in your place, I should throw the MS. into the fire. (*Douglass: Autobiographies* 12–13)

The framework for this representation is the classical model of citizenship. Phillips imagines the constitutional protections withheld from Douglass physically and spatially, as an "armory" and a "shield," and as property—a "spot" of land whereon one can be "safe." Similarly, as citizenship can be seen as a kind of fortress, its denial renders Douglass vulnerable to attack, "danger compassing [him] around." Such figures allude to Aristotle's standard distinction between citizen and slave: the citizen is both propertied and armed—that is, capable of protecting his family and his property—whereas the slave owns no property and depends for his security on his master's favor. Indeed, security—a "spot," to use Phillips's language, whereon one can say "I am safe"—is what qualifies the Aristotelian citizen for public participation. As Hannah Arendt explains, a man needed a "location . . . which was properly his own" in order to "participate in the affairs of the world." Conversely, "to have no private place of one's own (like a slave) meant to be no longer human": the lack of a protected privacy meant that one would be excluded from the public realm, and therefore unable to "attain the highest possibility of human existence" (*Human Condition* 29–30, 64).

Furthermore, the classical public realm was constituted through language. To draw again on Arendt, the difference between the public and private realms was also the difference between persuasion and violence, between using speech and using physical force (26–27). Exclusion from the public realm, then, meant that one was not only unprotected, subject to physical violence, but also silenced, prevented from representing oneself discursively.[15] In Phillips's passage the two are directly linked: it is Douglass's telling of his story that places him at risk and makes him vulnerable to capture, while it is self-censorship, "throw[ing] the MS. into the fire," that represents a chance of safety. Hence the distinction between citizen and slave is also—and crucially—manifest in the relation of one's words to one's person. The citizen speaks from a position of security and autonomy, protected from injury at the hands of either the state or the ungoverned passions of a mob; his words are abstracted and subjected to public scrutiny without placing his person at risk.[16] Douglass, by contrast, speaks only at the risk of injury; his words have direct and dire consequences for his person and are thus radically *attached* to him. Whereas speech enables the citizen to imagine a sphere of public interaction that is disembodied and thus free from physical force, for Douglass there is no such possibility. Speech for him is an act of exposure rather than protection, entailing physical risk rather than safety in abstraction.

But whereas in classical theory the slave's lack of a protected privacy—his incapacity for self-abstraction—precludes his public participation, the logical thrust of Phillips's passage is in exactly the opposite direction: it is Douglass's personal risk that makes his words so powerful, inducing his readers to approach them "with trembling." The fact that Douglass chooses to publish his narrative despite the "danger compassing [him] around" gives it a gravity and urgency that it would not otherwise have, just as the founding fathers' signing "with the halter about their necks" turns their public declaration into a powerful display of tyranny and resistance. Whereas in classical theory public speech is free when it is offered from a position of safety and security, it is Douglass's very lack of a protected privacy—the *un*freedom of his speech—that lends authority to his public voice.[17] And whereas classical theory opposes persuasion to physical force and violence, envisioning the public realm as disembodied, Douglass's public self, under the ever-present threat of physical harm, achieves its persuasive impact precisely through its bondage to his body.[18] That Douglass "publish[es his] declaration of freedom" only at great risk to himself raises the stakes of its publication, thereby heightening its drama and drawing the reader sympathetically in.

Another version of the same conflict involves the question of anonymity, as represented in Phillips's initial preference "to remain ignorant" of Douglass's "real name and birthplace." Eighteenth-century writers found fictions of anonymity and pseudonymity so enabling in part because they were mechanisms for imagining an intersubjective public space in which ideas could be judged and challenged independently of a speaker's personal reputation, and privacy could be protected.[19] But Douglass's anonymity is not a mark of his free public participation; on the contrary, it is a mark of his enslavement, a reminder that, unlike the citizen's, his speech is not protected. Douglass does not freely choose to publish anonymously or pseudonymously; rather, he is forced into anonymity as the kind of protective "shield" that the "Northern Law" does not provide for him. Moreover, in Phillips's passage, Douglass does insist on telling his name.[20] The desire that his true identity remain hidden behind a conveniently "vague description" comes not from Douglass himself, but from Phillips. And in contrast to Douglass's "honest" desire "to tell [his] name," Phillips's preference for an anonymous relationship comes off looking fainthearted and cowardly. So, again, Phillips succeeds in redefining an aspect of the classical public ideal such that what would have warranted Douglass's exclusion from public life is now a mark of his particular fitness. Anonymity—in the neoclassical imagination a figure for an impersonal and therefore free intersubjectivity—becomes in Phillips's passage a shield behind which fugitives are hidden and abolitionists can feel comfortable; and what from a neoclassical perspective signifies disinterested virtue becomes in Phillips's passage an act of cowardice.

The opposite of anonymity, as Phillips presents it, is personal presence, suggested both by the figure of the signature and by the repeated confusion of speech and writing.[21] If the distinction between speech and writing is understood as the distinction between presence and absence, then Phillips's elision of that difference encourages the reader to imagine writing as itself a kind of presence. His dizzying slide, over the course of four sentences, from "reading" Douglass's "book," to speaking personally with him, to listening to him "read [his] memoirs," to seeing the text of those memoirs, to reflecting on "honest men" who "*tell* their names"—a slide that continues on into scenes of "sign[ing]" and then publication—makes the reader unsure at any given moment whether Phillips is describing Douglass himself or Douglass's text. The effect is to imagine Douglass as somehow present within his text, reinforcing the idea that his words are not abstracted from, but rather attached to his person. The distinction between absence and presence, then, does not correspond easily to the distinction between writing and speech. Instead, it suggests opposing ways of imagining both writing and speech: on the one hand a discourse that is free by virtue of its abstraction from persons; on the other hand a discourse that places persons at risk.

Inasmuch as Phillips encourages us in the beginning of the paragraph to imagine Douglass as present within his text, the closing image of "throw[ing] the MS. into the fire" comes as a shock.[22] Of course Phillips does not say that Douglass ought to throw his manuscript into the fire; he only says what he should do in Douglass's place. So again, the emphasis, at least on the surface, is on their difference: Phillips the "free" man and Douglass the fugitive slave; Phillips the coward, unwilling to put himself at risk as Douglass does by publishing his *Narrative*. We might even infer from the image their different ways of relating to language: what seems an easy action for Phillips, who as a free man imagines his words as separate from his person, would be unthinkable for Douglass.[23] But the image of words that burn can also be read as an indirect reference to Douglass's powerful oratory, to the effect that words can have in a public sphere where persons are at stake. An audience "enkindled" by a powerful speaker was a common metaphor in the nineteenth century, used often enough in descriptions of Douglass's oratory.[24] Moreover, Douglass's *Narrative* ends with his accession as a public speaker, with his first major antislavery address to a mixed audience— a career that began, in Douglass's account, when his "soul was set all on fire" by reading the *Liberator* (*Autobiographies* 96). It is the very ambiguity of such imagery that makes it so useful for representing rhetorical strategies of exposure, which often—as in Phillips's passage—appear as the conscience of a rhetoric of protection, its earnest and volatile "other." As a religious and, specifically, Christian symbol, fire simultaneously represents worldly powerlessness and otherworldly power, calling up the apocalyptic fire and brimstone of a Puritan sermon, the tongues of fire at the Pentecost, the Protestant martyrs burned at the stake. The tradition of evangelical Christianity makes it possible to think of words that are burned as words that also burn into the hearts of others, thus, again, transforming the very things that exclude Douglass from citizenship— that constitute his worldly powerlessness—into marks of his peculiar power and righteousness as a public speaker.[25]

Phillips's letter, of course, was intended as testimony to Douglass's character, assuring readers that Douglass was known to someone (white and male) who was known to them. But it is also, to summarize my reading of it, engaged in a more complicated endeavor to legitimize Douglass's public voice by manipulating the very rhetoric in which white, male legitimacy is classically established. Inverting the premise that valid public participation requires a degree of autonomy and independence, Phillips uses images of vulnerability—the danger that compasses Douglass around, the Constitution's failure to secure a spot of safety for him, the burning manuscript, the halter about the founding fathers' necks—not to exclude the vulnerable or the endangered from public participation but, on the contrary, to intensify their public voices and actions, charging them with a depth and an urgency that is lacking in the abstract discourse of citizens, thereby heightening the impact on their audience. The very "catch-22" that would seem to have condemned Douglass either to a disabling imposture or to slavery and silence turns out, in Phillips's rendering, to authenticate his words and constitute his moral authority.[26]

Harriet Beecher Stowe and the Fugitive's Defense

A similar moment occurs in *Uncle Tom's Cabin* when George Harris, pursued by slave catchers, is led with his family and a few others to one of Phineas Fletcher's old hunting dens, a high, rocky fortress in the Ohio wilderness that "seem[s] to promise shelter and concealment" (250). But the promise of safety vanishes as the slave catchers find the den and vow to "ferret 'em out," and George emerges to confront his pursuers (252). He declares himself "a free man, standing on God's free soil," claims his wife and child as his own, and warns them that he is armed and prepared to defend himself (252). When they reply that both the law and the power are on their side, George bitterly acknowledges as much, but goes on to mount a defense of his actions that "for a moment [strikes] the party below to silence": "You mean to take my wife to sell in New Orleans, and put my boy like a calf in a trader's pen, and send Jim's mother to the brute that whipped and abused her before, because he couldn't abuse her son. You want to send Jim and me back to be whipped and tortured, and ground down under the heels of them that you call masters; and your laws *will* bear you out in it,—more shame for you and them! But you haven't got us. We don't own your laws; we don't own your country; we stand here as free, under God's sky, as you are; and, by the great God that made us, we'll fight for our liberty till we die" (253). As George delivers his "declaration of independence," we are told, "the glow of dawn gave a flush to his swarthy cheek, and bitter indignation and despair gave fire to his dark eye" (253).

Like Phillips's depiction of Douglass, Stowe's George makes his "declaration" with "danger compassing [him] around," the "whole armory of Northern Law" incapable of shielding him from the most outrageous abuses, even the "narrow and desolate" hunting den constituting for him no spot of safety. He speaks from a position of complete legal vulnerability, exiled from the protections of citizenship and exposed to whatever torture he cannot physically repel. His legal exposure is graphically represented by his position "out in fair sight, on the top of the rock," facing his coarse and brutal enemies in an utterly isolated, wild place (253). And the rocks themselves neatly evoke the unyielding strength and solidity of the law, as well as the barrenness of its promise for the slave. Furthermore, if the privileges of classical citizenship are granted only to those who have

the capacity to protect and provide for their dependents, then George's "declaration of independence" itemizes the systematic denial of that capacity to the
slave. The point I wish to emphasize here is that it is not simply George's commitment to an ideal of freedom and equality that makes his speech so compelling, capable of "[striking] the party below to silence." It is that commitment in
the context of his legal enslavement; it is the vision of a full and free life "under
God's sky" that has been thwarted and denied by the laws of the United States;
and it is especially the image of a loving family in imminent danger of being
torn apart, the law that should be protecting the domestic realm instead sanc-
tioning its violation. The key image of George's face flushed by the dawn and
his eyes enflamed with "bitter indignation and despair" generates the same emotionally charged tension: his fiery determination issues not simply from the divine promise of freedom, but rather from his facing the dawn with righteous
anger over the enormous injustice of his legal status as a slave.

This particular moment of eloquence, in which a slave or former slave moves
his listeners with a declaration of his independence—a powerful demonstration of
noble humanity struggling under the weight of tyranny and legal degradation—
appears with such frequency in antislavery fiction that we might well consider
it a literary convention. In Douglass's *The Heroic Slave,* published in 1853, the
aptly named Madison Washington unburdens his soul in a "whirlwind of anguish," offering "scathing denunciations of the cruelty and injustice of slavery"
and "heart-touching narrations of his own personal suffering," ending "each
speech by an emphatic declaration of his purpose to be free" (29). Having over-
heard Washington's soliloquy, Mr. Listwell is struck to "motionless silence";
it "[rings] through the chambers of his soul, and vibrate[s] through his entire
frame," and he becomes from that moment a committed abolitionist (29–30).
Later, having led his fellow slaves in mutiny, Washington compares his violent
seizure of the slave ship explicitly to the American Revolution: "We have done
that which you applaud your fathers for doing," he tells the surviving white sail-
ors, "and if we are murderers, *so are they*" (66). Even the racist sailor who recounts the uprising is "disarmed," forgetting "his blackness in the dignity of his
manner, and the eloquence of his speech" (66). In William Wells Brown's *Clotel,*
published the same year, George, sentenced to death for his participation in a
slave insurrection, explains to the court that he heard his master read the Declaration of Independence.[27] Then, in an emotional speech, he asserts that "the
grievances of which your fathers complained, and which caused the Revolutionary War, were trifling in comparison with the wrongs and sufferings of those
who were engaged in the late revolt," and his account of those wrongs and sufferings "[melts] nearly every one present . . . to tears" (212–13). The High Con-

jurers of Martin R. Delany's 1861–62 novel *Blake* pay tribute to "Nat Turner, Denmark Veezie, and General Gabriel" in the same paragraph that they proudly "claim . . . to have been patriots in the American Revolution" (113).[28] And the meeting of the council, convened to discuss the impending slave insurrection in Cuba, recalls the American revolutionaries in the cries of "Liberty or death!" as well as in Placido's clear invocation of both the spirit and the language of the Declaration of Independence: "We have petitioned and prayed for a redress of grievances," he tells the assembled crowd, "and not only been refused but spurned and ridiculed with greater restrictions placed upon us" (287, 288).

What is striking about these "declarations" is that their aim goes well beyond Phillips's description of Douglass, or even George Harris's "declaration of independence" to his would-be captors, both of which function primarily to heighten the speaker's eloquence. Here the Declaration is invoked as justification for armed insurrection. Thus do these moments of supreme eloquence also at the same time signify the failure of speech—the collapse of the civic ideal in which disputes can be settled through persuasion rather than violence, in which ideas can engage, as John Stuart Mill says, in "the rough process of a struggle between combatants fighting under hostile banners," while persons can remain protected (49). Clearly, it is a problematic moment for an antislavery movement that for the most part had to espouse a politics of nonviolence in order to gain popular support. But it is also, I would suggest, a direct result of the Declaration's logic, not only because of its explicit call to "alter or abolish" the colonial regime but also, more fundamentally, because of its strategy of claiming to speak for those who are excluded from the zone of civic protection. To the extent that protections establish the conditions for speech that is free by virtue of its abstraction from bodily life, the absence of protections will tend to posit the speaker as inescapably embodied, thereby denying him the means of resolving conflicts nonviolently. In other words, the same conditions that constitute this version of eloquence can also mark the speaker's exclusion from the realm of abstract civic exchange, leaving violent insurrection as his only alternative.

One consequence of the remarkable popular success of *Uncle Tom's Cabin* was the publication of a number of sentimental novels defending the institution of slavery and the Southern plantation system. In her 1854 novel, *The Planter's Northern Bride,* for example, Caroline Lee Hentz capitalizes on precisely this tendency of abolitionist eloquence to raise the possibility of violent insurrection in order to invert the terms of the abolitionist argument. Instead of countering abolitionism directly, or assuming that vulnerability renders one unfit for civic participation, Hentz appropriates the rhetorical form of the antislavery argument—in particular its emotionally charged recourse to scenes of injury and vulnerability, the yearning for freedom in the face of tyranny—for her own, proslavery ends. The novel's primary villain is a Garrison-like abolitionist named Brainard who foments violent insurrection in the South and gives fiery antislavery lectures in the North, twin activities that Hentz links by drawing on one of the abolitionists' own favorite tropes, speech that burns. After his Southern plot is exposed, Brainard flees to the North—a fugitive—and imagines the successes that await him on the antislavery lecture circuit: "Who says I have failed? . . . The flames I have kindled will not be quenched. They will burst out afresh, when people think they are gazing on ashes" (302). Here, what begins as an emphasis on the figurative "flames" of vengeance Brainard successfully "kindled" with his eloquence, as opposed to the literal fires of the failed insurrection, quickly becomes ambiguous. His prediction that "they will burst out afresh" seems to refer simultaneously to the figurative flames of anger that still smolder invisibly, and the actual flames of the future insurrection they will generate. To effectively literalize these figurative flames—or at least to bring them into a directly causal relation—is to conflate words and actions and to deny the abstraction of speech. Like the antislavery versions, Hentz's representation of Brainard's eloquence directly confronts the classical model in which speech is free by virtue of its abstraction from embodied action. But while the antislavery versions function to electrify the speech and heighten its urgency, Hentz's emphasizes the danger Brainard's enkindling eloquence poses to the potential victims of the violence it ignites.

Moreover, it goes without saying for Hentz that these potential victims are innocent, white Southerners. And so when Brainard goes on to "thank Heaven for the gift of eloquence!" envisioning the images "of flesh torn from the body with red-hot pincers, of children roasted alive, of women burned at the stake" that he will "manufacture" for his antislavery audiences, we are encouraged to imagine not the slave victims that Brainard intends, but rather the white victims of violent slave insurrection (303). This remarkable inversion, I would argue, is typical of Hentz's rhetorical strategy and her response to Stowe. Rather than develop her own competing framework of proslavery tropes, Hentz appropriates some of the most highly charged figures of antislavery rhetoric, emptying them of their antislavery significance. The enkindling abolitionist speaker, whose words burn into the hearts of the people, becomes in Hentz's account the incendiary agitator, fanning the flames of mob violence. Exploiting the very ambiguity that allowed a writer like Stowe to elevate the fugitive's defense into a climax of dramatic eloquence—the sense that George Harris's words exist at the boundary of abstract speech and embodied action—Hentz is able to associate Brainard with the threat of physical violence and the tyrant's reliance on force.

Even more fundamentally, Hentz deliberately uses the word "fugitive" to refer to Brainard (for example, 302). Although he is a fugitive from justice, seeking to evade the consequences of his actions, rather than a fugitive from tyranny, seeking a spot of safety, the word seems particularly pointed, fleeing as he does from South to North and then "testifying" to the horrors he "witnessed." Indeed, the climactic scene of his exposure at an antislavery rally can productively be read as rewriting the possibility that would have hung over antislavery lectures like those of Frederick Douglass before his freedom was purchased—the possibility that agents of his master would appear and, with the law on their side, remand Douglass to slavery. In Hentz's rewriting, the "fugitive" Brainard is exposed as he is speaking, the Southerner who had gone unnoticed in the audience comes forward, and even the unfaithful slave, Vulcan, who has been accompanying Brainard on the lecture circuit, gives "testimony" against him. Beginning "to feel the insecurity of his situation," Brainard appeals to the respected abolitionist Mr. Hastings "for redress, and protection from insult and outrage," but Hastings refuses him "the shield of his protection," saying, "I have no protection to offer an imposter and a liar" (324).

There are other scenes in the novel—such as the flight of the slave Crissy—that more obviously aim to empty the antislavery narrative of the fugitive slave seeking sanctuary in the North of its iconic significance. Related from a point of view we have come to recognize as typical proslavery propaganda, Crissy's escape is engineered by abolitionists who have manipulated her into thinking herself deprived, and tempted her with false visions of freedom in the North. But Hentz's description of her midnight crossing of the Ohio River—a scene laden with antislavery significance—adds this crucial detail: Crissy "had no outer covering to shield her from the night-damps,—her guardian and protector had not thought of that; why should he?" (162). Like Hentz's account of Brainard's exposure, this description casts the fugitive slave's flight in exactly the same terms Stowe and other antislavery writers use so successfully: as a drama of protection. What is decisive, of course, is Hentz's rearrangement of the elements in the drama. We need only recall Eliza Harris, after her harrowing escape and flight across the icy Ohio River, finding refuge in the warm and bountiful home of Rachel Halliday, to see how Stowe employs a drama of protection to narrate the plight of the fugitive slave. In the presence of Rachel's "ample, motherly form," we are told, Eliza experiences her first feelings of "security and rest" since embarking on her flight (158). Hentz, by contrast, conceives the slave's journey as moving from a loving home to homelessness and desolation, from parental kindness to an anonymous "guardian" who has no reason to care about her comfort. Hentz's ironic use of "protector" to refer to this callous and selfish man, who leaves Crissy exposed to the "night-damps" when he himself is dressed warmly, mirrors her larger project of hollowing out the standard antislavery motif of the fugitive slave who finds sanctuary in the North. Similarly, the abolitionist Hastings's refusal to offer "the shield of his protection" to the fugitive Brainard depicts the antislavery North not as a place of security, but as a place of exposure. In both cases, protection turns out to be a false promise—in the first instance, because it is a promise the abolitionist never intends to keep; in the second instance, because the fugitive's entreaty is reduced to a cynical ploy to evade the consequences of his crimes.

If Hentz challenges the antislavery drama of protection by questioning its assumptions about who really is in need of protection and where it can really be found, she also constructs her own positive drama of protection—one that anticipates the arguments for Jim Crow laws and lynching that become common later in the century. Clearly, the need to protect Southern families against the threat of slave insurrection is one such drama. But I would argue that a minor episode from Eulalia's past—recounted twice in the novel—is even more illuminating. Eulalia, the bride of the title, is the daughter of the abolitionist Hastings. Shortly before the events that open the novel, Hastings encountered a fugitive slave while he was traveling, "took him at once under his protection," and brought him into his home (22). Soon, however, Hastings's error became apparent: Eulalia fell ill, the slave grew "insolent and overbearing," and Hastings was "compelled to turn him out of the house" (23). As Mr. Brooks tells it, "since then, [Hastings] has had a double bolt fastened to his doors; and his dreams, I suspect, are haunted by black specters, armed and equipped for murder and robbery" (23). The story's significance, I would suggest, lies in the significance of the doors to Hastings's home. When Hastings opens his doors to the runaway slave, he leaves his family defenseless to the slave's pernicious influence; then he must expel the slave and lock the doors in order to restore his family's security. To protect the slave is to endanger the white family. In one respect, then, the doors are simply a self-evident symbol of household security: when they are open, the family is vulnerable; when they are locked, the family is safe. But the common-sense quality of the doors in this reading masks the way they also function as a barrier to racial mixing—in particular, to what will come to be known as "social equality." When Hastings opens his doors to the slave, what really happens is that he admits him on terms of equality, eliminating the protective barriers that maintain the racial hierarchy and, in particular, deny black men access to white daughters. Hence Eulalia's illness registers as contamination, the fear that her racial purity will be compromised. Moreland's later retelling of the episode makes it explicit: Eulalia's "intuitive delicacy and purity felt the contamination," he says, "and withered under its influence" (94). The doors are not simply barriers that protect the family's physical security; they also signify the laws and customs that maintain white supremacy and protect racial purity.

In the broadest sense, both sides in this argument over slavery make their case by claiming a particular vulnerability that is worthy of civic protection. For Stowe it is the slave family, the ties of marriage and parenthood that are legally liable to be torn apart at any moment, and especially the slave father's capacity to protect and provide for his wife and children; for Hentz it is racial purity, which she figures as both a positive good and also endangered by the abolitionists who naively open their doors to fugitive slaves and "take [them] under [their] protection." Indeed, I would suggest that unless whiteness is seen as both precious and delicate, under siege by an aggressive and invasive enemy, it cannot function as a justification for the laws of racial segregation and repression. Hentz, writing to defend the institution of slavery, has to be careful not to identify the threat as issuing simply from blackness. After all, proslavery rhetoric was equally invested in figuring the black slave as vulnerable and in need of the master's protection. So blackness is a threat in *The Planter's Northern Bride* only when it is incompetently or inadequately governed: in Moreland's commanding presence, the threat miraculously evaporates.[29] And most importantly, blackness is a threat when it is admitted on socially equal terms, when the protective barriers to racial mixing are relaxed and white daughters are put at risk.

Nevertheless, we can see in Hentz's answer to Stowe just how much both of their rhetorical strategies depend on maintaining the elements in a favorable tension, and just how easily they can slip into a position that potentially aids the other side. Stowe must demonstrate George's complete legal vulnerability without rendering him helpless to act nonviolently and incapable of rational deliberation; she must make his desperate words appear to cross over into the realm of embodied action so as to heighten their urgency rather than to trigger violence. Likewise, Hentz has to maintain a delicate balance between depicting the institution of slavery as a paternalistic sanctuary for the slave and depicting it as a security apparatus, designed to protect white purity and maintain an absolute racial hierarchy; between depicting the slave as deserving of the master's protection and depicting him as potentially treacherous. Placed into dialogue with each other, Hentz and Stowe illuminate both the power and the fundamental instability of rhetorics of protection. Both sides in this particular debate over slavery wish to claim a vulnerable embodiment without sacrificing the possibility of a peaceful outcome; both sides depict themselves as susceptible to violence, but unwilling to engage in violence except for purely defensive purposes. And both authors ultimately rely on dubious plot elements to bear out their claims. Stowe engineers George's escape without the infliction of significant violence (the slave catcher Tom suffers a flesh wound, which eventually leads him to live a better life). Hentz neutralizes the threat of insurrection while the slave owner Moreland—despite his supreme indignation—remains almost superhumanly restrained. At one point Moreland "[draws] forth the knife concealed in his bosom, . . . suffer[s] the moonlight to gleam upon it, . . . [and] shudder[s] at the temptation he had momentarily felt, to bury it in the false heart of Brainard" (299–300). If we are tempted to snicker at plot elements that appear so transparently contrived, it should also remind us how easily the momentum of the argument could be made to press in the other direction.

The antebellum debate over slavery has often been seen in terms of the conflict between liberty and security that liberalism supposedly generates. Abolitionism, the argument goes, was interested in widening the zone of liberty by extending it to slaves, while the defenders of slavery feared that freeing the slaves would result in general lawlessness, and saw the controls inherent in the institution of slavery as necessary to their own security. I would suggest that this way of framing the debate is inadequate. Figured negatively, liberty is itself necessarily dependent upon a system of security: in order for liberty to flourish, tyranny must be restrained, and so the antislavery promotion of liberty was equally invested in establishing and maintaining mechanisms of restraint and control. In other words, what from one perspective looks like protection, from another perspective will look like the exercise of power. Moreover, the abolitionist cause was engaged, on the one hand, not only in figuratively securing the abstract principle "liberty," but also in establishing physical security for the slaves. On the other hand, the proslavery cause foresaw in the end of slavery not just a general lawlessness but also a diminution of personal liberties. Even George Fitzhugh, who elsewhere explicitly took the side of security against liberty, warned that the campaign to abolish slavery would eventually threaten virtually every aspect of private life: "First domestic slavery," he wrote, "next religious institutions, then separate property, then political government, and, finally, family government and family relations, are to be swept away" (190). Here Fitzhugh characterizes the proslavery cause as the defender of what he considers the most sacred individual liberties: the freedom to worship as one chooses, to own and protect one's home, and to preserve the integrity of one's family. The obvious answer to Fitzhugh's claim would be that these are precisely the liberties that the slave is denied. But I wish to take a step back from the argument itself to ask how it is framed. Liberty and security do not appear here as opposing goods that need to be balanced against each other; rather, it is only when liberty is convincingly portrayed as in need of security that it can function as the basis for either the pro- or antislavery argument. Each side in this debate is trying to represent its own interests as endangered and worthy of legal protection, and the other side's interests as aggressive, invasive, and out of control.

THE COURTROOM AND THE SWAMP

Stowe's *Dred: A Tale of the Great Dismal Swamp*, published two years after Hentz's *The Planter's Northern Bride*, contemplates more directly than *Uncle Tom's Cabin* the possibility of violent insurrection. Like the scenes in *The Heroic Slave* and *Clotel*, *Dred* brings an ideal of protected citizenship into a charged tension with the slave's complete lack of legal protections, identifying that tension explicitly with Jefferson's Declaration of Independence and its justification of armed rebellion. Moreover, in keeping with liberalism's fascination with spatial metaphors, *Dred* represents that tension spatially, with the courtroom symbolizing the exclusionary ideal of abstract, civic deliberation, and the Great Dismal Swamp symbolizing a kind of alternative civic space. Excluded from the public sphere and denied the conditions for citizenship, the slaves retreat into the swamp, where they establish a meeting place whose rules turn the rules that govern the court upside down.

After fleeing to the swamp with his wife to escape the brutality of his new master-brother, Harry Gordon writes Clayton a letter defending his action. "I am now an outcast," he writes. "I cannot show my face in the world, I cannot go abroad by daylight; for no crime, as I can see, except resisting oppression" (544). His only hope of protection lies in becoming, like Dred, invisible to the white world; like Dred's disembodied voice on the last night of the camp meeting, the letter delivers its message of outrage and injury by virtue of its abstraction from Harry's person, the path by which it made its way to Clayton untraceable. But the swamp is a fraught space of protection, secure only because of its savage inaccessibility to whites, Dred's encampment "an island of security . . . amidst the wild and desolate swamp" (631). In stark contrast to Jefferson's independent yeoman farmer, the escaped slaves of the Great Dismal Swamp choose their spot because of its *un*suitability for cultivation. It is a region, the narrator explains, "of hopeless disorder, where the abundant growth and vegetation of nature, sucking up its forces from the humid soil, seems to rejoice in a savage exuberance, and bid defiance to all human effort either to penetrate or subdue" (275). It is precisely because this land will not support the kind of agrarian citizenship that Jefferson celebrates that the outcasts can find thereon a problematic security: more than simply undesirable to whites, the swamp seems actively to resist the labor essential to establishing a secure and prosperous domestic order, the foundation of liberal citizenship. And if classic liberalism envisions the law as the boundary that marks off the space of protected citizenship, here is a space that protects by virtue of its defiant lawlessness.

Harry continues his letter to Clayton by itemizing the differences between the slave's condition and that of the white American revolutionaries. "Their wives and families were never touched," he writes. "They were not bought, and sold, and traded, like cattle in the market, as we are" (544). But, like Douglass's Madison Washington and Brown's George, he does so not to diminish, by contrast, the significance of his own resistance to oppression, but to argue that the slave actually has a more authentic claim to American revolutionary status than did the founding fathers. "I have studied the Declaration of Independence," he writes. "The things mentioned there were bad and uncomfortable, to be sure; but, after all, look at the laws which are put over *us!* Now, if they had forbidden them to teach their children to read,—if they had divided them all out among masters, and declared them incapable of holding property as the mule before the plough,—there would have been some sense in that revolution" (544). If the Declaration bases the legitimacy of its claim to armed rebellion on the magnitude of the injuries suffered under the tyrant, then by its own logic American slaves have a vastly more legitimate claim to rebellion than did the American colonists. That George Washington is perceived as a more legitimate revolutionary than Denmark Vesey, Harry argues, is due solely to Washington's success, not to the underlying validity of the cause. Following the conventional pattern in abolitionist rhetoric, he envisions "Vesey and Peter Poyas, and all those other brave, good men," with the rest of the plantation's assembled slaves, being read the Declaration of Independence on the Fourth of July, and "dar[ing] to follow your example and your precepts" (545). And, as in representations as far back as *The Columbian Orator,* he envisions the white Southerners, incapable of comprehending Vesey's motive, shaking their heads and pointing out that he was well fed and clothed. "Well," Harry replies, "had not your people clothes enough, and food enough? and wouldn't you still have had enough, even if you had remained a province of England to this day?" (545).

Significantly, Harry's use of the example of the American Revolution, and in particular the Declaration of Independence, allows him to shift the focus of discussion from the slave's fitness for citizenship to the "injuries and insults" he has suffered (545). In as profoundly racist a society as the mid-nineteenth-century United States, few would have been willing to see Denmark Vesey as George Washington's equal in leadership or intellect. But when the point of comparison is the magnitude of the injustice and injuries inflicted by the regime they were fighting to overthrow, the resemblance can be convincing even to someone who believes in white superiority. The proslavery claim that slaves are unfit for independence is simply not at issue here, just as the colonists' capacity for self-government is not part of the Declaration's rationale, only the British government's failure to secure the colonists' rights to life, liberty, and the pursuit of happiness. And when Harry imagines himself arguing with a defender of slavery, it is not about the ability of slaves, but rather the failure of the institution to recognize that slaves, as human beings, have rights worthy of protection. Once the argument turns to the feeding and clothing of slaves, it has already become an argument about protection: the question is how well slaveholders have lived up to their paternalistic responsibility to defend their slaves against the threats of cold and starvation. It is then but a short step for Harry to suggest that there are regions of life aside from the mere bodily that are worthy of preservation, and injuries that are not always registered physically—injuries that the slaveholders, like George III, have inflicted on precisely those subjects they were paternalistically bound to protect.

But Harry's emphasis on the ways in which slaves have been thwarted in their desire for a degree of security for themselves and their families does more than just shift the focus of the argument away from the racist presumption of black inferiority. It enables him actually to recast such thinking into a powerful argument for the abolition of slavery. Viewed against the classical conception of the republican citizen—a property owner, educated, capable of defending his home and family from attack, and therefore entitled to a share in public life—Harry's description of the slave amounts to a systematic denial of the essential qualifications for citizenship. Not only is the slave "declared . . . incapable of holding property as the mule before the plough," he is also "sold, and traded" as property. He is "forbidden . . . to teach [his] children to read" and ever at risk of having his wife and family abused or taken. And Harry's own circumstance, banned from "show[ing his] face in the world" and unable to "go abroad by daylight," is the negation of the citizen's guaranteed privilege of public participation. In other words, what defenders of slavery cite as the reasons that slaves cannot be citizens, Harry recasts as the systematic exclusion of slaves from citizenship, an exclusion established and enforced by the laws of the land. Seen in light of Harry's logic, Dred's transient community of outcasts in the Great Dismal Swamp—denied the conditions for establishing a privatized domestic realm and an individuated selfhood—offers a vivid representation of the slave's position in American life. It is only because it cannot sustain a self-sufficient farm and homestead in the American style that the land is available to them, and only because the laws of the land cannot extend into in the swamp that these outlaws have a degree of security. And yet their desire for home and safety is continually evident in their determined, but ultimately futile, efforts to establish them in this wild and inhospitable place.

Shortly after writing his letter to Clayton, Harry receives the tragic news that his sister had been sold and, in desperation, has killed her two children. With his future growing ever bleaker, and Lisette his only strong tie to the world, he and Dred discuss the impending midnight assembly of slaves and fugitives. "When they come to-night," says Dred, "read them the Declaration of Independence of these United States, and then let each one judge of our afflictions, and the afflictions of their fathers, and the Lord shall be the judge between us" (564). Echoing Harry's implication that, when judged on the magnitude of their injuries, the slaves are more justified in rebelling against their oppressive government than were the Founding Fathers, Dred's emphasis on "afflictions" offers both a means of cultivating righteous anger and a way of legitimizing their rebellion by invoking America's founding text. That night the conspirators gather around the grave of a fugitive slave who was torn apart by the slave catchers' dogs, and Harry tells them about the Founders, who "resolved that they would be free" and "signed a paper, which was to show all the world the reason why. You have heard this read by them when the drums were beating and the banners flying," he tells them. "Now hear it here, while you sit on the graves of men they have murdered!" (567). After reading the text—which he refers to as "the grievances which our masters thought sufficient to make it right for them to shed blood"—Harry charges them with judging for themselves whose grievances are worse (568). And what follows is the spontaneous, heartrending testimony of the assembled slaves, stories of families torn apart and slaves tortured and brutally murdered, all sanctioned by law, leaving no doubt which way the judgment must fall.

At this moment in the novel, we can see the tension between the ideal of protected citizenship and the spectacle of injury—the tension at the very heart of liberal civics—reaching a crisis point, the point at which there appears to be no outlet other than violence. When the "quadroon young man" tells the other conspirators the story of his mother, who "begged [her master] to protect her" from a certain unscrupulous man, but instead of protecting her he sold her and she "went crazy," we can see, surely, the grave injury that was done to this precious life and the master's appalling callousness to the woman whom we might assume is the mother of his child (569). But we can also see the absolute inefficacy of the slave's speech, the denial of a just hearing for her grievances, and the ultimate loss of her capacity to reason. It is a graphic illustration of the slave's systematic exclusion from the realm wherein conflict can be resolved through reasoned negotiation, through persuasion rather than force. The avenue whereby she should have been able to petition for a remedy turns out to be the very instrument of her undoing. The incident dramatizes in the extreme Jefferson's claim in the Declaration that "in every stage of these oppressions we have petitioned for redress in the most humble terms: our repeated petitions have been answered only by repeated injuries" (Jefferson 22). Clearly, the implications here are problematic for Stowe's gradualist politics. Not only does the scene vividly demonstrate, by enlisting this slave's eloquent testimony in support of their "right . . . to shed blood," that such eloquence always threatens to spill over into the realm of violence. It also, by incorporating this story of violated womanhood and aggrieved motherhood into a clandestine meeting of insurgents, exposes the problematic and unstable alliance between the sentimental response and outrage. What in *Uncle Tom's Cabin* could be contained by the reader's tears at Tom's saintly forgiveness of his tormentors, and her relief at George Harris's eventual escape, here—despite the similarities in their stories of suffering and injury—seems closer to a call for armed rebellion.

Scenes in which slaves are precluded from defending themselves through reasoned argument are common in antislavery literature, and do occasionally lead directly to violence: we need only think of the incident in Douglass's *Narrative* when he petitions his master for protection from Covey's brutality, the denial of which results in his and Covey's epic battle. But probably the clearest illustration of their exclusion from civic life is the fact that their testimony was generally inadmissible in Southern courts, and the parallel plotline in this portion of Stowe's novel develops this theme of the slave's unprotected status from the perspective of North Carolina law. After being beaten and shot by the man to whom she had been contracted, Milly returns to Canema and Clayton agrees to bring her case to court. He comes to see it as a test case for his vision of reform, intending to use it, as he says, "to prove the efficacy of the law in behalf of that class of our population whose helplessness places them more particularly under our protection" (382). In the trial Clayton's eloquent portrayal of the events "carrie[s] the whole of his audience with him," and the jury decides the case unanimously in Milly's favor (389). Just as *The Columbian Orator* contends that "the compassionate lawyer [who] . . . advocates the cause of the suffering widow, or injured orphan, . . . *must* be eloquent," so Clayton's defense of Milly succeeds by appealing to the powerful desire to protect the helpless and vulnerable (Bingham 247, emphasis in original).[30] His eloquence arises directly from the spectacle of Milly's legal vulnerability, from what Clayton emphasizes as her "*entire dependence*," manifested in "the fact that [she] has no refuge from our power" (Stowe, *Dred* 388, emphasis in original). Moreover, the absence of a "refuge" from physical violence is mirrored in Milly's exclusion from the refuge of the court, in the fact that Clayton must find white witnesses who can testify in her behalf. The strategy is consummate in its circularity: Clayton grounds Milly's legal defense in her defenselessness, and his eloquence before the court depends upon her legally mandated silence.[31]

Not surprisingly the judgment in Milly's favor is shortly overturned on appeal, in a decision rendered by Clayton's own father. Judge Clayton's logic, based on the actual 1829 opinion in *State v. Mann,* written by Justice Thomas Ruffin for the North Carolina Supreme Court,[32] bears an uncanny resemblance to Clayton's in its repeated emphasis on the slave's absolute subjugation to the master's will. As Clayton portrays the slave as having "no refuge from our power," so his father stresses the master's "uncontrolled authority over the [slave's] body." "The power of the master must be absolute," he contends, "to render the submission of the slave perfect" (448). But whereas Clayton reasons that the slave's powerlessness entitles him to protection under the law, his father points out that to grant the slave legal protection is to undermine the master's absolute authority. "We cannot allow the right of the master to be brought into discussion in the courts of justice," he says. "The slave, to remain a slave, must be made sensible that there is no appeal from his master" (449). Judge Clayton's argument reveals and explicates the conflict between an ideal of civic protection and an ideal of mastery: the master's autonomy *requires* that the slave have no refuge from his power, for any legal protection accorded the slave necessarily constitutes an intrusion into the master's domain. At issue are the criteria for admission to the courtroom and entitlement to legal protection: where Edward Clayton would admit human beings on the basis of their vulnerability to injury and their lack of any other means of self-defense, the judge would admit only masters. And when Judge Clayton claims that "the right of the master [must not] be brought into discussion," he is merely invoking one of the law's most elemental functions, that of delineating and enforcing the boundaries of essential selfhood, across which no authority can trespass, and within which there can be no compromise. Both arguments, moreover, emphasize the slave's utter defenselessness, the father's so as to justify the slave's exclusion from civic life, the son's so as to appeal to the jury's desire to protect a helpless thing. "I had hoped," says Clayton, responding to his father's decision and bitterly declaring his retirement from the legal profession, "that [slavery's] laws were capable of being administered as to protect the defenceless. This illusion is destroyed. I see but too clearly now the purpose and object of the law" (450). As the judge explains it, of course, the "purpose and object" of the law *is* protective: it is to ensure "*the security of the master and the public tranquility*" (450, emphasis in original). But it protects the slaveholders and the status quo at the expense of those whom

Clayton sees as the most vulnerable members of the society. To the extent that the very idea of protection imagines the defense of the weaker party against the stronger, then, Judge Clayton's ruling appears perverse, a distortion of the protective impulse into something whose effect is to shield the perpetrators of gross brutalities from having to answer for their crimes. The judge's ruling appropriates the language of protection in order to sanction mastery—which, as Judge Clayton affirms, necessarily entails the forcible subjugation of the slave—and in order to screen the conduct of masters from public scrutiny and public judgment.

This rhetorically charged moment in which protection is transformed from a defense of the vulnerable into a safe hiding place for wrongdoers is evident elsewhere in Stowe's fiction. In *Uncle Tom's Cabin,* for example, we are shown that the same law that exposes George Harris to abuse also protects those who profit from the institution of slavery. The very ideal of protection—a sacred cause from George's perspective—is corrupted when it is the slaveholder who is being shielded from accountability for his crimes. When George first learns that he is being pursued by slave catchers, and that the slave catchers are authorized in their actions by the Fugitive Slave Law, we are asked to imagine what a man might look like "whose wife was to be sold at auction, and son sent to a trader, all under the shelter of a Christian nation's laws" (244). We can clearly hear the ironic hollowing out of the word "Christian"; I would add that the word "shelter" is ironized here as well. A shelter evokes a feeling of safety from impending danger, a warm and dry harbor from a raging storm. But here we get a jarring inversion of those connotations: it is not the man whose family is to be torn apart, but rather his persecutors that are being "sheltered," as though the storm were given protection in its errand of battering the helpless victims. The shelter has become a harbor for violence and iniquity, a hiding place wherein villains can protect themselves from the consequences of their immoral actions.

A similar moment occurs in *Dred* as the slave Monday testifies at the midnight meeting of the conspirators. After Harry reads the Declaration of Independence and recounts the events of Milly's trial—"that judicial decision which had burned itself into his memory, and which had confirmed and given full license to that despotic power"—Monday rises to tell his brother Sam's story (569). Sold to "white trash" to pay off wedding debts, Sam was accused of theft by his new master; as punishment he was tied up and cut, slashed, hacked, burned, and scalded until finally he died. The case was taken to court, the master found guilty of second-degree murder and sentenced to five years in prison, but the conviction was overturned in the upper court. As Monday explains, "dey said 'dat it had been settled, dat dere couldn't be noting done agin a mas'r fur no kind of beating or 'busing of der own slaves. Dat de master must be protected, even if 't was ever so cruel" (570). Lapsing momentarily into Standard English, Monday echoes the court's pledge to protect the master and—as the narrator of *Uncle Tom's Cabin* does with "the shelter of a Christian nation's laws"—renders it bitterly ironic. But here it is more than just the concept of protection that is ironized: we have, in effect, two parallel versions of civic space. There is the courtroom, which admits only masters to its protective zone and sanctions violence against those who are excluded, and there is the "refuge" of the Dismal Swamp, inhabited by those who are without any legal protection. Both are spaces where witnesses are called, testimony is given, and judgments are made; indeed, dark, insecure and ghostly, the latter can be seen as a negative version of the former.[33] By the standards of the courtroom, everything that transpires in the swamp is illegitimate. But by the standards of the novel, it is the courtroom that has corrupted not only the ideal of protection but also the ideal of justice itself—the very ideal it was established to uphold.

In *Race, Slavery, and Liberalism in Nineteenth-Century America,* Arthur Riss takes issue with the commonly held assumption that a progressive political agenda requires an abstract model of "personhood" in which gendered and racialized elements of identity necessarily exist apart from the self that participates freely and equally in civic affairs. He offers Harriet Beecher Stowe as an example of a writer who represents slaves as "persons" worthy of civic protection and, at the same time, as having essential racial characteristics. In a reading of George Harris's letter defending his decision to settle in Liberia, for example, Riss contends that George declines a home in the United States—despite what George calls "the claim of an injured race for reparation"—because he does not conceive of citizenship apart from his racial identity (80–81). In fact, Riss argues, George's reference to "reparation" marks the turning point in his logic, from a "rhetoric of equal rights" to reasoning that more closely resembles affirmative action, in which discriminations based on race are fully compatible with a vision of social justice. Like Riss, I read Stowe's abolitionism not as an effort to represent slaves as capable of self-abstraction, but rather as proposing an alternative version of civic space. And to the extent that a racialized embodiment signifies one's vulnerability to injury—and therefore entitles one to, as George says, "the claim of an injured race"—we might see what Riss identifies as "the distance between Stowe's racialist understanding of human rights and the formalism of contemporary liberalism" in the distance between the swamp and the courtroom (81). At issue is what it is that entitles one to recognition. From the perspective of the court, Milly has no "personhood" that is worthy of recognition because she does not exist independently of her master: her body is entirely subject to his will.

From the perspective of the swamp, however, it is precisely the helplessness of a slave like Milly that entitles her to "the claim of an injured race."

Nevertheless, Stowe clearly does not propose the swamp as a model to be emulated; she does not, in other words, abandon the ideal of a civic realm that protects the vulnerable. Rather, we can see the force of Stowe's argument in the tension between courtroom and swamp, each one bringing into relief what is lacking in the other, and each one representing the other's desire. If the swamp lacks the legal protections and the legal legitimacy of the courtroom, the courtroom lacks the compassion and the capacity for human empathy of the swamp. Stowe does give us glimpses of an ideal synthesis—in the initial verdict in Milly's favor, which is subsequently overturned by Judge Clayton, for example, and in the scene in *Uncle Tom's Cabin* where Senator Bird rethinks his support of the Fugitive Slave Law in the presence of Eliza and her little boy. The problem with public deliberation as Senator Bird had conceived it, Stowe's narrator explains, is that it is too abstract: "his idea of a fugitive was only the idea of the letters that spell the word" (100–101). If the abstraction of language enables nonviolent public deliberation, it also promotes a cold rationality and an insensitivity to human suffering. The "real presence of distress," we are told—"the imploring human eye, the frail, trembling human hand, the despairing appeal of helpless agony"—works a kind of "magic" on the good senator, revealing to him that true justice must also have a sentimental component (101). The dynamic field in which arguments like Stowe's are advanced, then, holds out two promises: the promise of safety for the vulnerable, and the promise of what we might call sentimental vulnerability for the safe. And the force of the argument is in the sustained tension between the two versions of public participation and the dual impulses it creates, the movement toward the other. Inasmuch as the two promises tend to undo each other, the distinction has to be maintained. But inasmuch as the positions are hardened into an absolute opposition—inasmuch as the protected abstraction of the courtroom and the legal vulnerability of the swamp become mutually exclusive—the chance of a peaceful resolution to the problem of slavery is severely diminished.

It is this latter possibility that is contemplated with horror in Stowe's *Dred.* As I have suggested, the novel reaches a potential impasse at the scene of the midnight meeting: Clayton's reformist project of finding within the courts legal recourse for Milly's injury has failed miserably, the final decision making absolutely clear their complete exclusion from the law's protective agency, and the plot seems to be racing inevitably toward violent insurrection. The swelling chorus of stories of injury, the slaveholders in each case protected from having to answer for their brutality—as compelling as it is rhetorically—simply leaves no possible outcome other than violence or submission. To exclude the slaves entirely from civic protections is to cut off any possibility of a nonviolent resolution; it is to condemn them to a life of pure embodiment. As the meeting reaches its crescendo, Dred rejects Hannibal's call for vengeance, asserting that their righteous army will neither torture their masters nor defile their women. "But we will slay them utterly," he declares, "and consume them from off the face of the earth!" (575). The deus ex machina appears in the form of Milly, singing "in a wild and mournful tone" of the loving Lamb of Calvary bleeding and dying on the cross (575). Her desperate plea to them to forgive their injuries and "love yer enemies" succeeds in putting a temporary stop to the insurrection— "Woman, thy prayers have prevailed for this time!" says Dred. "The hour is not yet come!" (577). But the Christian vision of spiritual transcendence through bodily suffering is ultimately no more capable of bringing this American story to a satisfactory resolution than it is George Harris's in *Uncle Tom's Cabin*. For both Harry and George the only solution is exile, communities that afford them civic protections and secure domestic lives outside the boundaries of the United States.

DECLARATIONS OF IRONY

As a rhetorical figure that draws its energy from a jarring disjunction of words and meaning, irony offered antislavery activists a powerful means of exposing slaveholders' hypocrisy. However, when Samuel Johnson famously asked how it is "that we hear the loudest *yelps* for liberty among the drivers of negroes," he was not simply highlighting the hypocrisy of tyrants who would presume to cry for liberty. By putting "*yelps*" into the mouths of the slave drivers, he was also mocking those who falsely claim injury and exposing them as actually having inflicted injury on the defenseless. Johnson's irony capitalizes on the unresolved tension at the heart of declarations of independence: the tension between the protective abstraction of public discourse and the grievances that such documents catalog. We can see a similar use of irony in William Lloyd Garrison's 4 July 1829, speech to the American Colonization Society. "Every Fourth of July," he said, "our Declaration of Independence is produced, with a sublime indignation, to set forth the tyranny of the mother country, and to challenge the admiration of the world. But what a pitiful detail of grievances does this document present, in comparison with the wrongs which our slaves endure!" (Lowance 99). Like Stowe's Harry Gordon, here Garrison suggests that the magnitude of the slaves' grievances gives them a more legitimate claim to rebellion than the American colonists had. But Garrison's statement also mocks the founders' tone of "sublime indignation," and their anticipation of the world's admiration, in light of their "pitiful grievances." Its dual effect is both to elevate the slaves' cause and to diminish the founders' and, especially, its ritual reiteration every Fourth of July. If writers like Phillips and Stowe appropriate the Declaration's earnest patriotism and indignation for the antislavery movement, Garrison's ironic rendering empties it out. Moreover, like Samuel Johnson's, Garrison's critique plays on the tension between protection and vulnerability characteristic of liberal civics: to point out the hypocrisy of those who would indignantly claim injuries from a position of relative safety is to expose the underlying ambiguity on which declarations of independence depend. Taken to its extreme, it would delegitimize the speech of protected citizens and turn the public sphere as it was delineated by the founders inside out.

This section will consider how irony was strategically deployed in antislavery rhetoric in response to the two general problems I described in my readings of Stowe. The first problem is how to identify the antislavery cause with the cause of negative liberty, and thereby to recognize the slave as having rights that are both worthy of and in need of protection. This is the general project in which we can see both Johnson and Garrison engaged: diminishing one's opponents' claims to represent an endangered liberty complements one's claiming it for oneself. The impact of both the argument and the irony is still greater if, like Johnson, one can at the same time identify one's opponents as the true tyrants. But there is also a problem with too rigid or unyielding an identification: one must avoid, to follow Stowe's metaphor, getting stuck in the Great Dismal Swamp. The relation between protection and vulnerability must be a dynamic one; they must neither collapse into each other, nor harden into a mutually exclusive opposition. The possibility of safety for the vulnerable must not be foreclosed, nor can the protected be allowed to become too comfortable. It is largely in the service of this second imperative, I will argue, that Frederick Douglass uses irony in his 1852 speech "What to the Slave Is the Fourth of July?" repeatedly turning his own position of exteriority into an opportunity for a renewed vision of inclusiveness, which is, in turn, opened up to critique. For Douglass irony entails not just the hollowing out of proslavery discursive tropes, but a kind of negative dialectics, a progressive de-signifying and re-signifying, turning to his advantage the dynamics of the very discursive realm from which he was excluded.[34]

Before turning to Douglass, however, I wish to examine the function of irony in Horace Mann's 1850 "Speech on the Subject of Slavery in the Territories."

Despite having long been associated with the antislavery movement, Mann had generally tried to avoid weighing in on the slavery question during his first two years in Congress. However, in response to Henry Clay's proposed Compromise of 1850, Mann embraced the antislavery cause with a vengeance, delivering to the House of Representatives a biting indictment of slavery and of America's failure to implement the principles of the Declaration of Independence.[35] Incorporating both direct and indirect references to the Declaration and the nation's founding, the speech offers an apocalyptic vision of America's immediate future if the Compromise were to become law. Like John Winthrop's "A Modell of Christian Charity," in which he imagined "the eies of all people . . . vppon vs," and the Declaration itself, which asserted "a decent respect to the opinions of mankind" and explicitly "appeal[ed] to the supreme judge of the world," Mann envisions "the civilized nations of the earth" as "a ring of lookers-on" (Miller and Johnson 199; Jefferson 23, 19; Mann 201).[36] "All civilized men stand around us," he told Congress. "It is an august spectacle." But while Winthrop hoped New England would prove to be an example to all people, and the Declaration anticipated a world that was potentially sympathetic to its cause, Mann vividly describes the reverse: "When new chains are forged and riveted, when new realms are subdued by haughty taskmasters, and overrun by imbruted slaves, do their plaudits greet your ears and rouse you to more vehement efforts? All the reverse; totally the reverse. They are now looking on with disgust and abhorrence. They groan, they mock, they hiss. The brightest pages of their literature portray you, as covered with badges of dishonor; their orators hold up your purposes as objects for the execration of mankind; their wits hurl the lightnings of satire at your leaders" (201). Citing Adam Smith's *Theory of Moral Sentiments,* Mann points out that "the judgment of men" plays a role in enforcing norms of conduct by producing either "the pleasure of being approved, or the pain of being disapproved" (201). But the "august spectacle" he describes in this passage goes far beyond mere disapproval: with jeremiad-like intensity, he imagines his fellow members of Congress as objects of "disgust and abhorrence," the civilized nations forming a menacing ring around them, hissing and mocking their hypocritical claim to be part of the civilized world. *The Scarlet Letter*—which Mann's brother-in-law Nathaniel Hawthorne would publish about a month later— depicted a spectacle of public shaming that was believed, "in the old time, to be as effectual an agent in the promotion of good citizenship, as ever was the guillotine among the terrorists of France" (59). Hawthorne's irony aside, the suggestion that there is an undercurrent of violence in these rituals of public shaming applies equally well to the scene Mann describes. With its figurative hurling of lightning bolts, Mann's scene is closer to a vengeful fantasy of divine retribution than it is to the polite, international court of public opinion that the Declaration imagines.

From one perspective, we can see this strategy of shaming the slaveholder as the counterpart to the strategy of enlisting sympathy for the slave. Indeed, Mann's strategy bears a certain similarity to the outrage Stowe generates at the law that protects "*the security of the master,*" as Judge Clayton in *Dred* puts it, or the master who can sell George Harris's wife and son "all under the shelter of a Christian nation's laws." If the slave's eloquence derives from his legal vulnerability, the master's shame results from his perpetration of violence with legal impunity. And if the thrust of the slave's cause is toward the establishment of protections that are currently lacking, the thrust of the master's shaming is, in two respects, toward exposure. First, figures such as Mann's imagine the slaveholder as exposed not only to the world's gaze but also to the world's derision. Mann's language—the "brightest pages," the "lightnings of satire"—suggests shining an unforgiving light onto something ordinarily in the shadows. Surrounded by the civilized nations, the slaveholder has nowhere to hide; the law may well shield him from prosecution in the courts, but cannot shield him from public scorn and condemnation. Second, the very concept of civic protection is ironized when it is tyranny that is being protected. The slaveholder's claim to the protections of citizenship is transformed from something honorable and compelling, like the founders' in the Declaration, into something cowardly and hypocritical.

In his "Speech on the Institution of Slavery," Mann then goes on to perform just such an ironic rendering of the founders' claims in the Declaration of Independence:

> We hold these truths to be self-evident, that men are not created equal; that they are not endowed by their Creator with inalienable rights; that white men, of the Anglo-Saxon race, were born to rob, and tyrannize, and enjoy, and black men, of the African race, to labor, and suffer, and obey; that a man, with a drop of African blood in his veins, has no political rights, and therefore shall never vote; that he has no pecuniary rights, and therefore whatever he may earn or receive, belongs to his master; that he has no judicial rights, and therefore he shall never be heard as a witness to redress wrong, or violence, or robbery, committed by white men upon him; that he has no parental rights, and therefore his children may be torn from his bosom, at the pleasure or caprice of his owner; that he has no marital rights, and therefore his wife may be lawfully sold away into distant bondage, or violated before his eyes; that he has no religious rights, and there-

fore he shall never read the Bible; that he has no heaven-descended, God-
given rights of freedom, and therefore he and his posterity shall be slaves
forever. We hold that governments were instituted among men to secure
and fortify this ascendancy of one race over another. (216)

Here we see the familiar list of grievances, amounting to the absolute exclusion
of black men from participating in the nation's civic life and the destruction of
their private life. But by incorporating the slaves' grievances into the Declaration's statement of principles, this passage assumes a very different tone. The
antislavery and women's rights declarations, as well as the original on which they
are modeled, all clearly distinguish the cause of liberty from the force of tyranny, and all speak on behalf of a tyrannized constituency. But Mann's version
is written in the voice of the tyrant. The grievances, which in the original inspire
outrage and offend our sense of justice, are jarringly phrased as principles to be
embraced and proclaimed. Instead of defending a precious and vulnerable liberty against the encroachments of power, Mann's version asserts an aggressive
and hierarchical power, and defines it in explicitly racial terms. The effect is the
doubling of the voice characteristic of irony, the disjunction of the words' surface meaning from their ultimate significance or impact.[37] And, by emptying
the actual language of the Declaration of its meaning—by ironizing its "self-
evident truths"—Mann enacts the Compromise of 1850's betrayal of the nation's founding principles.

Ironic doubling—the form that is at odds with its content—has implications for the speaking self, for the kind of listening it requires and, more generally, for the kind of public world it posits. Unlike sincere speech with its illusion of transparency, ironic speech is deliberately insincere. This does not, of
course, mean that it is deceptive; indeed, ironic speech like Mann's is successful only inasmuch as it is seen to be insincere. Mann's listeners are supposed to
hear how the words of the Declaration have been twisted and wrenched from
their original significance, and how Mann is forced into saying something that
he finds deeply offensive. If sincere speech conveys the unity of inside and outside, ironic speech conveys the untenable coexistence of contradictory—even
warring—elements. One of the reasons this passage is so successful rhetorically,
I would suggest, is that it functions in a way that reflects the functioning of the
Fugitive Slave Law. As Mann speaks words that directly contradict his principles, so the Fugitive Slave Law would force Northerners to act in support of
an institution with which they are in profound disagreement. Both establish a
jarring disjunction between corrupted external behavior and betrayed internal
conviction.

Moreover, that disjunction is manifested in Mann's speech not only internally within the speaker but also sectionally, as the conflict between Southern
tyranny and Northern principles. It is specifically the South that has rewritten
the Declaration, changing it from a defense of liberty and equality into a profession of racial tyranny and inequality, and forcing it into the mouths of Northerners. And, in fact, the speech as a whole is haunted by the specter of civil war,
a "spectacle" Mann says he "cannot contemplate . . . without a thrill of horror"
(269). He envisions "this once glorious union . . . rifted in twain from east to
west, with a gulf between us wide and profound, save that this gulf will be filled
and heaped high with the slaughtered bodies of our countrymen" (269). As a
trope that is characterized by irreconcilable internal conflict and disunion, irony
served to represent not only Mann's personal predicament but also his apocalyptic vision of civil war. However, to imagine the ironic disjunction as the ir-
resolvable conflict between Southern law and Northern principle was to imply
that compromise would be impossible. And so Mann's speech in opposition to
the Compromise of 1850 could actually have had the effect of hastening its passage, exacerbating sectional partisanship, and convincing skeptical Southerners
that Clay's so-called compromise would actually constitute a Southern victory
(Messerli 509–19).

Frederick Douglass, too, claimed that irony was peculiarly appropriate to
the national political climate in the years following the Fugitive Slave Act. "At
a time like this," he said in his 1852 speech "What to the Slave Is the Fourth of
July?" "scorching irony, not convincing argument, is needed" (196). But despite
their common antislavery agenda, Douglass used irony for a different purpose
and to a different effect. Even though irony always has a personal dimension in
its conception of a speaker at odds with his or her speech, Mann's fundamental entitlement to participate in the national debate was never in question. As a
black man and former slave, however, Douglass faced a very different set of assumptions. Earlier in this chapter I pointed out that a slave would, by definition,
have been excluded from the public realm as it was delineated in classical republican theory. Bound to a life of bodily labor and denied a legally sanctioned
"spot of safety," a slave would have been conceived incapable of achieving the
self-abstraction necessary for independent public deliberation. Abolitionists like
Garrison and Phillips envisioned a different kind of public presence for the fugitive slave. Instead of challenging the racialized exclusivity of the classical republican model, this alternative version drew upon the slave's bodily bondage and
legal jeopardy to charge his voice with an urgency and intensity that a protected
white citizen could not achieve. Hence, to the extent that embodiment and self-
abstraction constituted a mutually exclusive opposition, the fundamental dis-

tinction between slave and free remained intact, even though—taking their cue from the Declaration of Independence—the Garrisonians radically revalued the terms.

Although he clearly recognized the exclusivity of the classical republican model, Douglass also resisted the role that the Garrisonians envisioned for him. In a much-cited passage from *My Bondage and My Freedom,* he describes John A. Collins, general agent of the Massachusetts Anti-Slavery Society, advising him to speak with "a *little* of the plantation manner," effectively urging him to play more convincingly the part of the illiterate slave. "'Tis not best that you seem too learned," explained Collins (*Autobiographies* 367).[38] Admitting that such advice was "actuated by the best of motives, and . . . not altogether wrong," Douglass nonetheless asserts his intention to "speak just the word that seemed to *me* the word to be spoken *by* me" (367, emphasis in original). We can read Douglass's desire to script his own performance as signaling his desire to challenge, rather than capitalize on, the racialized distinction of slave and free. More generally, we can see his decision to devote more of his time to editing the *North Star* than to speaking on the abolitionist lecture circuit, and even his decision to reject Garrison's view of the Constitution as a proslavery document, in light of his resistance to the way the Garrisonian abolitionists conceived his public appearance. If the Garrisonians saw a strategic advantage in establishing an embodied and legally vulnerable public persona for Douglass, these decisions can be seen as moving in the opposite direction, choosing the greater abstraction of print and envisioning the supreme law of the land as at least potentially inclusive and protective. And so Douglass found himself faced with competing models of public selfhood, neither of which he could fully embrace. At one end of the spectrum was the neoclassical version of abstract and disinterested public participation, which was historically limited to propertied white men; at the other end of the spectrum was the eloquent fugitive in search of asylum, which was defined by its exclusion from the neoclassical version and would have required Douglass, to quote Robert Fanuzzi, "to perform his exclusion from the public sphere of citizenship, which in turn became his token of inclusion" (211).

The rhetorical figure Douglass employed most often to express this unresolved contradiction between speech and enslavement was irony: whether he was the speaker who, ironically, was enslaved, or the slave who, ironically, was a speaker, the two coexisted for him as form and content that were profoundly at odds.[39] In his Fourth of July speech, Douglass repeatedly called attention to the unbridgeable gulf between himself and his audience, pointing out that his history of enslavement made it impossible for him to celebrate the nation's founding unequivocally. But the difference he identified was not simply the difference between himself as an outsider and his audience of insiders. It was also the difference between his own sharply conflicted relation to American liberty and his audience's wholehearted and unconditional devotion to it. Moreover, Douglass saw his conflicted relation to American liberty replicated in his conflicted presence before the audience. Just as his inner allegiance to liberty had been thwarted by America's history of slavery, his sense of himself as a full participant in the civic discourse had been thwarted by a white audience that saw him through their own distorted and distorting lens. His "second-sight," to apply Du Bois's phrase, revealed an untenable duality where the dominant white culture saw only one dimension. And his strategy of shifting from one formal position to another, each of which he in turn emptied out, was one way for him to challenge that fixed, one-dimensional role established for him by his white audience's gaze.

I wish to examine two specific examples in Douglass's Fourth of July speech of this progressive shifting of vantage points, looking first at his treatment of paternalistic configurations of authority. Father figures, of course, played a major role in Fourth of July rhetoric, as the tyrannical George III against whose authority the colonists rebelled, and as the founders themselves, whom Americans venerated.[40] But father figures also loomed large in pro- and antislavery discourse. Douglass himself had taken the proslavery image of the master as benevolent father figure and recast it as utterly corrupt and dysfunctional, particularly in cases where the master was also the slave's biological father. His 1845 *Narrative* notably depicted such fathers as having to choose between "sell[ing their] own children to human flesh-mongers," and standing by while "one son tie[s] up his brother . . . and [plies] the gory lash to his naked back" (*Autobiographies* 17). Moreover, Douglass was at the time engaged in establishing his own autonomy from the paternalistic authority of the Garrisonian wing of the antislavery movement. John Louis Lucaites has pointed out that, having been in the making since about 1847, Douglass's Fourth of July speech was taking shape during precisely the period of Douglass's separation from the Garrisonians (55). And probably nothing signaled that separation as deliberately as Douglass's affirmation of the Constitution as "a glorious liberty document," and his claim that Northerners had "allowed themselves to be . . . ruinously imposed upon" in believing the Constitution to be proslavery—a direct challenge to one of Garrison's core principles (204). It is in this context of fraught father-son relations, both literal and figurative, that we can read Douglass's account of the founders and the history of American independence in "What to the Slave Is the Fourth of July?" In the speech, Douglass takes a series of contrary positions that build to an ironic crescendo. In a glaring departure both from conventional Fourth of

July rhetoric and from its antislavery variations, he begins with a measured account of the colonists' break from Britain from the point of view of the British "home government": "in the exercise of its parental prerogatives, [it] impose[d] upon its colonial children, such restraints, burdens and limitations as, in its mature judgment, it deemed wise, right and proper" (190). We might expect to hear the words "mature judgment" ironically, given that the judgment being described is that of George III. But Douglass does not permit his listeners a comfortable ironic distance from the British perspective. He goes on to identify the "fashionable idea of this day"—in particular the belief in "the infallibility of government, and the absolute character of its acts"—not with the founding fathers, but with the British perspective (190). America in 1852, he suggests, has come to represent exactly the "idea" against which the founders fought, and so the real irony is to be heard in midcentury Americans' veneration of their founders. It is "exceedingly easy," Douglass says, to "discant on the tyranny of England toward the American Colonies" without really considering what such an assertion entails (190). Comparing such people to the children of Jacob, who "contented themselves under the shadow of Abraham's great name, while they repudiated the deeds which made his name great," Douglass tells his audience, "You have no right to enjoy a child's share in the labor of your fathers, unless your children are to be blest by your labors" (193). Indeed, he says, "the cause of liberty may be stabbed by the men who glory in the deeds of your fathers" (190).

The implications here are complicated. Turning the conventional Fourth of July narrative upside down, Douglass reimagines the founders as good children, respectful but unable to abide the wrongs they perceived, and his contemporaries as bad children, capitalizing on their fathers' achievements while betraying their principles. He takes issue—as we would expect—with the patriarchal ideal, the father who demands blind obedience. But he also takes issue with the sentimentalized ideal of the father as protector, who keeps the child "under the shadow of [his] great name," and its counterpart, the child who takes refuge in his father's shadow. While most of the declarations of independence I have examined in this chapter denounce fathers who have injured the children they were supposed to protect, Douglass takes issue with the very model of parental authority to which such denunciations subscribe. His depiction of paternal and filial relations shifts the focus away from the father's duty to protect his children and the son's right to his father's protection. Rather, he envisions the good father as one who sets an example by his resolute adherence to principle, and the good son as one who, like the founders, will be remembered not as a son to his father, but as a father to his sons. In an analysis of Douglass's critique of paternal-

ism in *My Bondage and My Freedom* and "The Heroic Slave," Eric J. Sundquist
has argued that Douglass creates a fictional self who "makes himself his own
father." That persona, Sundquist explains, is "composed at once of the absent
father who so absorbs his attention . . . of the black rebel-slave who leads others to freedom and converts a white audience to antislavery, and of the Founding Fathers, whose rhetoric of democratic liberty punctuates Douglass's writing
after 1848 and begins fully to flower in the break with Garrison over the proper
reading of the Constitution of the United States" ("Frederick Douglass" 124).
One aspect of the myth of the founders that so appealed to Douglass, I would
suggest, is their transformation from rebellious sons into respected fathers. As
such, they offered not only a model for Douglass's own public persona but also
a means of criticizing contemporary white Americans' contentment with bask-
ing in the glory of their founding fathers.

   In the Fourth of July speech, then, Douglass adopts what Sundquist calls the
founders' "rhetoric of democratic liberty," but only as a position from which he
can paradoxically criticize the ubiquitous Independence Day "demonstrations
of joyous enthusiasm," and never without an ironic consciousness of the slave's
exclusion (192). Indeed, no sooner does he praise the founders' "solid manhood" in adhering to the principles of liberty, than he declares himself outside
"the pale of this glorious anniversary!" "The rich inheritance of justice, liberty,
prosperity and independence, bequeathed by your fathers, is shared by you, not
by me" (194). The criticism of his audience is continued here, somewhat more
subtly, in Douglass's identification of liberty as a "rich inheritance," suggesting again that they are living passively off of the achievements of their fathers
rather than earning such riches for themselves. But Douglass's blunt declaration
of his exclusion from that inheritance also prepares for the dramatic intensification of irony. Up to this point, Douglass has performed what amount to two
ironic inversions of the conventional Fourth of July narrative, both of which
can be seen in terms of paternal and filial relations. First he assumed the perspective of the British crown, only to identify it with that of his audience, associating them with the conservative father rather than the rebellious children.
Then he allowed them to assume the children's perspective, only to distinguish
it from that of the founders, whose legacy he reconceived as one of responsible
fathering. Now, explicitly assuming the perspective of the slave, Douglass uses
his exclusion from the legacy of the founders to present that legacy with the
"scorching irony" he says the historical circumstances call for. From the slave's
perspective, he says, "your celebration is a sham; your boasted liberty, an un-
holy license; your national greatness, swelling vanity; your sounds of rejoicing
are empty and heartless; your denunciation of tyrants, brass fronted impudence;

your shouts of liberty and equality, hollow mockery" (196). From the slave's perspective, the principles celebrated on Independence Day are words without meaning—or, more accurately, forms belied by their real content. Like Horace Mann, Douglass uses irony to dramatize the irreconcilable conflict between the nation's principles and its current historical course—a conflict that is mirrored in Douglass's own divided self. Turning respectively to the internal slave trade, the Fugitive Slave Law, and the hypocrisy of the church in America, his speech builds in ironic intensity, culminating in a reading of the famous words from the second paragraph of the Declaration, by now thoroughly emptied out. And, like Mann, Douglass reimagines the Declaration's appeal to the world's judgment in the current historical context: "the existence of slavery," he says, echoing both Winthrop and his Biblical source, "makes your name a hissing and a bye-word to a mocking earth" (203).

But Douglass ends the speech with yet another shift in perspective, and a corresponding shift in tone. Returning to the subtler ironic displacements of the earlier section, he turns his gaze toward the future and sees an increasingly unified and interconnected world. "Long established customs of hurtful character could formerly fence themselves in, and do their evil work with social impunity. Knowledge was then confined and enjoyed by the privileged few, and the multitude walked on in mental darkness. But a change has now come over the affairs of mankind. Walled cities and empires have become unfashionable. . . . Oceans no longer divide, but link nations together. From Boston to London is now a holiday excursion. Space is comparatively annihilated.—Thoughts expressed on one side of the Atlantic are now heard on the other" (205). To the extent that the Declaration of Independence severed transatlantic ties and dissolved the "Political Bands" connecting America to England, Douglass here imagines the future as a fortuitous reversal of the founders' project of independence. He depicts independence negatively, as provincial isolation and backwardness, contrasting it with an enlightened cosmopolitanism. Ralph Waldo Emerson's 1837 "Concord Hymn" figured the beginning of the Revolutionary War as the "shot heard round the world"; Douglass envisions not shots but "thoughts" crossing the Atlantic, and crossing in the opposite direction. To the founders, Britain represented the tyranny that was poisoning their future; to Douglass, Britain offers a model to be emulated, a nation that abolished slavery and recognizes the black man's humanity, the hope for the future of mankind. Unlike the unmistakable, stinging irony of his reading of the Declaration's self-evident truths from the perspective of the slave, this passage couches its critique in a hopeful, forward-looking tone. But it nevertheless constitutes an ironic re-reading of the Declaration in its own right—a rendering of the founders' project of independence as obsolete.

Douglass's revisionist history here is played out spatially: if in the seventeenth century liberty had to flee European oppression to the New World, the nineteenth century calls for a critical look at America from the outside.[41] What had been imagined as a sanctuary is now, in Douglass's rendering, a "walled city" or "empire," insular and confining. But the spatial pattern Douglass traces— a flight or exile that initiates a founding; the refuge that turns adversely inward and must be escaped—also describes a thought process. Irony replicates the impulse to escape, sending an audience outside a word's immediate meaning for its significance. Moreover, although irony often simply illuminates hypocrisy, for Douglass it can also point toward a potential renewal of meaning. Both of the examples I have been examining—Douglass's strategic shifts among various paternal and filial positions and his critique of American independence from a global perspective—suggest such redefinitions. In the first example, Douglass breaks out of the usual pattern of argument in which, just as the colonists' injuries from the king's abuses and usurpations underwrite their claim to public attention, the slaves' injuries and vulnerabilities constitute the ground on which the antislavery movement is built. That pattern of argument sets itself against a failed paternalism—a father figure who injures the subjects he is charged with protecting—replacing it with another system of protections, a benign paternalism that establishes the "spots of safety" within which the vulnerable can find sanctuary. Douglass, by contrast, imagines a nation of fathers who look forward to future generations rather than children who look to a paternal figure for protection. As Eric Sundquist argues in his reading of Douglass's 1876 speech at the dedication of the Freedman's Lincoln Monument, he "probes the limits of paternalistic rhetoric even as he accepts a familiar role" (131). But Douglass goes on from there in the Fourth of July speech, first to emphasize his exclusion from the legacy of the founders, and then to use that position of exile to posit a new vision of global interconnectedness and cosmopolitan exchange. His exclusion from the "self-evident truths" of the Declaration leads to his two ironic rereadings of that document and to a new perspective on the meaning of America's founding.

On multiple levels Douglass's rhetoric brings protection and vulnerability— inside and outside—into a dynamic and productive relation. The speaking role that the Garrisonians envisioned for Douglass would have highlighted his vulnerable embodiment and his exclusion from the sphere of civic protection, dramatizing liberty's search for a sanctuary from tyranny. But, in a country that was predisposed to see all slaves as inarticulate and incapable of critical thought, the Garrisonians chose to emphasize Douglass's exclusion at the expense of his potential for full civic participation, tending thus to reinforce the distinction between citizen and slave rather than to unsettle the categories. Douglass's break with the Garrisonians can be seen as a second flight away from a fixed, externally imposed role and toward another as yet undefined role. It is an Emersonian move, akin to what Richard Poirier has called "troping," the "turning" of words in a way that "promises . . . to save us from being caught or fixed in a meaning or in that state of conformity which Emerson famously loathed" (*Renewal of Literature* 17).[42] Poirier points out that the crucial element of troping is the action itself: "it is never any particular trope that matters, but rather the act of troping," and "action is to be located in the movement toward but never *in* a result" (17, 49, emphasis in original). Emerson himself used the metaphor of embodiment in "The Poet," describing the poet's drive "to escape the custody of that body in which he is pent up" (460). Like Emerson, Douglass figures his progress as a series of escapes from bodily bondage. But for Douglass it is not simply a search for sanctuary, because his account also subverts the very concept of protection: what from the outside promises refuge for an aggrieved liberty, turns out to be yet another form of confinement.

2

Unmasking Slavery

Angelina Grimké's Rhetoric of Exposure

We have torn off the mask, and brought to light the
hidden things of darkness.

—Angelina Grimké

Discussion, as the manifestation of intelligence in political life, stimulates
publicity; by its means sore spots are brought to light that would otherwise
remain hidden.

—John Dewey, *Liberalism and Social Action*

In 1776 Thomas Paine asked the readers of *Common Sense,* "Hath your house
been burnt? Hath your property been destroyed before your face? Are your wife
and children destitute of a bed to lie on, or bread to live on? Have you lost a parent or a child by [British] hands, and yourself the ruined and wretched survivor?
If you have not, then are you not a judge of those who have" (91). Some eighty-
five years later, Harriet Jacobs made a remarkably similar appeal to the readers
of *Incidents in the Life of a Slave Girl:* "happy women, whose purity has been
sheltered from childhood, . . . whose homes are protected by law, do not judge
the poor desolate slave girl too severely!" (384). Both passages directly address
readers who are presumed to be in positions of comparative safety, and both as-
tutely undercut those positions of safety by associating them with harsh, critical
"judg[ment]," as opposed to sympathetic identification with the victims of injury. Such rhetorical strategies function to open up a sphere of public participation to groups (American colonists, slave women) that have been denied legal
protections. And while Paine and Jacobs both reinforce an ideal of safety and
protection, it is their evocation of a scene of *un*protected privacy—and their

bringing that scene before the judgmental attention of their reading public—that in each case charges the moment with its persuasive power.

Clearly, there are also significant differences between Paine's and Jacobs's appeals. For one, whereas Paine—speaking to men rather than women—figures the endangered privacy as property, wife, and children, Jacobs figures it primarily as sexual "purity." And, even more fundamentally, whereas Paine is taking on the cause of others whose lives have been devastated by the British, Jacobs is speaking for herself. It was by no means clear in the mid-nineteenth century that invoking "the cause of the suffering widow, or injured orphan," as *The Columbian Orator* put it, would entitle widows and orphans to claim a public role for themselves.[1] At issue is the complicated relation among three things: systems of political oppression like slavery and patriarchy, our sense of privacy as a precious thing always at risk of violation and the protective impulses that that sense generates, and our tendency to see our own tender interior—our affective life—reflected in the suffering widows and injured orphans of the world. Each of the three writers considered in the chapters that follow—Angelina Grimké, Frances E. W. Harper, and Henry James—brings that constellation of elements together in a different way and with different effects, and each one tells another part of the story of the liberal public sphere in the nineteenth century.

At the heart of this development is the conflation of the actual injuries experienced by disenfranchised groups with our sense of our own vulnerable interior and our own precarious dignity—a conflation that is both crucial to and problematic for the reformers' cause. At its most basic level, romantic eloquence provided a model for the public representation of privacy, and to associate private selfhood with such conventionally private concerns as slavery and the treatment of women was to make romantic eloquence serve the reformers' project of bringing those concerns to the public attention. Furthermore, the very resistance to exposing such matters to public scrutiny could be turned to the reformers' advantage: just as Emerson imagined the private self as triumphing over a confining and constricting social order and completing itself in its defiant self-expression, so the reformers, by figuring oppression as repression, imagined their cause as the victory of openness over secrecy and concealment. And just as the private self is most compelling when it is thwarted and opposed in its desire for liberty, so the spectacle of stunted development and damaged lives—what James sarcastically has his fictional women's rights activist Olive Chancellor call "the historic unhappiness of women"—constitutes a central aspect of the reformers' appeal (James, *The Bostonians* 142, also 33).[2] Perhaps most of all, to draw a parallel between the vulnerability of the private self and that of such disenfranchised groups as women and slaves was to establish an empathetic and identificatory bond between the audience and the object of its attention. Repeatedly we see the reformers fostering in their audiences a tenderness of heart and associating that tenderness with the wounds suffered by society's most vulnerable members, encouraging them to see reflected in those wounds their own inner pain and turmoil. It was a powerful strategy, at once eliciting openness and heartfelt compassion for the oppressed and generating commitment to the reformist political agenda out of an audience's own instinct for self-protection.

But the strategy did not come without potential complications for the reformers' cause. It linked the project of securing protections and alleviating actual injuries to the cultivation of our sense of inner injury, thus placing the ends at cross purposes with the means. It capitalized on the belief that there is something inherently private about the treatment of women and slaves, even as it strove to bring those issues into the public discourse. And, most importantly, it depended upon a problematic blurring of literal and figurative, actual and imagined. By persuading listeners to experience the actual injuries of disenfranchised groups as their own inner vulnerability, strategies of self-exposure tended to elevate the imaginary over the actual—indeed, to literalize the figurative and vice versa, encouraging citizens to imagine themselves as much outsiders to the zone of civic protection as were the literally disenfranchised.[3] Repeatedly we see the reformers stressing that abstract reason is not sufficient to comprehend the injuries perpetrated under slavery, that such things can only be experienced. Although privileging authentic, experiential knowledge would appear on the surface to reinforce the divide between citizenship and slavery, reformers often used such constructions not to highlight the inaccessibility of such knowledge to citizens but, on the contrary, to engage citizens experientially, and to erode their feelings of protection in abstraction. It transformed the boundary between abstraction and experience from something that protected citizens from suffering bodily consequences for their speech into something that prevented citizens from knowing the truth, from a border to be fortified into a barrier to be overcome.

This chapter examines Angelina Grimké's antislavery rhetoric and feminist activism both for their radical potential to challenge the exclusion of slaves and women from civic life and for their potentially problematic implications for citizenship and gender. Her last major public address, given in Philadelphia on 16 May 1838, offers a dramatic example of her mastery of strategies of self-exposure. She delivered the address above the din of a violent anti-abolitionist mob—a mob that, the following night, would burn the newly built Pennsylvania Hall for Free Discussion to the ground. "As the tumult from without increased, and the brickbats fell thick and fast," William Lloyd Garrison recalled,

"[Grimké's] eloquence kindled, her eyes flashed, and her cheeks glowed" (qtd. in Ceplair 303).[4] In vivid contrast to the civic humanist ideal of protected speech and rational public deliberation, Grimké's "eloquence" appears to thrive in this tumultuous environment of violence, under the menacing threat of the brickbats. Her glowing cheeks—a bodily sign of both indignation and ire—anticipate the "kindling" effect of her speech as well as the fire that will ultimately destroy this Hall for Free Discussion. But more than simply dramatic effect, the chaos provided Grimké with an analogy for the personal insecurity that slavery institutionalized: "What if the mob should now burst in upon us," she asked after a particularly noisy interruption, "break up our meeting and commit violence upon our persons—would this be anything compared with what the slaves endure?" (320). This degeneration of the public sphere into mob violence, Grimké suggests, strips us all momentarily of our citizenship, leaving "our persons" vulnerable and therefore incapable of self-abstraction into free speech. Moreover, it is the listeners' bodily experience of vulnerability that makes them capable of imagining the suffering of the slave in all its inabstractable magnitude. Abstract reason, Grimké insisted, was insufficient to understand the "truth" of slavery; its "horrors," she told her Pennsylvania Hall audience, "can never be described" (319). A truer understanding depended instead on the irrational faculties of sentiment and imaginative sympathy, on the capacity to put oneself in the slave's position, to overcome one's "callous[ness]" and "insensibility" and "*feel* the truth" (320, emphasis added). Vulnerability of heart was something to be cultivated rather than protected against—something even to be wrought, as in Grimké's jeremiad-like image of the abolitionists "scattering 'the living coals of truth' upon the naked heart of this nation" (322).[5] And so, because the republican model of free discourse falls short when it comes to speaking about slavery, Grimké was able to turn the atmosphere of violence in Pennsylvania Hall to her advantage. By stripping the abolitionist crowd of its security, the anti-abolitionist mob provided them with exactly the kind of bodily knowledge without which slavery could not be understood; by turning the abstract cause of the slaves' self-protection into the immediate danger to the abolitionists' own self-protection, the mob was unwittingly made to bolster the cause of abolition.

Grimké's responses to the persistent argument that woman's natural defenselessness incapacitated her for public speaking likewise turned the very thing that her opponents used against her into a mark of her particular qualification. In 1837, for example, a widely circulated pastoral letter—published in the *New England Spectator* and read from the Massachusetts Congregationalist pulpits—made just such an argument. Woman's "power," declared the ministers, "is in her dependence, flowing from the consciousness of that weakness which God has given her for protection." When a woman disregards her "weakness," however, and "assumes the place and tone of a man as a public reformer," she also relinquishes the "care and protection" that is due her as man's dependent.[6] Grimké responded to such arguments not by refuting their premise, but by appropriating it and turning it to her own ends. Woman's "power" is indeed "in her dependence," she maintained, for the Christian ideal of sacrifice requires her to depend wholly on Christ, exposing herself to public humiliation, without regard for worldly protection, for the sake of her belief. And not only does a woman's vulnerability mark her for a special kind of public role; it also constitutes a standard of public conduct for men. "Are [men and women] not equally defenceless, equally dependent on Him?" Grimké asked in her *Letters to Catharine Beecher*. "What did Jesus say to his disciples, when he commissioned them to preach the gospel?—'Behold, I send you forth as SHEEP in the midst of wolves'" (191). All of these figures of public vulnerability—"SHEEP in the midst of wolves," "coals" on the "naked heart of [a] nation," the threat of "violence upon our persons"—imagine an ideal public self that is "defenceless" and exposed, subject to physical violence, a public self for whom "protection" implies callousness. In contrast to the ministers' neoclassical assumption that "weakness" is incompatible with a public position, Grimké delineates a public space that is characterized by personal insecurity, and therefore peculiarly suited to women. When Grimké's critics wrote that the "FEMALE CHARACTER [is threatened] with wide-spread and permanent injury" when a woman appears in public, they intended it as both a justification and a reinforcement of her exclusion from public life.[7] For Grimké, however, it was precisely that kind of "injury" that qualified women for public life, "commissioning" them to incarnate the cause of abolition in ways unavailable to protected citizens.

Angelina Grimké's appropriation of a rhetoric of self-exposure for political reform provided women and slaves with a model for imagining themselves as public—a model that drew upon and actually favored their condition of representing, as opposed to having, privacy—and also enabled them to deliver slavery and other domestic relations from the unchangeable, apolitical, ahistorical sphere of private life into politics and history.[8] Nevertheless, the same elements that Grimké used to construct her public persona could be rearranged into an argument opposing women's civic participation and condemning public oversight of master-slave relations. Because privacy must deny its dependence on public representation even as it is publicly and discursively constructed, strategies like Grimké's are potentially vulnerable to charges of hypocrisy and immodesty. In order to be effective, Grimké had to represent herself not as someone actively seeking a public spotlight, but as having been irresistibly drawn into her public role by the urgency and extremity of the slaves' situation, not as someone engaging in self-promotion, but as having sacrificed her privacy for a greater public good. In other words, Grimké had to manage the tension inherent in liberal privacy—which comes into being through public representation, and yet must simultaneously demonstrate its reticence, its natural tendency to recoil from public exposure—to her advantage. A particular published exchange between Grimké and Catharine Beecher will illuminate both the pattern of criticism to which Grimké's project was vulnerable and Grimké's skill in retaking control over the terms of the debate.

Catharine Beecher's Rhetoric of Protection

Early in 1837 Catharine Beecher published *An Essay on Slavery and Abolitionism, with Reference to the Duty of American Females*—addressed specifically to Angelina Grimké—attacking the tactics of the American Anti-Slavery Society and, in particular, the public participation of women in abolitionist activities. Her critique of such women centers on the distinction she makes between the means of influence appropriate to men and to women.[9] "A man," she contends, "may act on society by the collision of intellect, in public debate; he may urge his measures by a sense of shame, by fear and by personal interest; he may coerce by the combination of public sentiment; he may drive by physical force, and he does not outstep the boundaries of his sphere. . . . [But] woman is to win every thing by peace and love; by making herself so much respected, esteemed and loved, that to yield to her opinions and to gratify her wishes, will be the free-will offering of the heart" (100–101). Man's sphere, quite simply, is one of aggressive debate and opposing interests; women, as Beecher says elsewhere in her essay, are "mediators," whose sphere is one not of partisanship, but of "peace" and harmony (128). The gendering of private and public spheres was a familiar argument, as was the idea that women who crossed the boundaries of the domestic sphere also crossed the boundaries of their gender. Women like Mary Wollstonecraft and Harriet Martineau were commonly referred to as "female men" or "semi-women, mental hermaphrodites," and Beecher herself had launched just such an attack on Frances Wright in her 1836 *Letters on the Difficulty of Religion,* criticizing Wright's "great masculine person, her loud voice, her untasteful attire" and "the bare-faced impudence" of her practice of "mingling with men in stormy debate" (Ryan 134; Welter 40).[10]

But Beecher's *Essay on Slavery and Abolitionism* is remarkable precisely for its refusal to focus on the spectacle of an "unsexed" female on the lecture platform, however "intolerably offensive and disgusting" that may be. Rather, having made her point about masculine and feminine means of influence, Beecher turns her attention from women per se to the gendered category of the personal. Freedom of opinion, she contends—something both necessary and fundamental to a democracy—depends on a public sphere that is devoid of the personal. While it is every man's duty to promote his opinions with all the facts and evidence and reason at his command, he should avoid "attacking the character or motives of the *advocates* of false opinions, or of holding them up, individually, to public odium" (116–17). The abolitionists who attempt to bring the private, domestic lives of Southerners under public scrutiny, therefore, are for Beecher endangering the very foundation of democracy: they corrupt the public sphere with personal issues, passions, and selfish motives, displacing reason and the common good. And not only do they violate the privacy of those Southerners whose domestic relations they scrutinize; their tactics also reveal their own lack of self-restraint. Beecher writes, "a man is not fitted for the duties of a reprover"— not fitted, that is, to enter the public debate—"until he can bring his feelings under . . . control" (149). In order for the public sphere to function, the passions and interests must be secured and cordoned off, kept under control; the unrestrained mingling of public and private threatens not only the social order but also the very integrity of private selfhood.

It is worth taking a moment to point out the remarkable ease with which Beecher shifts her focus from women who petition Congress for abolition to the consequences of making personal attacks a part of the public discussion, for the implied analogy assumes that the private self is in some sense feminine.[11] That assumption gives Beecher's argument both its underlying unity and its force: it enables the connection between masculine self-control and women's confinement in the domestic sphere, between the exclusion of the personal from public debate and the exclusion of women from the public sphere. Moreover, Beecher's recasting of the boundary between the sexes as the boundary between private selfhood and the public discourse raises the stakes of its dissolution. Women who cross the boundaries of their sphere are not simply grotesque spectacles; rather, their actions have consequences for the whole of society, for manhood as well as for themselves.

In a particularly revealing passage, Beecher suggests that Northerners imagine themselves in the position of Southerners, having their private faults broadcast to the world.

How would the husbands and fathers at the North endure it, if Southern associations should be formed to bring forth to the world the sins of North-

ern men, as husbands and fathers? What if the South should send to the
North to collect all the sins and neglects of Northern husbands and fathers, to retail them at the South in tracts and periodicals? What if the
English nation should join in the outcry, and English females should send
forth an agent, not indeed to visit the offending North, but to circulate at
the South, denouncing all who did not join in this crusade, as the defenders of bad husbands and bad fathers? (144–45)

Beecher's vision here gets its force not from images of "female men," but from
suggestions of violated masculinity. Men, in her hypothetical North, are at-
tacked as "husbands and fathers"—a phrase repeated four times—in their most
intimate roles, the very roles that represent both sovereignty over women and
children and mastery of their own affective selves; it is an exposure of the intimate and the private that amounts to a subversion of masculine selfhood. And
the other side of this vision in which the private has become public is the "cir-
culat[ing]" female agent from England. Clearly, hers is not the virtuous public
sphere of reasoned, disinterested discourse, but the vulgar and sensationalized
publicity of the periodical press. The double meaning of the word "retail" suggests that the "sins and neglects of Northern husbands and fathers" are not only
recounted in detail to strangers; they are also sold. She pries into the private lives
of men, not only exposing them to the invasive gaze of a reading public but also
commercializing them, making them into commodities on the marketplace. She
bullies and meddles; her "crusade" has no modesty, no respectful sense of a space
that should rightfully be protected from public scrutiny.

During the last six months of 1837, in the midst of a demanding speaking
tour, Angelina Grimké published a series of thirteen letters in the abolitionist
press responding to Beecher's criticism. Her defense of women's right to speak in
public is especially interesting because its effect is to destabilize the distinction
Beecher makes between public and private and, therefore, to dislodge it from its
grounding in gender difference. In a key moment, Grimké responds to Beecher's point about the means of influence appropriate to women: "This principle
may do as the rule of action to the fashionable belle, whose idol is *herself;* whose
every attitude and smile are designed to win the admiration of others to *herself;* and who enjoys, with exquisite delight, the double-refined incense of flattery which is offered to *her* vanity, by yielding to *her* opinions, and gratifying
her wishes, because they are *hers*" (Ceplair 189, emphasis in original). Beecher
had faulted "female advocate[s]" for "choos[ing] to come upon a stage," therefore subjecting themselves to public censure just as "the book of an author, or
the dancing of an actress, or any thing else that is presented to public observa-

tion" (121). Here Grimké faults the "fashionable belle" for what is in effect the same thing: making an "idol [of] herself." If Beecher's domestic woman exerts influence "by making herself . . . respected, esteemed and loved"—that is, by making herself the object of a man's respect, esteem, and love—then she is indeed self-consciously "public" in the sense that she acts for a male audience, albeit an audience of one or two rather than hundreds. Grimké's attribution of a kind of theatricality to what Beecher defines as feminine influence speaks directly to Beecher's critique of the "female advocate," who places herself on a "stage" and asks to be judged as the public judges "the dancing of an actress." For if Beecher's domestic woman appears, by contrast, self-effacing and passive, "dependent and defenseless," Grimké reveals such "attitudes" and postures to be mere show, "designed to win the admiration of others." Her influence is in actuality a sexual and theatrical influence, designed to manipulate others by manipulating the way she appears to them.

In such moments, Grimké gestures toward redefinitions of privacy and publicity—redefinitions that loosen the terms from their moorings in gender difference. Such publicity as Grimké envisions in the "fashionable belle" is not limited to a specific sphere of society; rather, it is an attitude of self—indeed, an attitude of selfishness, as indicated by Grimké's repetition of the italicized *her*. That sphere of society Beecher deems "public" is therefore no different in kind from that which she deems "private," for whatever happens on the stage or platform or in the theater can happen as well in the parlor.[12] Elsewhere in her writings Grimké suggests that the elements of domesticity are themselves merely show, designed to conceal the terrors of slavery. She describes, for example, a wealthy and respectable Charleston woman who, after the 1825 revival, "opened her house to social prayer-meetings." But "the room in which they were held in the evening, and where the voice of prayer was heard around the family altar, and where she herself retired for private devotion thrice each day, was the very place in which, when her slaves were to be whipped with the cowhide, they were taken to receive the infliction" (Ceplair 340–41). Here all the elements of the peaceful domestic scene—prayer, devotion, the "family altar," everything that in the rhetoric of Beecher and others[13] was supposed to provide safety and respite for the private soul—are shown to be public spectacle, hiding the slaves' punishment from public view. "Every thing cruel and revolting," Grimké continues, "is carefully concealed from strangers, especially those from the north" (345). Duplicity and hypocrisy flourish in private places in ways that would not be possible under the public eye.

The images of enclosure that abound in Grimké's writings are, by and large, not images of peaceful retreat, of safety and sanctuary, but prisons and tombs.[14]

The passage quoted above continues with a description of one Southern family who had to borrow slaves from neighbors to wait on their table, "because their own slaves had been so cruelly flogged in the workhouse, that they could not walk without limping at every step, and their putrefied flesh emitted such an intolerable smell that they were not fit to be in the presence of company" (Ceplair 345). The facade of domestic tranquility here conceals broken bones and rotting flesh; "it is a whited sepulchre full of dead men's bones and uncleanness" (345). Grimké uses the same trope elsewhere, when she proposes that "Anti-Slavery Societies are taking away the stone from the mouth of the tomb of slavery, where lies the putrid carcass of our brother. . . . Did He come to proclaim liberty to the captive, and the opening of prison doors to them that are bound, in vain?" (69). And in her fourth letter to Beecher she speaks of "springing a mine beneath the great bastile [*sic*] of slavery" (160). Of course, it was neither original nor especially remarkable to use prison as a metaphor for slavery. But Grimké takes these metaphors in an unusual direction: repeatedly, her emphasis is not just on confinement, but on concealment. Her object is not just liberty for the captive, for it is the exposure of slavery to public view that provides comfort and deliverance. Bringing the invisible and unknown violence of Southern domesticity into the public discourse—the central tactic of abolitionism—is, in Grimké's metaphors, opening the tomb, exposing the putrid and pestilent to fresh air and sunlight, liberating the captive, and bringing the dead back to life.

These images are in stark contrast both to Beecher's nightmare image of unrestrained, invasive female surveillance, and to her sense of a sacrosanct, inviolable privacy to which that surveillance proves a threat. Although liberalism gives rise to both Grimké's and Beecher's treatments of privacy, each woman chooses to emphasize a different aspect of its contradictory significance. Beecher's version of privacy is a precious and vulnerable region of life that must be protected from public scrutiny, and public supervision of that region is not only immodest and indecent, but threatens to erode the very foundations of selfhood. For Grimké, however, privacy is already theatrical and therefore necessarily available to publicity. Her project of unmasking the terrors of slavery—the brutal punishment, torture, miscegenation, and murder that are carried out behind closed doors and out of the view of Northern visitors—presupposes that the domestic is performative rather than constitutive, designed to attract rather than avert attention. Moreover, exposure is itself spectacular, for the exposé—like the raising of Lazarus from the dead—draws its audience even as it breaks open the nightmarish cell that is privacy. Grimké's treatment of the domestic here does not preclude the existence of another, deeper space of privacy; indeed, I will argue that it depends upon such a space.[15] But by removing slavery from the realm of privacy, she identifies it as a very public, very material institution that can and must be eradicated.

REPRESENTATIVE REPUBLICANISM

Frequently Grimké resorts to an ideal of sincerity in her critique of Beecher's notion of privacy.[16] A postscript she appended to her thirteenth and final letter to Beecher concludes her response with precisely that tactic.

> P.S. Since preparing the foregoing letters for the press, I have been informed by a Bookseller in Providence, that some of thy books had been sent to him to sell last summer, and that one afternoon a number of southern-ers entered his store whilst they were lying on the counter. An elderly lady took up one of them and after turning over the pages for some time, she threw it down and remarked, here is a book written by the daughter of a northern dough face, to apologise for our southern institutions—but for my part, I have a thousand times more respect for the Abolitionists, who openly denounce the system of slavery, than for those people, who in order to please us, cloak their real sentiments under such a garb as this. (203)

Contrasting the abolitionists' sincerity and Beecher's hypocrisy, the abolition-ists' self-exposure and Beecher's self-concealment, here Grimké claims for her-self the moral ground of integrity. Beecher's *Essay*—a "garb" under which her "real sentiments" are "cloak[ed]"—displays the same duplicity as the "fashion-able belle": it is opaque rather than transparent, designed "to please" rather than to express truth. Moreover, Grimké implicitly contrasts the abolitionist tactic of exposure with Beecher's defense of privacy: the elderly Southern lady, it seems, does not want protection from the prying eyes of abolitionists as much as she wants "open[ness]."

Sincerity, however, can be a double-edged sword. It is an enabling concept for Grimké inasmuch as it collapses the distinction between public and pri-vate and makes a feminine public voice conceivable. But it becomes problem-atic inasmuch as it is marshaled in *opposition* to a performative or theatrical model of selfhood—inasmuch, that is, as it lays claim to perfect transparency.[17] Once Grimké attacks Beecher's "book," or the "fashionable belle," or the re-spectable Charleston woman's domestic arrangements, for what is in effect their materiality—their concealment of a secret self behind that which is visible to the public—then she is left with the problem of her own materiality. Moreover, Grimké's body was a *woman's* body—something she was reminded of in virtually every account of her lectures, by supporters and detractors alike. In February of 1838 Grimké was invited to speak before a committee of the Massachusetts legislature that had been appointed to consider antislavery petitions. Her rhetorical strategy in that speech merits close attention, for in it she not only fashions her personal presence in opposition to the patently sexual body of a woman; she also establishes the nature of the attention her male audience will pay to her speech.

Grimké begins her address with a reference to Esther, another woman whose calling it was to petition the governing power on behalf of an oppressed people.[18]

> The Queen of Persia,—if Queen she might be called, who was but the mistress of her voluptuous lord,—trained as she had been in the secret abominations of an oriental harem, had studied too deeply the character of Ahaseurus not to know that the sympathies of his heart could not be reached, except through the medium of his sensual appetites. Hence we find her arrayed in royal apparel, standing in the inner court of the King's house, hoping by her personal charms to win the favor of her lord. . . . She felt that if her mission of mercy was to be successful, his animal propensities must be . . . wrought upon—the luxurious feast must be prepared, the banquet of wine must be served up, and the favorable moment must be seized when, gorged with gluttony and intoxication, the king's heart was fit to be operated upon by the pathetic appeal. (310–11)

Grimké's Esther is a "public woman" in two respects: she concerns herself in the public affairs of her country, and she effectively prostitutes herself, using her body to play upon the king's "sensual appetites." Although Grimké was simply drawing on the common characterization of women who ventured beyond their domestic duties, her emphasis on Esther's sexuality must have been shocking. All the conventional language and imagery of sex is there: the oriental setting, the titillating detail of Esther's "training" in "secret abominations," and Ahaseurus, with his "animal propensities," "gorged with gluttony and intoxication," the very image of excess. And as shocking as this vivid description of a woman using sex to achieve her ends must have been, Grimké's audience must have been equally struck by the contrast between the two "public women": Esther "arrayed in royal apparel" and Angelina "in her simple gray Quaker dress, her delicate features framed by a white neckerchief"; Esther's Judaism and Angelina's devout Christianity; Esther's sensuality and Angelina's chastity (Lerner 6). Despite their similar "mission[s] of life and love," it is this contrast that Grimké builds upon, for the contrast will clear the way for a new model of publicity—

one that is neither encased in a sexual body, nor abstracted from the "hearts" and "sentiments" of persons (Ceplair 311).

It is significant that Esther works her influence in "the King's house," using her "personal charms" to gain her object. Indeed, she is not terribly different from Catharine Beecher's woman, who "make[s] herself so much respected, esteemed and loved, that to yield to her opinions and to gratify her wishes, will be the free-will offering of the heart" (101). But Beecher's domestic hearth has, in Grimké's version, become an "inner court," with its suggestion of secrecy and corrupt dealings; the wholesome meals have become "the luxurious feast" and "the banquet of wine"; the "cultivat[ion]" and "refine[ment]" that, for Beecher, constitute feminine influence have become "train[ing] . . . in the secret abominations of an oriental harem." The tainted spin Grimké puts on these domestic details works for her in two ways. First, like her critique of the "fashionable belle," it reveals the manipulative sexuality and theatricality that underlie such versions of the domestic. But, more importantly, it establishes the opposition not as that of "public woman" to "private woman," but rather between two distinct versions of publicity.

Grimké concludes the opening paragraph of her speech by building on exactly that contrast:

> I feel that it would be an insult to the Committee, were I to attempt to win their favor by arraying my person in gold, and silver, and costly apparel, or by inviting them to partake of the luxurious feast, or the banquet of wine. I understand the spirit of the age too well to believe that you could be moved by such sensual means—means as unworthy of you, as they would be beneath the dignity of the cause of humanity. Yes, I feel that if you are reached at all, it will not be by me, but by the truths I shall endeavor to present to your understandings and your hearts. The heart of the eastern despot was reached through the lowest propensities of his animal nature, by personal influence; yours, I know, cannot be reached but through the loftier sentiments of the intellectual and moral feelings. (Ceplair 311)

Having established Esther's public strategy as corrupt, Grimké proceeds to establish a publicity for herself based on republican virtue. Persian luxury—the wine, the feast, the gold and silver—is contrasted with the dignity and austerity of nineteenth-century Massachusetts. The despotism of Ahaseurus—his "inner court" and "golden scepter"—is contrasted with the republican state legislature. And the sensual—gluttony, intoxication, and sexual indulgence—is contrasted with "the loftier sentiments of the intellectual and moral feelings." Unlike Esther, who "array[s her] person in gold, and silver, and costly apparel," Grimké refuses to call attention to her female body; her petition is not private— "not . . . by me"—it is, rather, to the "understandings" and "hearts" of her audience, through the moral and intellectual medium of public appeal.

Grimké was well aware of how necessary it was for sexual difference to be left out of public discourse if women were to be taken seriously as public figures. In the eleventh of her series of letters to Beecher she had responded to Beecher's assertion that "all the generous promptings of chivalry, all the poetry of romantic gallantry, depend upon woman's retaining her place as dependent and defenseless" (101–2). Grimké's reply is striking for the vehemence of her language: "[Woman's] noble nature is insulted by such paltry, sickening adulation, and she will not stoop to drink the foul waters of so turbid a stream. If all this sinful foolery is to be withdrawn from our sex, with all my heart I say, *the sooner the better*" (Ceplair 190, emphasis in original). For Grimké it is precisely the conventions of "chivalry" and "romantic gallantry" that degrade relations between men and women, because such conventions are built upon a heightened consciousness of sexual difference. "When human beings are regarded as *moral* beings," she wrote in her twelfth letter to Beecher, "*sex,* instead of being enthroned upon the summit, administering upon rights and responsibilities, sinks into insignificance and nothingness" (195). However, the dethroning of sex depends upon the audience's consciousness rather than the speaker's, and perhaps the most remarkable aspect of Grimké's speech to the Massachusetts legislators is her fashioning of her audience. For if Grimké compares herself to Esther, she implicitly compares the legislators in her audience to Ahaseurus—a comparison that she makes explicit in the closing sentence of the paragraph: "The heart of the eastern despot was reached through the lowest propensities of his animal nature . . . ; yours, I know, cannot be reached but through the loftier sentiments of the intellectual and moral feelings." Hence the contrast that Grimké has developed on so many levels—Eastern and Western, royal and republican, private and public, corrupt and virtuous—culminates by contrasting Ahaseurus's lustful gaze, ever conscious of sex, with the elevated gaze of her contemporary audience. Such an overdetermination leaves Grimké's hearers no room to choose their camp; she has them precisely where she wants and needs them.

By bringing her focus to rest on the gaze of her audience, Grimké implicitly makes a point about the power of public opinion to determine the possibilities for women in public life. The primary barrier Grimké sees for herself is not the nature or ability of women themselves. Rather, it is the expectations of men and the disposition of public attention to women—"the wall of public opinion," as she described it in an 1837 letter to her friend Jane Smith, "which lies right in the way of woman's true dignity, honor & usefulness" (272). If Beecher distinguishes the chivalrous gaze of a gentleman from the lecherous gaze of a seducer, Grimké makes no such distinction. For her, both depend on the "lowest propensities of [man's] animal nature"; both "enthrone [sex] upon the summit." Such consciousness inevitably condemns woman's influence in public affairs to the sensual tactics of Esther rather than the moral and intellectual appeal of Angelina Grimké. Grimké's rhetorical creation of her audience—her fashioning of them as above the "sensual means" of Esther ("means as unworthy of you," she says, "as they would be beneath the dignity of the cause of humanity")—is more than just flattery, more even than another tactical move to distinguish herself from Esther. It is testament to her realization of the defining role of public opinion in women's participation in public life.

And so, although Grimké raises the gaze of her audience above the "sensual means" of Esther, she does not thereby raise it above all means available to the senses. Despite her call to her audience to focus on the "lofty" and disembodied "truths" that are the substance of her message—despite, that is, the essentializing drift of her rhetoric—Grimké comprehends her presence as fundamentally public. For, in fashioning the attention of her audience, she also necessarily fashions herself; her Quaker garb is no less a costume than Esther's "royal apparel"; her chastity a no less public posture than Esther's sensuality. Republican "virtue" is indeed itself performative, its distinguishing features as visible, in their own way, as the opulent trappings of monarchy. Fully aware of the reason she was getting so much public attention, Grimké used her female body to her advantage: she presented herself to her audience as a deeply personal, distinctly feminine speaker, a "spectacle of sincerity."[19]

Epistolary Publicity

The turning point in Angelina Grimké's life had come two and a half years earlier when she wrote a letter to William Lloyd Garrison declaring her support of his radical stance against slavery. At the time she was living with her sister Sarah in the home of some Philadelphia Quakers, having resolved that she could no longer stay on her family's plantation in Charleston, South Carolina, where she would directly benefit from a slave economy. The Orthodox Friends with whom she lived deeply disapproved of Garrison's brand of abolitionism, and Grimké knew that her letter would mean a breach in her relationship with them and eventually with the Society of Friends. She posted it only after several nights of anguished prayer. A few weeks later she was visited by an elder Friend who showed her a copy of Garrison's paper, the *Liberator*. Garrison had published her letter in its entirety—without her permission, and with her name attached.

That the Grimké name had appeared in the abolitionist press became the focus not only of the severe reprimands Angelina received from those around her, but of her own thoughts about the incident as well. "To hav my name," she wrote in her diary, "not so much *my* name, as the name of Grimké associated with that of the despised Garrison, seemd like bringing disgrace upon my *family*, not myself alone" (31, emphasis in original). It would have been customary for Garrison to have published the letter anonymously or with a pseudonym attached. Anonymous and pseudonymous publication had been standard in the eighteenth century, justified by the contention that the ideas themselves should be the focus of a reader's attention, not the character of their author; it illustrates what Michael Warner has called the "principle of negativity," "the apparent absence of a personal author in printed language," on which its validity as public discourse depended (*Letters of the Republic* 43).[20] But Garrison clearly saw an advantage to identifying the author of the letter as the daughter of a prominent slaveholding family, the "sister," as he refers to her in his introduction, "of the departed GRIMKÉ."[21] The letter would have its greatest impact, he knew, not as abstract reason, but as personal testimony. That the character and family and interests of the author should be so central to the meaning of the text for its readers indicates a different understanding of its nature than the one Warner describes: instead of a critical publicity based in the exclusion of private interests from public discourse, Garrison draws on a publicity of exposure, whose source and ground is ostensibly personal.

Grimké herself reacted initially with surprise and embarrassment. It had, of course, occurred to her that the letter might be published, but, she said later, "I had no idea, if it was, that my name would be attached to it" (qtd. in Lumpkin 85). "Blushing & confusion of face were mine," she wrote in her diary, "& I tho't the walls of a prison would hav been preferable to such an exposure" (Ceplair 31). The Quaker elders urged her to write to Garrison disavowing some of the sentiments expressed and disapproving the letter's publication. But Grimké would not recant; she would not, after all, choose the "prison" of silence and Quaker discipline over the pain and embarrassment of exposure. "I feel willing to bear all," she wrote, "if [the letter] was only made instrumental of good" (31). And less than a year later she was finishing her *Appeal to the Christian Women of the South* and writing to Sarah that it was to be published "with my name attachd, for I well know my name is worth more than myself & will add weight to it" (34). Revealingly, the *Appeal* begins by addressing not the abstract issue of slavery but, in a highly personal tone, Grimké's motives for writing, her character and her interest. "RESPECTED FRIENDS," she writes, "It is because you have known me, that I write thus unto you" (36). And to those who "have never seen me, and never heard my name, . . . I feel an interest in *you*" (36–37).

It is significant that this fiction of personal presence arises from Grimké's experience of forcible exposure, her "blushing & confusion of face," for it is as a violation of privacy—often represented as a violation of bodily integrity—that Grimké's "publicity" comes into being. Her letter to Garrison, for example, is haunted by the spectacle of physical violence against abolitionists—a martyrdom that she comes to associate with her own exposure as its author. As her letter to Garrison expresses the hope that "we . . . [will be] willing to suffer the loss of character, property—yea, and life itself, in what we believe to be the cause of bleeding humanity" (26); her letter to Sarah shortly after publication reads, "I feel as though my character had sustained a deep injury," and asks "whether *this* suffering was not the peculiar kind required of *me*" (Ceplair 29).[22] The remarkable thing is not that Grimké associated her emergence into publicity as a published author and her commitment to "the cause of bleeding humanity" with the "deep injury" that had been sustained by her "character"; such associations were staples of the conservative argument, warnings to women of the consequences of their assuming a public role. The remarkable thing is that Grimké chose "injury" over protection, realizing that a public posture of vulnerability was, paradoxically, her strength. Such a self-conception turned protection into cowardice and deception, thus setting in motion a process of *un*masking that revealed an ever-reducible persona and, in the process, played to the curiosity of her public.

Of Grimké's many references in her letter to the "violent proceedings" against abolitionists, the one she refers to specifically is the flogging of Amos Dresser. Dresser was a student at Lane Theological Seminary who, on a trip to the South to sell "Cottage Bibles," distributed some antislavery tracts to sympathizers. When he arrived in Nashville, Tennessee, his box was searched and the antislavery material found. As Larry Ceplair explains, Dresser's " 'trial' [before Nashville's Committee of Vigilance] resulted in a verdict of 'guilty' and a sentence of twenty lashes on his bare back laid on by a heavy cowhide in the public square. He left in disguise the next morning, carrying only the clothes on his back" (27 n.). His story was published in the *Liberator,* and eventually as a pamphlet titled *The Personal Narrative of Amos Dresser.* It is easy to see why Dresser's story struck a chord with Grimké: in it are all of the elements of the rhetoric of self-exposure. He begins by keeping his tracts hidden in a box and distributing them in secret, so that he will be protected from the Southern laws against such activity—

protected by his dissociation from the text of his beliefs. When his true connection to the tracts is revealed, he is sentenced to be flogged: his public exposure as the source of the antislavery literature results in the public exposure and punishment of his body. But it also marks a radical change in both his attitude toward his public self and his way of participating in the antislavery cause. His apparently sensible anonymity in the beginning of the story becomes the humiliating "disguise" in which he must leave town. And the humble "clothes on his back," which may hide his wounds from the public gaze but cannot restore his public dignity, stand in awkward contrast to the flogging of his "bare back" in the "public square," a violent display that draws an audience to his cause even as it makes a spectacle of his offense. And when he returns to the North he abandons the tactic of anonymity altogether in favor of the tactic of exposure: the publication of his "personal narrative" under his own name and, consequently, the exposure of the brutality of the Southern system. His own exposure and martyrdom have, in effect, empowered him to expose the injustice of slavery.

Nevertheless, letters and personal narratives and even names—despite their fiction of personal presence—are, after all, public representations. It is significant that immediately before her mention of Dresser Grimké writes, "Let us endeavor, then, to put on the *whole* armor of God" (27)—a metaphor that calls attention not only to a kind of body, but specifically to that body's protective qualities rather than its vulnerability. Echoing Grimké's own rhetoric, Blanche Glassman Hersh has more recently described Grimké thus: "Responding only to the demands of an inner voice, she seemed naturally endowed with the kind of protective shield that other reformers worked hard to acquire" (263). At the very least, it is mixing metaphors to see an "inner voice" as a "protective shield." Yet the inside-out tension in the figure is exactly the tension in the ideal of sincerity, for sincerity is, after all, a public strategy—one whose efficacy, paradoxically, diminishes the "hard[er]" one seems to "work . . . to acquire" it. Moreover, Grimké was, as I have argued, acutely conscious that her work was with audiences, that her object was to change—or "rectify," as she put it in her letters to Catharine Beecher—"public opinion" (Ceplair 155). When Beecher accused her of "*coercion* by public opinion," Grimké responded, "we know that when public opinion is rectified at the North, it will throw a flood of light from its million of reflecting surfaces upon the heart and soul of the South" (175).[23] The difference in their language is both characteristic and revealing: what Beecher portrays as a use of force, Grimké portrays as a bringing to light. But it is exactly Grimké's denial of her rhetoric as forcible that gives it its force; it is her figuring of it as a transparent expression of truth—a "reflecting surface" that calls attention not to itself but to the image it mirrors—that makes it effective public strategy. And the paradox is at least as evident in Grimké's public appearances as in her writings: even her most ardent admirers repeatedly resorted to language that evoked force and even coercion to describe her public speaking. "Angelina Grimké's serene, commanding eloquence," wrote the abolitionist Robert F. Wolcutt, "enchained attention, disarmed prejudice, and carried her hearers with her"—the distinctly material effects of a rhetoric that denies its materiality (qtd. in Lumpkin 145).

Grimké's figure of public opinion's "million of reflecting surfaces" is a key image, suggesting as it does surface without depth and endless iteration, as well as absolute visibility. It is an image of pure publicity, akin to the world of Beecher's monstrous woman surveyor, with the important distinction that in Grimké's figure there is no irreducible privacy, neither the "heart and soul of the South" nor the surveyor herself. Ideally, everything is subject to the "flood of light" that is publicity, and therefore available for viewing. But Grimké's rhetoric also depended upon the existence of a private realm, if only as the space out of which the things of darkness could emerge into the light. Moreover, her letters show that she was disturbed by the charge that there might be private, selfish motives behind her public success, and it is not surprising that those doubts were at times disabling for her as a public speaker. In an October 1837 letter to Grimké, shortly before declaring his love for her, the antislavery activist Theodore Dwight Weld wrote with disgust of the apparent tendency of abolitionists "to be seeking fame and notice"; he warned of "the immense temptations, desire for applause, ambitious pomp and circumstance, the sickening eulogies of Speakers" (qtd. in Lumpkin 183–84). As Grimké's biographer Katharine Lumpkin has argued, it must have been clear to Grimké that the criticism was directed at her. Five months later, she was writing to Weld about her appearance at the Massachusetts State House: "I think it was good," she wrote, and then, suddenly recoiling from her assessment, "I expect you to help me . . . crush down the first things of *pride* and self gratulation. . . . I am sorely tempted to believe *I* have had a *triumph* this afternoon, but I pray to be delivered from such sinful, presumptuous thoughts" (qtd. in Lumpkin 156, emphasis in original). Significantly, after Weld's initial suggestion that a "desire for applause" underlay Grimké's public appearances, Grimké could not have him present in the audience when she spoke. According to Lumpkin, "she would tell him, 'Yes, come if the Lord wills it,' but then she would write, 'O please do not come.'" When Weld pressed her for a reason, she responded, "Only because I have felt since I knew you such a crushing sense of my own inferiority that it has seemed impossible to rise above it" (Lumpkin 184).

Weld's own struggle against ambition, by contrast, drove him into a kind of anonymity. "As I look over our ranks," he had written in his October 1837 letter to Grimké, "I sometimes ask myself how many of these brethren and sisters would do *just as much* in the abolitionist cause if they worked utterly in the dark, and they were never known as writers, speakers, the poets, the officers, the leaders?" (qtd. in Lumpkin 184, emphasis in original). Already Weld had himself renounced public speaking—despite being known as a "spellbinding" orator—presumably due to an ailing throat. And two years later he would edit one of the most influential antislavery pamphlets ever published, *American Slavery as It Is,* anonymously. When Grimké had refused to dissociate herself from her letter to Garrison, and when she had boldly attached her name the following year to her *Appeal to the Christian Women of the South,* she had seen anonymity as a cowardly choice. But for Weld anonymity was the necessary "proof" of his humility. One significant difference, of course, lies in the reception of the audience: while Grimké's "character" had sustained "injury" from her exposure as author, Weld anticipated only praise. Indeed, Grimké's public "presence" was and is in some fundamental way a martyred presence, rejected by her native South for her abolitionism, by her adopted faith for her outspoken radicalism, and by much of her public—even many fellow abolitionists—for her feminism. But even more basically, Weld's retreat to anonymity entails the fantasy of an irreducible privacy, a domain of the personal that can and should be kept "utterly in the dark," and whose exposure can only corrupt the public discourse.

The antithetical faces of liberal privacy afforded Grimké a dramatic and dynamic structure within which she could fashion both her antislavery crusade and her sense of herself as a woman on the lecture platform. As a region of life that must continually be produced publicly and reinscribed as irreducibly private, liberal privacy generates a logic of exposure: it underwrites both the impetus to bring everything under the light of public inquiry, and the fiction that there is still more to be revealed. Grimké's treatment of the ostensibly invisible and unspeakable things of life—slavery, domesticity, feminine virtue—as performances, as masks that not only can conceal an underlying corruption but also attract the very fascination they pretend to avert, capitalized on the hypocrisy inherent in liberal privacy, which must deny its public face even as it depends on it. Yet Grimké could also assume liberal privacy's attitude of self-righteousness, its claims of privilege and respectability and its outrage at those who would violate it. She held out the tempting possibility of feminine "virtue" even as she revealed it, too, to be performative; she presented her message as a transparent expression of truth, directed not at her audience's senses but at their "understandings" and their "hearts," even as her rhetoric's momentum called that transparency into question. The precariousness of Grimké's bold rewriting of the conventions of liberal privacy is perhaps nowhere as evident as in her own venture into domesticity. She was thirty-three years old and at the height of her power as a public speaker when she married Weld; the 14 May 1838 ceremony took place just two days before her dramatic address at Pennsylvania Hall. But, despite both partners' intentions to the contrary, that address, it turned out, would be her last until the Civil War, as she routinely declined the invitations to lecture that continued to come after her marriage. Biographers and historians have disagreed as to the specific reasons for Grimké's abrupt withdrawal from public speaking, but they have generally treated it as a kind of defeat, a surrender to ill health and increasingly oppressive domestic responsibilities.[24] Her public years, the reasoning goes, constituted her challenge to women's confinement in the domestic sphere, while what Grimké herself referred to as her "hidden life" demonstrates, sadly, her inability to sustain that challenge for more than a few years, as well as the overwhelming power of the conventions she was up against.

Yet this tendency to divide Grimké's life into opposing "public" and "domestic" phases—the former radical and heroic, the latter retrogressive—conflicts with the way Grimké viewed her marriage to Weld, at least initially. "Now I verily believe that [Sarah and I] are *thus* doing *as much* for the cause of woman as we did by public speaking," she wrote to her friend Anne Warren Weston two months after the wedding. "For it is absolutely necessary that we should show that we are *not* ruined as domestic characters, but so far from it, *as soon* as duty calls us home, we can & do rejoice in the release from public service, & are as anxious to make good bread as we ever were to deliver a good lecture" (Ceplair 326, emphasis in original). Grimké's emphasis on the "absolute" necessity of "proving that public lecturing does not unfit woman for private duties" is significant in two paradoxical respects (330). First, it clearly demonstrates that, for Grimké, publicity is not opposed to, but rather dependent upon one's "[fitness] for private duties"; housekeeping is not a retreat from her "public service" but its necessary complement. In other words, woman's effectiveness in public, Grimké believed, would require her to cultivate rather than discredit her conventional, domestic guise, to reinforce her audience's confidence in her as an able housekeeper.

At the same time that she promotes herself as "not unfit . . . for private duties," however, Grimké exposes domesticity as spectacle, treating it—much as she does in her antislavery writings—as a performance, here intended to "show" an observing public that "lectur[ing]" and "mak[ing] good bread" are not incompatible, but complementary. Earlier in the same letter Grimké imagined her "enemies" rejoicing, "could they only look in upon us from day to day & see us toiling in domestic life, instead of lecturing to *promiscuous* audiences" (326). While prudishly disapproving of Grimké's public lecturing, these enemies would nevertheless "look in" at her private life; their voyeurism differs from the attention of "*promiscuous* audiences" only in its hypocritical insistence on a fiction of private space. The problem, of course, is that Grimké's "household affairs"—however fictional or performative they may in theory have been—were no less oppressive: the rigorous Graham vegetarian diet, the constant stream of houseguests, a series of difficult pregnancies, simply left little time for her antislavery work. If, like "the rituals of sentimentalism" in Ann Douglas's account, Grimké's rhetoric of exposure promotes "privacy" as "a convention to be violated" and "invests exposure with a kind of final significance,"[25] then it is a process at once more radical and more thorny than Douglas suggests: for while Grimké's radicalism lay in her stubborn insistence on violating privacy, on treating everything—including her own domestic life—as potentially public, she also needed to perform a more conventional privacy in order to hold her public's attention, to play to her public's prejudices even as she proceeded to empty them out.

3

Melting into Speech

Frances E. W. Harper and
the Citizenship of the Heart

Intelligence does not generate action except as it is enkindled by feeling.
  —John Dewey, *Liberalism and Social Action*

The principle of moderation in punishment, even when it is a question of
punishing the enemy of the social body, is articulated first as a discourse of
the heart.
  —Michel Foucault, *Discipline and Punish*

On 24 December 1860, a convention of South Carolina delegates adopted the
"Declaration of the Immediate Causes Which Induce and Justify the Secession of South Carolina from the Federal Union," a document modeled explicitly on the Declaration of Independence, detailing for "the Supreme Judge of
the world" the systematic disenfranchisement of the state by the federal government. Citing President-elect Lincoln's opposition to slavery, the delegates
claimed that his inauguration the following March would deprive "the slaveholding States" of their "power of . . . self-protection," leaving them vulnerable
to a federal government expressly "hostile to the South, and destructive of its
beliefs and safety." Among other evidence, they pointed to the practice in some
Northern states of "elevating to citizenship, persons who, by the supreme law
of the land, are incapable of becoming citizens." The stark opposition implicit
in the delegates' logic is that to enfranchise blacks is to disenfranchise white
Southerners.

   The passage of the Thirteenth and Fourteenth Amendments and the period of Reconstruction thus offered the conditions under which white Southerners could figure their own cause as that of an aggrieved liberty in search of

protection in ways that had not been possible before.[1] This cultivation of a new rhetoric of protection in support of the Southern cause—along with the notion that black citizenship was in and of itself injurious to whites—in turn affected how the case for black citizenship could be made. This chapter turns to the writing of Frances Ellen Watkins Harper, including her 1892 novel *Iola Leroy* and its fictional examination of the historical transition from slavery to black citizenship. Harper's great innovation, I will argue, was to turn the white rhetoric of protection against itself, capitalizing on the interdependency of protection and vulnerability to depict an ideal of self-protection collapsing under the weight of its own internal contradictions. The figurative language of Harper's poetry and some of her more imaginative prose pieces is rich with such moments: repeatedly we see the "solid seeming" world of public forms, to use Emerson's language, being dissolved and, obversely, vulnerability being transformed into strength and solidity. Some of her favorite tropes defy reason, turning inside out and outside in, imagining fortresses dissolving under a gaze, or "weakness" as a protective "shield" ("The Lake City Tragedy," *Brighter Coming Day* 384).[2] For Harper, such openings meant that the material injustices of the world were always vulnerable to exposure, and that even the most lowly and despised could potentially occupy the "throne of power."[3] But they also—especially in her writings after the end of Reconstruction—allowed her to raise questions about self-protection as a civic ideal, about whether it was possible or even desirable as a foundation for civic participation. As the defenders of segregation and Jim Crow, whether directly or in coded language, increasingly appropriated a sentimentalized rhetoric of protection, Harper developed her own strategies both for casting doubt on their underlying assumptions and for constructing a model of civic space that would be genuinely inclusive.

Some of Harper's most extravagant imagery appears in "The Triumph of Freedom—A Dream," which was inspired by John Brown's martyrdom and first published in 1860, the year Abraham Lincoln was elected president and South Carolina declared its secession from the Union (*Brighter Coming Day* 114–17). Written in the first person, the piece begins with an idyllic vision of Nature that quickly turns into nightmare when a spirit appears to "show [the narrator] the goddess of this place." Through a series of revelations, the narrator comes to see that the apparent serenity is really just a facade for an underlying horror: the goddess's white robe turns out to be stained with blood, and her "glittering throne" is supported by piles of quivering hearts. The narrative lingers over its grotesque descriptions of the various piles of hearts—the "little hearts" of "a hundred thousand new-born babes," the "agon[ized]" hearts of "desolate slave mothers," the "bruised and seared" hearts of men and "withered hearts . . . in which the manhood has never been developed," and the "young, fresh hearts," streaming blood, of girls "sold from the warm clasp of their mothers' arms to the brutal clutches of a libertine or a profligate." Aside from their Gothic resonance, the exposed hearts of slaves function in two ways here. First, by imagining the figurative "heart" of the institution of slavery as the literal hearts of slaves, Harper brings body and spirit, tangible and intangible, exterior and interior, into a complex interplay. Bodies turn out to be strangely ethereal and transparent, while interiors turn out to be strangely material. There can be no hiding in such a place; whatever is behind or underneath the surface will inevitably make itself known and felt. And so, when the blood-stained goddess feels herself exposed, the "earnest eye" of Agitation "searching into the very depths of her guilty soul," and she begs her worshippers to "hide me beneath your constitutions and laws—shield me beneath your parchments and opinions," we know that the request is futile, that the seemingly immutable "constitutions and laws" will yield to Agitation and dissolve just like all the other appearances.

The second way in which the piles of hearts function is more conventionally sentimental. Again, it has to do with the powerful move of turning a thing inside out, or turning a thing into its apparent opposite—in this case, turning the black heart of slavery into the exposed hearts of black slaves. That move, for Harper, becomes a figure for the way in which her rhetoric is intended to work on the hearts of her readers: beneath an uncaring surface, they discover their own vulnerable hearts. Just as (in the dream) the institution of slavery is undone by exposing the wounded hearts of its victims, the public apathy upon which it depends is undone once the public is made to feel the cruelty of slavery in its own heart. Thus is exposure turned into self-exposure, and the bleeding heart of the black slave turned into the vulnerable heart of the nation. Freedom triumphs, then, not through its abstraction from the realm of violence, as in classical republicanism, but rather through citizens' identification with the victims of violence—indeed, through their recognition of *themselves* as injured by injustice. Freedom triumphs not through the guarantee of personal security and self-protection, but rather through the universal acknowledgment of vulnerability. For Harper, speech is not separate from the material world of bodily existence; on the contrary, speech is most powerful precisely when it is crossing over that boundary, either from or into materiality. The grand celebration at the end of "The Triumph of Freedom" offers just such an image: the "anthems of praise" and "songs of deliverance," the narrative explains, are "just such songs as one might expect to hear if a thousand rainbows would melt into speech." That image of rainbows melting into speech challenges the oppositions upon which the classical model of public discourse depends, blurring world, language, and speaker, and defying rationality. The letter Harper sent to John Brown as he awaited his conviction and execution for the Harpers Ferry raid is similarly extravagant in its defiance: "Virginia has no bolts or bars through which I dread to send you my sympathy," she wrote, imagining "sympathy" as capable of transgressing both the laws of Virginia and the laws of physics (*Brighter Coming Day* 49). And, in yet another reason-defying reversal, she portrayed "Universal Freedom" using the bodies of Brown and his men as "her first stepping stones to dominion"—the same figure with which she drew "The Triumph of Freedom" to an end. Here Freedom is not simply capitalizing on the injustice that she opposes; she has herself become "the dominant power of the land."

Four decades later, as Jim Crow laws proliferated and lynching reached an appalling peak, Harper was still experimenting with figures of protection and vulnerability—in particular, with the potential for reform she found in their creative instability. But now, with lynching being carried out in the name of protecting the vulnerable, Harper approached such tropes with more skepticism, endowing them with bitterness and irony as often as triumph. In 1899 Harper wrote a poem responding to a lynching in Lake City, South Carolina, in which a mob set fire to the home of the black postmaster and began shooting as he attempted to quell the flames, killing him and his infant daughter. "The Lake City Tragedy" draws from the inflammatory rhetoric that was routinely deployed to justify such crimes—the image of vulnerable white womanhood, and the language of purity and pollution—and turns it against the perpetrators: in Harper's account, it is "Carolina" whose name has been "blurred . . . With blood," and whose sons have "trail[ed] / Their manhood in the dust" (383–85). Ultimately, however, "The Lake City Tragedy" is about the failure of sentiment, and the failure of the sort of vision for national renewal she presented in her piece on John Brown. At the crucial moment in the poem, Harper imagines the black family's sudden terror, realizing that their home is encircled by "The fiery breath of kindled flames."

> The trembling mother clasped in vain
>   Her babe, whose innocence
> And weakness, should have been a shield;
>   Its feebleness, defense.

The idea that innocence could disarm aggression—especially sexual aggression—was a staple of sentimental literature; here Harper emphasizes its counterintuitive quality by yoking together the apparent opposites around caesuras. But the refiguring of vulnerability *as* protection, elsewhere an empowering move for

Harper, is in this stanza something else. Not only is it something that "should have been" but was not; the idea itself becomes cruelly meaningless when we are presented with an infant threatened by fire. If elsewhere it represents the possibility of real transformation, here it elicits outrage and suggests the enormity of the obstacles. And if elsewhere the spectacle of injury exposes the tender heart of the nation, "The Lake City Tragedy" aims at a different kind of exposure: the shameful exposure of these men who perpetrated their crime "veiled in darkness" to the unforgiving light of the nation's judgment.

RACE, REPUBLICANISM, AND THE SEGREGATION DEBATE

Before turning to *Iola Leroy,* I wish to examine the mainstream debate over segregation law and the rhetorical strategies employed both in support of and in opposition to the legally enforced separation of the races. Recalling the rationale for the Fourteenth Amendment to the Constitution in his *Plessy v. Ferguson* dissent, Justice John Marshall Harlan framed the central issue as a question of protection. Even though "the words of the amendment . . . are prohibitory," its intent and its effect are protective, he argued citing the court's own language, establishing an "immunity" for "the colored race—the right to exemption from unfriendly legislation against them distinctively as colored" (Plessy 537, 556). The logic is familiar: to justify a law is to present whatever it shields as vulnerable, and whatever it restrains as aggressive and invasive. And so the "prohibitory" language of the amendment does not mean that it imposes severe or authoritarian restrictions on the states, because all it prohibits is "unfriendly legislation" designed to infringe the civil rights of "the colored race." To the other side in the debate, it is the states' segregation laws that are protective, and the federal law that must be prevented from invading the states' rights. This latter point is made explicitly by Justice Henry Billings Brown in the *Plessy* decision: the Fourteenth Amendment "does not invest Congress with power to legislate upon subjects that are within the domain of state legislation," he argues, but only to offer means of redress when their rights have been violated (Plessy 537, 546–47). Brown goes on to deny that the Louisiana statute in question infringes on the civil rights of Negroes, but he stops short of positively claiming that it is protective. Although his argument is constructed so as not to require an active defense of segregation laws, it is nevertheless an intriguing omission, because it would seem to invite a challenge on that basis. And, indeed, Harlan's dissent takes advantage of precisely such a strategy: the idea that whites are somehow so delicate as to need a law to protect them from coming into contact with blacks, he suggests, is ridiculous. The state enactments in question, he concludes, "proceed on the ground that colored citizens are so inferior and degraded that they cannot be allowed to sit in public coaches occupied by white citizens. That, as all will admit, is the real meaning of such legislation as was enacted in Louisiana" (Plessy 537, 560).

If the idea of white vulnerability and black degradation is not part of the official legal justification for segregation laws—and can even support the other side, so improbable and offensive it appears when it is made explicit—it is advanced in countless other ways, through the concepts of racial purity and contamination, in the specter of the black rapist and racist stereotypes of black masculinity, and in the ubiquitous metaphor of the South as a delicate white woman, to offer just a few examples. Segregationist discourse, then, often evinces a duality: it relies heavily on figures of white vulnerability at the same time that white vulnerability is officially denied as the reason for legal separation of the races. The national debate over segregation laws that reached a culmination in *Plessy v. Ferguson* is rife with coded language and evasions, but I will argue that these questions of protection and vulnerability—what the law exists to shield and what it exists to restrain—also constitute a major subtext, often at odds with the very argument being advanced. A decade before *Plessy v. Ferguson,* the *Century Illustrated Magazine* published a series of articles by two white Southerners, George Washington Cable and Henry Woodfin Grady, debating segregation laws. It is an illuminating exchange, not only for its creative approaches to the concept of civic protection but also for its references to the explicit and the implicit, to silence, speech, and the unspeakable.

Cable's "The Freedman's Case in Equity," opposing the legally enforced segregation of the races, appeared in the January 1885 edition of *Century Illustrated.* With the air of a white Southerner speaking confidentially to other white Southerners, Cable urges an honest and open self-examination and concludes that such an inquiry will yield a basic truth: segregation laws are an attempt to legislate a social hierarchy along racial lines, and to enforce it as it was under the institution of slavery. Such laws aim "to preserve the old arbitrary supremacy of the master class over the menial without regard to the decency or indecency of appearance or manners in either the white individual or the colored" (414). We must acknowledge the error of slavery, he insists, and abandon these efforts to reestablish it in a different form. But ultimately Cable's message is a hopeful one for white Southerners: once these artificially imposed distinctions are abandoned, the natural social hierarchy will be permitted to emerge, which of course will be favorable to the white race. In fact, Cable sees his position as the only possible one for those who truly believe in white supremacy. To legislate a racial hierarchy, he suggests, is to admit that white supremacy requires the support of law in order to exist at all. Addressing the idea that there is an instinctive repugnance to racial mixing, Cable writes: "if there is such an instinct, so far from excusing the malignant indignities practiced in its name, it furnishes their final condemnation; for it stands to reason that just in degree as it is a real thing it will take care of itself" (418). Cable's logic implies that the superiority of the white race *cannot* be imagined as vulnerable, threatened by an encroaching blackness, because to imagine whiteness as in need of legal protection is effectively to deny its natural superiority.

In his reply to Cable, "In Plain Black and White," published in *Century Illustrated Magazine* three months later, Grady does not address this particular point directly. Instead, he mischaracterizes Cable's position as one that favors racial mixing.

> A careful reading of Mr. Cable's article discloses the following argument: The Southern people have deliberately and persistently evaded the laws forced on them for the protection of the freedman; this evasion has been the result of prejudices born of and surviving the institution of slavery, the only way to remove which is to break down every distinction between the races; and now the best thought of the South, alarmed at the withdrawal of the political machinery that forced the passage of the protective laws, which withdrawal tempts further and more intolerable evasions, is moving to forbid all further assortment of the races and insist on their intermingling in all places and in all relations. (910)

Clearly, Grady's primary strategy is to present the question of legally enforced segregation as a "plain black and white" choice between racial "assortment" and racial "intermingling." If Cable is not for segregation, then, he must be for racial mixing. Such an argument assumes that there is no interracial contact that is not intimate; there is no possibility of a civic realm in the classical republican sense—where interactions are by definition abstract and impersonal—that can accommodate Negroes.[4] In this respect, Grady looks back to the older logic of civic exclusion, in which racialized subjects are marked as inescapably embodied and thus incapable of the self-abstraction requisite for civic participation. To "force" such subjects into white public spaces is necessarily to force whites into intimate contact with them.

By using the language of "force," however, Grady also enacts his own drama of protection, and it is worth taking a closer look at how his argument is also played out as a contest over vulnerabilities that are worthy of legal protection. The Fourteenth and Fifteenth Amendments not only officially recognize the freedmen as having rights that are worthy of legal protection; they also imply that without constitutional protection those rights would be in danger of violation, and the Fifteenth Amendment explicitly identifies "race, color, or previous conditions of servitude" as the reason for that vulnerability. In other words, there is an implicit racialization of the struggle of liberty against tyranny: if the liberty in need of protection is identified as black, then the tyranny in need of restraint can be assumed to be white. Grady's muddled rendition of Cable's argument reveals just how offensive he finds this logic to be. Twice he refers to the Fourteenth and Fifteenth Amendments as "protective" of the freedman, but immediately denies any moral authority such a characterization might carry by describing them as having been "forced" on "the Southern people" by "the political machinery" of Reconstruction. On one level, such references simply redirect the focus from segregation to states' rights. But in doing so, Grady also identifies "the Southern people" as vulnerable to an intrusive federal government, rewriting the drama of black protection against white tyranny as a drama of Southern (white) protection against Northern tyranny. Indeed, in Grady's account, the "protective" amendments are made into just another instrument of Northern aggression, and their "persistent . . . evasion" by Southerners is recast as a flight from oppression and brutality. The "states' rights" formulation, in short, is a way to align "the Southern people" with the cause of an aggrieved liberty, rather than with racial tyranny. Nevertheless, as I shall examine in more detail shortly, the segregation laws themselves are not aimed at protecting white Southerners from an intrusive federal government. And so Grady must make an apparent leap of logic: his argument assumes that to protect blacks from racial aggression is necessarily to "insist on [the races'] intermingling in all places and in all relations." The protection of blacks, in short, means the violation of whites.

Five months later, Cable published his response. "The Silent South" reiterates his earlier argument that social relations between the races must not be legally enforced; rather, they must be allowed to establish themselves naturally. But Cable goes further than in his previous article in theorizing his position in terms of the distinction between the civic and the social realms. Proponents of segregation law like Grady, he claims, "are . . . making the double mistake of first classing as personal social privileges certain common impersonal rights of man, and then turning about and treating them as rights definable by law—which social amenities are not and cannot be. . . . All the relations of life that go by *impersonal right* are Civil relations. All that go by *personal choice* are Social relations" (677, emphasis in original). Cable's insistence on establishing an absolute boundary between impersonal civil relations and personal social relations is the classical republican fantasy of a civic realm that is free by virtue of its abstraction from the personal. And his insistence that personal social relations do not require legal protection—indeed, that they are inevitably distorted when they are defined by law—is the fantasy of a realm of personal privacy into which the state must not be permitted to intrude. Nevertheless, Cable's own argument offers evidence that this classical republican model is perfectly compatible with a commitment to white supremacy. To inscribe race relations in the social realm, and therefore to declare race relations off limits to legal enforcement, is to forbid integration as well as segregation. And so, despite Cable's certainty that white supremacy does not need legal protection from challenges by blacks, his logic would also prohibit federal law from interfering with the "natural" supremacy of the white race. As he puts it, "the social integrity of the races . . . [will take] care of itself" (683).

On the surface, then, Cable presents his opposition to segregation laws as an argument against the assumption that the white race needs legal protection—against, in his words, "the idea that the social integrity of the races requires vigorous protection from without" (683). But a closer look reveals that Cable's argument relies on an implicit logic of protection. It is not simply that race relations do not need to be legally proscribed; it is that any attempt to codify such relations into law amounts to an invasion of the social realm by the state. Cable's example is revealing. Positing Mr. A. and his lady friend attending a concert, he distinguishes their civil right to be there from their social relationship with each other, which requires mutual consent. If no one can be prevented from exercising his civil rights, no one can be required to engage in social relations. Here, Cable imagines both the civil and the social realms defensively, and the "boundary line" between them as protection against invasion: "Mr. A. and his companion's social relations," he writes, "are, under these rulings, as safe from invasion as they were before; nay, even safer, inasmuch as the true distinction is made publicly clearer, between the social and the civil relations" (678). Cable's model allows him to distinguish the interests that are vulnerable and in need of protection from those that are invasive and in need of restraint—the crucial move in the rhetoric of protection. Any legal attempt to draw the boundary between civil and social other than where it really exists, he suggests, is inherently invasive of one or the other realm. He must, therefore, present that boundary as self-evident; otherwise, his argument becomes circular. Of course, the boundary between civil and social is anything but self-evident—Cable, for example, locates education in the social, rather than the civil, realm. But by drawing the boundary along what he presents as intrinsic societal rather than racial lines, Cable effectively redefines racial prejudice, from something that must be legally imposed to something that must be protected from interference by the state.[5]

If Cable and Grady turn out to be much closer politically than they admit, figuratively much of their language is almost identical. In particular, I would like to examine their common recourse to the metaphor of the South as a violated and silenced woman. In "The Freedman's Case in Equity," Cable uses the figure sparingly, portraying the (white) South as internally conflicted, and calling upon her to "stand . . . on her honor before the clean equities of the issue" (418). The problem, he suggests, is that those Southerners "who see the wrong and folly of [the segregation laws], silently blush for them, and withhold their open protests only because their belief is unfortunately stronger in the futility of their counsel than in the power of a just cause" (414). But for Cable such self-censorship is ultimately corrosive: adopting a trope that anticipates the language of Southern Gothic, he warns against those who wish to consider the legacy of slavery a "dead and buried issue." "What the impatient proposal to make it a dead and buried issue really means," Cable claims, is "to recommit it to the silence and concealment of the covered furrow" (409). If it is allowed to remain "suppressed," the "moral question" will only "incubate," eventually to return in a more virulent form (409). If Cable only subtly implies the threat to a woman's honor in his depiction of the South as a woman who silently blushes at what he elsewhere calls a "violat[ion]" (418), Grady takes it up as an organizing principle for his essay. Indeed, it is precisely Cable's claim to be speaking for the silent South that so infuriates Grady, who portrays it instead as "[bearing] false witness against her" (916). "She cannot let pass unchallenged a single utterance that, spoken in her name, misstates her case or her intention," he writes (909). At stake are nothing less than "her honor, her dear name, and her fame" (917). Not only does each man in this debate claim to be giving voice to the voiceless, we also have what are effectively dueling claims to be defending a modest, white woman's honor.

Grady is the more strident of the two in this respect because his position in favor of segregation law more readily evokes the image of a white woman whose "honor" is in need of protection. Although he is careful to avoid explicitly raising the figure of the black rapist, Grady takes every opportunity to imply such a threat. In the midst of describing "the negro's" shyness, for example, he unaccountably imagines him "forc[ing] himself into the ladies' car" (915). And, recounting a failed effort to integrate the Methodist Episcopal Church in the South, he explains that the bishop who tried "time and again [to] force the experiment" was eventually "driven to the conclusion that but one thing could effect what he had tried so hard to bring about, and that was miscegenation. A few years of experiment," Grady adds, "would force Mr. Cable to the same conclusion" (911). To equate the social mixing of races with the sexual mixing of races, and repeatedly to use words like "force" and "driven" in the equation, is to invoke the black rapist of white women, while at the same time pretending not to engage in such inflammatory rhetoric. Moreover, it is to suggest that segregation laws are established ultimately to protect the "honor" and purity of white women—and thereby the white race—from black sexual aggression and contamination.[6] While there is nothing particularly surprising about this construction, it is nevertheless illuminating to see it as an effort to marshal a logic of protection to the segregationist cause. By implicitly entrusting white racial purity to a sexually endangered woman, Grady maps white dominance onto female weakness, enabling him to evade the apparent contradiction between white vulnerability and the assertion of white superiority. But Grady's repeated insistence that the real threat issues from white Northerners, like the Methodist Episcopal bishop, even as he identifies *racial* integrity as what is at stake, is equally telling: it demonstrates that the opponents of "social equality" were as committed to denying the threat that blacks posed to whites as they were to amplifying it.

One other figure in Grady's essay in which a feminized South must defend her racial/sexual integrity against an invasive white North is worth examining here, in part because Cable picks it up in his reply. Imagining the South establishing a boundary beyond which zealous carpetbaggers may not go in determining race relations, Grady writes: "'Thus far and no farther,' she said to her neighbors, in no spirit of defiance, but with quiet determination. In her weakest moments, when her helpless people were hedged about by the unthinking bayonets of her conquerors, she gathered them for resistance at this point. Here she defended everything that a people should hold dear. There was little proclamation of her purpose. Barely did the whispered word that bespoke her resolution catch the listening ears of her sons" (916).[7] At the heart of this overdetermined image is a precious and vulnerable thing ("everything that a people should hold dear") threatened with violation. It is at once a mother threatened with rape, a home threatened with invasion, and a people threatened with conquest. The violating power is both military and political, both the Northern troops and the policies of Reconstruction. But, as many permutations of liberty's struggle against tyranny as there are in this figure, both liberty and tyranny are always racialized white. The divide is variously figured in terms of gender, or region, or state versus federal, but emphatically not race. And yet, it is precisely the racial divide that is at stake. Put another way, the segregation laws at issue in Grady's essay do not protect any of the versions of liberty imagined here from any of the versions of tyranny imagined here: they do not protect the South from Northern tyranny, or the states from federal tyranny, or white women from the tyranny of white men.

Significantly, Cable cites exactly this passage from Grady as evidence of their agreement ("Silent South" 675). That Cable sees this image of a feminized South under siege as perfectly compatible with his antisegregationist position underscores the extent to which flash points like states' rights or the tyranny of Reconstruction or vulnerable white womanhood entail a deflection from arguments for segregation. Nevertheless, the *un*acknowledged counterpart to this image is the specter of the black rapist, as we see in our close reading of Grady's essay. There is nothing in Cable's essays aimed directly at challenging the ideology of black sexual aggression and racial contamination; indeed, in "The Freedman's Case in Equity" he effectively eliminates it from the scope of his inquiry. "If this be a dark record," he writes, referring to the grossly disproportionate imprisonment of the black population, "what shall we say of the records of lynch law? But for them there is not room here" (417). However, there are moments that can be read as indirectly disrupting the assumption that white women are sexually threatened by black men. In "The Silent South," for example, he recounts the story of a "colored person . . . of lady-like appearance and deportment" who was forcibly ejected from a car designated by the railroad for whites only, even though there were some unruly passengers in the colored car, and even though no one in the white car objected. In court, the railroad was found liable for damages, but only because they did not provide separate first-class accommodations. "For laying violent hands upon a peaceable, lady-like, and unprotected woman," Cable declares, "nothing" (686). Here Cable tells a familiar story of injury, leaving the dominant discourse's assumptions about gender and class intact, and reversing the conventional racial roles. That Cable's idea of social refinement can accommodate a few genteel colored women means, clearly, that it does not follow strict racial lines. But his willingness to make exceptions for "lady-like," presumably light-skinned, colored women does not compromise his overall belief in white superiority, nor does it have any bearing on that sphere of life he deems "social," the boundaries of which even the "lady-like" would not be permitted to cross.

Ultimately, Cable's ostensible progressivism leaves white male authority comfortably intact. Like Justice Harlan, he exposes the inherent contradiction entailed in figuring segregation laws as protective. But, by relocating the racial hierarchy from the legally delineated civic realm to the social realm of free choice, he effectively replaces one logic of protection with another logic of protection, albeit a defensive one. And, by drawing a wide circumference around the social realm, Cable effectively fortifies the status quo, protecting the structures of racial inequality from any interference by the state. His republican fantasy envisions a limited civic realm of disembodied abstraction, and a vast, "natural" social order that happens to divide along racial lines. If a few, refined colored people can afford tickets to a concert, or first-class train tickets, then Cable is willing to accept their presence as long as they don't impose themselves socially. Such minor breaches of the racial hierarchy, after all, do not threaten the legal and economic structures, or the larger web of standards and assumptions that limit black access to such positions, and mark such refinement as essentially white.

Similar accusations have been made against Frances Harper's project of racial uplift. She, too, has been charged with promoting a hierarchy of refinement and taste that turns out to replicate an attitude of white superiority.[8] In his much-discussed criticism of Harper, for example, Houston A. Baker Jr. has called *Iola Leroy* "a courtesy book intended for white reading and black instruction," which promotes "a bright Victorian morality in whiteface" (*Workings of the Spirit* 32, 33). According to Baker, writers like Harper, in their desire to court a Northern white public, both dilute their critique of what he calls "whitemale hegemony," and abandon the "southern, vernacular, communal expressivity of black mothers and grandmothers," imagining in its stead a "mulatto utopia" (36). Indeed, by depicting mulatto characters who choose rather to identify with the black race than to assume positions in white society, Harper would seem to confirm Cable's reassuring conviction that social segregation will "take care of itself" without legal enforcement. In other words, she could be seen as subscribing to a model like Cable's, in which a "separate but equal" order is sustained by relocating it from the civic to the social realm, and thereby naturalizing it. I will argue, however, that such readings miss the more comprehensive way in which Harper challenges these racialized structures of civic engagement and the constitution of the civic realm. In her fictional accounts of African American citizenship, Harper does indeed construct racial and gender difference in such a way that abstraction and autonomy are marked as specifically white and male. But her didactic stories of virtuous civic conduct and enlightened public service function not as validations of white male authority, but as critiques of an exclusive, white and male version of citizenship and the logic of protection on which it relies: against white privilege and protection she offers an ideal of black self-exposure; against male duplicity, female transparency. Instead of simply engaging in a debate over which group's interests are the more vulnerable and in need of civic protection, then, Harper puts forth a model of civic participation that calls the terms of such a debate into question. And instead of replicating a racial hierarchy that privileges whiteness, Harper depicts racial discrimination as the source of the civic sphere's debasement.[9]

BLACK "REPRESENTATIVE PUBLICNESS" AND THE BODY OF THE FREEDMAN

At the center of Harper's vision of African American citizenship and a successful Reconstruction is the problem of representation. Before turning to the question of the freedman's representation in the body politic, however, *Iola Leroy* considers the conditions for self-representation before emancipation. As the novel opens, we find ourselves in the midst of a conversation: two slaves who are walking back to their masters' plantations from the market are discussing the freshness of the butter. As the conversation continues, they give their report to other slaves that they meet along the way, all of whom are unusually relieved to hear of the freshness of the morning's produce. Then the narrator explains: the conversation is not really about the state of the produce market; rather, it is "a phraseology [invented] to convey in the most unsuspected manner news . . . from the battle-field" (9). The slaves who stayed on the plantations during the Civil War seemed on the surface to be carrying on as usual, absorbed in domestic concerns, "but under this apparently careless exterior there was an undercurrent of thought which escaped the cognizance of their masters" (9). Thus from the outset Harper gives us slaves who have depth of character, who present a face to the world that is cut off from the "undercurrent[s] of thought" accessible only to the initiated.

The slaves' secret means of communication works, of course, by virtue of the disjunction between sign and referent: the produce market is *not* the battlefield, and so they can speak freely without arousing their masters' suspicion. Within the corrupt institution of slavery, free speech is possible only through *mis*representation. It is what Thomas Gustafson calls the "Thucydidean Moment": "a moment when . . . the social contract—the bond of faith, affection, and compromise sustaining harmony between man and man—is broken by political strife and linguistic duplicity" (71). The absence of a founding "social contract" in slavery is registered in Harper's novel as the linguistic breakdown Gustafson refers to as "the unfastening of words" (87). There is a key story about Tom Anderson, who learns to read on the sly and, in order to prevent his master's surmising, greases the pages of his book and hides them in his hat. "Then," as Robert Johnson explains, "if his master had ever knocked his hat off he would have thought them greasy papers, and not that Tom was carrying his library on his head" (44).[10] Like the "phraseology" invented for conveying information about the Civil War, the "greasy papers" misrepresent Tom's active intellect as a kind of vulgar materiality; both play to the white assumption that slaves are domestic and utilitarian creatures, capable of seeing things only for their immediate, physical uses and not as abstract representations of something else. Slave masters assume that slaves live their lives in a world of things-in-themselves, excluded from abstract reasoning, from the rational life of the mind that is achieved through literacy. For the slaves in *Iola Leroy*, however, the appearance of mere functionality becomes a cover for precisely that rationality from which they are presumed to be excluded: a cover for both literacy and intellectual involvement in the political affairs of the nation—in effect, for civic lives. And it is the abstraction of language—the fact that words *can* be "unfastened" from the things they represent and misread as something else—that permits the slaves to carry on active civic lives even within the institution of slavery.

Always at stake in such situations—implicitly, if not explicitly—is the slave's body. Misrepresentation is necessary in the first place, clearly, because slaves are subject to bodily punishment if their desire for liberty is exposed; linguistic abstraction, for them, is therefore directly tied to self-protection. Moreover, because the mask that slaves must wear is the mask of a purely material or bodily existence—that sphere of life Arendt refers to as "necessity"—their bodies often become the primary focus of that misrepresentation. In another related incident, Tom explains how he was able to overhear a meeting of some Confederate generals on his master's plantation: "Well, I war laying out on de porch fas' asleep an' snorin' drefful hard. Oh, I war so soun' asleep dat when Marster wanted some ice-water he had to shake me drefful hard to wake me up. An' all de time I war wide 'wake as he war" (17). The stereotype of the lazy slave, "fas' asleep" on the porch, here becomes the mask behind which Tom's curious intellect can carry on undisturbed. As with the coded language, in which political concerns are masked as domestic ones, and the "greasy papers," in which literacy is masked as a gross materialism, Tom's secret is safe because his facade conforms to white expectations and is therefore unlikely to be penetrated. And moreover, just as in the two other situations, Tom's nap misrepresents intellectual existence as physical existence. It is a performance of bodily indulgence and mental oblivion: what appears to be Tom's surrender to his body's desire for sleep is really Tom's controlled use of his own body. Self-discipline appears in the guise of indolence, acute consciousness in the guise of unconsciousness.

The connection between freedom and duplicity is made even more explicit in a secret conversation among the slaves about leaving the plantations to join the Union army. Even though Uncle Daniel, as he claims, "lubs de bery name of freedom," he chooses not to leave because of a promise he made to look after his master's wife and children—and, we later learn, a bag of money—while "Marse Robert" was away fighting for the Confederacy. Tom reminds him how rarely white folk keep their promises: "I don't trust none ob dem," he says. "I'se been yere dese fifteen years, an' I'se neber foun' any troof in dem" (25). But Uncle Daniel is adamant; three times he declares, "I promised him I'd do it, an' I mus' be as good as my word" (18, 19, 28). To bind himself to his "word" is in this case to remain enslaved, to renounce the kind of freedom that is achieved through misrepresentation, even though that is the only kind of freedom available to him. Furthermore, as Uncle Daniel explains his reasons for staying it becomes clear that there are also ties of sentiment binding him to the plantation. His telling of the death of his dear mistress, "Marse Robert's" mother, pulls all the conventional sentimental strings, with Miss Anna looking "sweet" and talking "putty" despite her frailty, extracting a tearful promise from Uncle Daniel to "be good to your Marster Robert," and finally "jis' fad[ing] away like a flower" (21). Miss Anna's girlish innocence and purity situate her deathbed scene plainly in the tradition of Stowe's Little Eva, and mark Uncle Daniel as a kind of Uncle Tom, whose vulnerability to sentiment sanctifies him, but at the same time prevents him from ever realizing freedom in this world.

Sentiment, then, appears here as another form of bondage. And, like bondage to one's word, the ties of sentiment imply a certain ideal model of interpersonal relations in which the face one presents to others is a true representation of one's inner self. Sentiment, we might say, imagines one's public face as bound to a unitary, essential self, and is therefore antithetical to the sort of deceptions that Robert Johnson and Tom carry out. And, because the primary locus of sentiment has conventionally been home and family, the suppression of sentiment often appears as the determination to leave home. The early chapters of *Iola Leroy* establish this particular pattern of binary oppositions with extraordinary clarity. One the one hand are the slaves who choose to remain on the plantation, represented most fully in Uncle Daniel and his wife Aunt Katie, thoroughly sentimentalized characters, whose goodness and purity are described in Christian terms, and who seem incapable of deception.[11] Aunt Katie has a face that "expresse[s]" her soul: when Robert Johnson asks her whether she feels bitterness toward her white owners she replies, with a "touching . . . look of resignation and hope" and a "simple child-like faith," "the Lord says we must forgive" (28). On the other hand are Robert Johnson and Tom Anderson, who resist such "touching" appeals with skepticism and humor. Robert "laugh[s] carelessly" at Uncle Daniel's description of Miss Anna's death, saying, "Oh, I don't take much stock in white folks' religion" (21). And Tom responds to Uncle Daniel's tearful acceptance of "Marster Robert's" charge to look after his wife and children by commenting that Uncle Daniel's "tear bags must lie mighty close to [his] eyes" (25). Breaking the bonds of slavery, for Robert Johnson and Tom, also means steeling oneself against the influence of sentiment.

When at last the Union army advances to within reach of the community, Robert Johnson senses that "freedom [is] almost within his grasp": "All the ties which bound him to his home," the narrator observes, "were as ropes of sand, now that freedom had come so near" (35). Implicit in that statement is a larger and more comprehensive theory of bondage and freedom, established by Harper in the first four chapters of the novel. Slavery is, of course, being "bound" to one's "home" in the obvious sense that a rigid system of laws and law enforcement prohibited slaves from moving freely from place to place. The Union army dissolves that "tie" by offering armed protection—in effect, an alternative "home"—for slaves who choose to leave the plantations. But slavery is also being "bound" to a life of necessity—precisely the life that, in classical theory, is relegated to the private realm—a life focused entirely on bodily existence, ruled by violence rather than persuasion, where the meanings of things are plain and immediate and singular, never in doubt. In terms of language, slavery binds or fastens signs to the things they represent, thereby disabling language of its capacity to establish a realm apart from the physical, a realm of abstract reasoning and fluid meanings, where influence can be liberated from the bondage of physicality. And, in terms of selfhood, slavery binds one's face to an immutable and unitary essence. Because it is the disjunction of public and private selfhood that establishes interiority, slaves are therefore theorized as without depth, artless, and thus necessarily incapable of deception. Freedom, in contrast, is the breaking of all these bonds—the bonds of coercion and sentiment that tie the slave to his home, as well as the bonds that imprison him in the realm of necessity by tying his mental processes rigidly to the tangible and bodily world. For Robert Johnson, freedom is liberation from the private realm into the public realm of linguistic abstraction and representative selfhood, a liberation the narrator describes, significantly, as the proof of his "manhood" (36).

However clearly Harper advances this neoclassical model of freedom in the first four chapters, though, *Iola Leroy* eventually abandons it for another model of citizenship—a model that requires the reestablishment, rather than the rupture, of ties to home and heart. A minor but crucial character in this respect is Ben Tunnel who, with Uncle Daniel, chooses to remain on the plantations during the Civil War. Unlike Uncle Daniel, however, Ben Tunnel is deeply conflicted about his decision. Proud and defiant, profoundly embittered by his experience under slavery and resentful of white domination, he nevertheless rejects "firm[ly]" Tom's and Robert's urgings to desert because of the responsibility he feels to his mother. In a "touching" speech he tells the others of his betrayal by the woman he loved, and his determination to "stick by" his "dear old mammy . . . as long as there is a piece of her" (30, 31). The last we see of him, he is "hushing his heart's deep aspirations for freedom in a passionate devotion to his timid and affectionate mother" (31). Harper sets up Ben Tunnel's predicament in the familiar terms: to remain in bondage is to submit to sentiment and the claims of home. But after emancipation, Ben is the man elected to represent his community in Congress. Aunt Linda and her husband Salters tell the story thus:

> "Ben got inter a stream of luck. Arter freedom com'd, de people had a heap of fath in Ben; an' wen dey wanted some one to go ter Congress dey jist voted for Ben ter go. An' he went, too. An' wen Salters went to Washin'ton to git his pension, who should he see dere wid dem big men but our Ben, lookin' jist as big as any ob dem."
> "An' it did my ole eyes good jist ter see it," broke in Salters; "if I couldn't go dere myself, I war mighty glad to see some one ob my people dat could. I felt like de boy who, wen somebody said he war gwine to slap off his face, said, 'Yer kin slap off my face, but I'se got a big brudder, an' you can't slap off his face.' I went to see him 'fore I lef,' and he war jist de same as he war wen we war boys togedder. He hadn't got de big head a bit." (167–68)

Significantly, it is Ben Tunnel—the man who rejected "freedom" in the terms in which it is established in the beginning of the novel—who goes further than any of the novel's other characters in national politics. At stake is nothing less than the viability of political representation: Ben's resolute attachment to "home," while preventing him from escaping slavery as Robert and Tom do, is what qualifies him to carry out the work of Reconstruction.

One of the ongoing problems for theorists of representative government— one that emerged in the debates over the state constitutions and, later, the federal Constitution—was how to ensure the fidelity of representation without disabling representative government.[12] How, in other words, could a public official faithfully represent his constituents and still maintain his distinction and independence from them? Aunt Linda and Salters's account of Ben Tunnel's relation to his constituents highlights precisely this tension between sameness and difference. Ben looks "jist as big" as any of the big men in Washington, and yet he is "jist de same" as when he and Salters were boys, his "head" no bigger than when he was a slave. My political representative, says Salters, cannot be "myself," but he can be one of "my people." It is Ben's difference from his constituents that signals his effectiveness as a representative: he represents their better selves; he is the "big brudder" who can be invoked for the little people's protection. But it is Ben's sameness to them—and to what he was before being elected to Congress and even before being emancipated—that secures their "fath." Moreover, with its emphasis on the sense of sight, Salters's account can also be read as a kind of mirror scene in which he goes to Washington and recognizes him*self* when he sees his representative. Thus is the moment of identity formation—when one sees an objective image that both is and is not oneself—related to one's entrance into civic life and, in particular, the American electoral process.[13] It is a moment, clearly, of special significance for the freedmen, who as slaves were denied political representation as well as—in theory—representative selfhood. And in Harper's version, the emphasis is necessarily on the signifier's identity with, rather than abstraction from, its referent. For Salters, it is his recognition of Ben Tunnel—or, more precisely, his recognition of himself in Ben Tunnel— that marks the moment's significance for him. Its impact lies not so much in how "big" Ben has become as in how constant he is, how much "the same" as he has always been. And so Ben Tunnel's capacity to represent his constituents is a direct consequence of his own integrity of character, the fidelity of his own self-representation. Salters's analogy that likens Ben to the "big brudder" whose "face" cannot be "slapped off" is significant because it suggests not just a scene of protection from neighborhood bullies but also a "face" that is indivisible from whatever is behind it.

In important ways, the tension inherent in representative politics both reproduces and engages the tension inherent in representative selfhood. For political representation to work as it is supposed to, constituents must have confidence in the fidelity of their representatives without their being bound to the people's will. Similarly, representative selfhood entails a public self that faithfully reflects one's inner self without being bound to it, thus constructing a selfhood with both integrity and depth. And in *Iola Leroy*, the emphasis is necessarily on integrity of character, just as it is on the fidelity of political representation, for it is integrity rather than depth that distinguishes the freedman from the slave. Even while enslaved Robert and Tom could achieve literate, politically engaged lives through *mis*representation: what remains lacking in slavery, and what therefore must be the work of Reconstruction, is the reattachment of visible and public signs to their private referents—to their "homes," as it were. It is the necessary counterpart to a vision of freedom-in-abstraction, to the slaves' "phraseology," and to Tom's "greasy papers" and his feigned nap. Furthermore, Harper's portrayal of Ben Tunnel demonstrates the direct bearing of personal integrity on the freedmen's confidence in the representative process. For them to believe they are not misrepresented, they must believe Ben Tunnel is not misrepresenting himself. Again, citizenship is imagined as involving a countermovement to the impulse to freedom established in the novel's Civil War chapters—a countermovement toward transparency, a reattachment to the personal.

What is striking about Harper's depiction here of the movement from enslavement into freedom is that it is aimed in a counterintuitive direction. I have been arguing that liberalism constructs a mutually constitutive opposition between a protected self-abstraction and a vulnerable embodiment, and that civic exclusions can be challenged by capitalizing on the tensions that opposition generates. The general pattern in my readings thus far has been to posit citizenship as a zone of protection, and noncitizenship as vulnerability to injury. For Stowe, for example, the Great Dismal Swamp represents a kind of civic exile, a capacity for empathy that can potentially renew American civic life, but also a bondage to bodily life that—at its extreme—affords no possibility for civic expression other than violence. By contrast, Harper envisions civic insidership as already embodied and vulnerable to injury. Too skillful a capacity for self-abstraction is for Harper a reason to be excluded from the body politic; it offers freedom on the wrong terms, a version of freedom available even to slaves through the corruption of language and self-misrepresentation. To secure the people's confidence in representative government, Harper stresses accountability over abstraction: both Uncle Daniel and Ben Tunnel, after all, successfully make the transition from slavery to freedom, suggesting that the failure to sever one's ties to home and thus prove one's "manhood" is not, after all, detrimental to achieving citizenship after emancipation. Robert Johnson, meanwhile, must reestablish his ties to home by finding the mother who was sold away from him during slavery, and Tom Anderson, whose case I will consider in more detail shortly, dies in a heroic effort to protect a company of white Union soldiers. The same ties that bound slaves to a life of necessity and bodily existence turn out to be crucial to citizenship after emancipation, returning, it could be argued, in the guise of self-discipline.[14]

The suggestion that American citizenship is not, after all, simply an escape from bodily existence—that it is in fact *embodied* in some fundamental way—arises again and again in *Iola Leroy,* from Tom's heroic death to Harper's treatment of the question of racial passing. Before going on to consider those issues, however, I wish to take one final look at the problem of representation in public life and its implications for the body. Salters's rendering of Ben's representation of the community in terms of sight—as a moment of *seeing* that does his "ole eyes good"—suggests, as I have argued, that for him it is a moment of recognition, the moment that lies at the heart of political representation because it secures the confidence on which representative government relies. But for Ben it is a moment of *being seen*. His capacity to represent his community depends upon the actual or implied presence of an audience of constituents; he must appear before them and display his representative selfhood publicly for them to recognize. This surprising moment of spectacle at the heart of Harper's version of representative politics suggests a relation to what Jürgen Habermas calls "representative publicness," a theatrical display of authority characteristic of both feudalism and the "refeudalization" of society that results from the bourgeois public sphere's deterioration. The feudal lord, writes Habermas, "displayed himself, presented himself as an embodiment of some sort of 'higher' power. . . . [R]epresentation pretended to make something invisible visible through the public presence of the person of the lord" (7).[15] His publicity was, therefore, "stag[ed]," "dependent on the presence of the people before whom it was displayed" (8, 10). In a similar way, maintains Habermas, twentieth-century mechanisms of publicity generate a kind of representative publicness: successful public officials impart an "aura of personally represented authority" that is a function of their "reputation" (200, 201).

Habermas clearly distinguishes this "representative publicness," on the one hand, from "representation in the sense in which the members of a national assembly represent a nation," the former being "inseparable from the lord's concrete existence, that, as an 'aura,' surround[s] and endow[s] his authority" (7). Representative politics, on the other hand, imagines public authority as separate from the "concrete existence" of the persons who wield it, and thus is for Habermas entirely consistent with the abstract and critical disposition of the bourgeois public sphere. But Harper's portrayal of Ben Tunnel's representative authority blurs that distinction in several significant respects. Most importantly, Ben's public presence cannot be understood simply as a representation of an impersonal abstraction; it is also, as I have shown, fundamentally linked to his personal integrity. It points not just beyond himself to the people's will, but also inward, to an immutable, essential self. And it is that quality, more than any other, that makes Ben Tunnel's authority different from—and subversive of— the authority of representative politics as Habermas theorizes it. Because integrity gestures to the private self, and can be known to others only by its inherently unreliable outward signs, Ben's representative authority is necessarily a matter of his constituents' confidence. As we have seen, Ben must present an integral rather than a divided self: his face must render visible his invisible depths and expose his private heart. But he can do that only by differentiating himself from the deceptive and the duplicitous—from, in Ben's case, the self-interested politicians with "big heads" who leave home and forget where they came from, or who change themselves into something other than what they were. In contrast, Ben's public face must be seen as authentic, not just a manipulable appearance but the real thing, a thing that cannot be "slap[ped] off"; his "invisible" self, to apply Habermas's terms, must be made "visible" in his public presence and perceived as "inseparable from [his] concrete existence." His public authority thus appears as a kind of "aura," an authenticity not of noble blood or lineage, but of self. And so although Ben's version of representative selfhood is inescapably an appearance—it exists, that is, in the eyes of others and must, therefore, be described from the outside—it must simultaneously deny that is so. It is a display that must not be perceived as such.

For Habermas "representative publicness" is associated with the body of the king, and it is worth taking a moment to consider the way American representative politics has been imagined in relation to monarchy. I have been arguing that Ben's capacity to represent his constituents depends upon his embodiment of an essential selfhood, and that the more inseparable his visible presence is from that essential selfhood—the more integrity of character he emanates, in other words—the more confidence he can inspire in his constituents, and the greater will be his public authority. Inasmuch as Ben's public authority consists in his successfully convincing his constituents that he is worthy of their confidence, then, he will always be striving to deny that it is a performance. If representative publicness is, as Habermas writes, "staged" and "dependent on the presence of people before whom it [is] displayed," then Ben's public face must be perceived as independent of an audience, a matter of essence rather than display. And yet Ben's visible presence before his constituents is neither incidental nor superfluous; it is, rather, the very basis of an authority that rests upon the people's confidence.[16] Nevertheless, Ben is not like a king in the sense that the king directly embodies the "higher power" of the realm; Habermas is quite correct to draw a distinction between that vision of public authority and representative politics, which explicitly precludes that kind of "sacred and inviolable" embodiment.[17] Although at first glance a face that cannot be slapped off might appear to be an image of inviolability, it is actually just the opposite. Ben's face cannot be slapped off because it is not a mask: it cannot be detached from the inner self that it exposes. His private heart is, to apply Habermas's phrase, "inseparable from [his] concrete existence." To try to slap off such a face would be to do violence not just to the body but also to the inner self from which it is inseparable. Thus we begin to see exactly how strange a figure of protection this is: the "big brudder" who is invoked for the boy's protection, whose face is apparently offered up for slapping in place of the boy's, is himself the very image of vulnerability. It is a figure more of sacrifice than of protection, and could indeed be read as Ben's sacrifice for the protection of his constituents.

The most vivid story of self-sacrifice for the protection of others in *Iola Leroy* is the story of Tom Anderson's death in battle. Harper advances the novel's Civil War chapters primarily through a series of conversations between Robert Johnson and Captain Sybil, a young man from Maine who joined the Union army "to free the slave" despite the ardent pacifism of his Quaker mother (49). As the news of Tom's fatal injury is brought to them, they are in the midst of a discussion about race prejudice among Northerners. Robert has been relating a series of incidents that characterize bigotry as white callousness, and he even takes an opportunity to point out the comparatively subtle prejudice in Sybil's own remark that it is "a burning shame to have held a man" as light-skinned and articulate as Robert in slavery. Robert replies that it is no "worse [than] to have held . . . the blackest man in the South," thereby exposing the racism that underwrites Sybil's liberal sympathy for Robert (44). The exchange suggests that Sybil's notion of sympathy—to look in the slave for a whiteness with which he can identify—will never solve the problem of race prejudice, because it still implies a rejection of blackness. It seems like an obvious point, but over the next few pages Harper takes it in an unusual direction. Just as in the earlier chapters she established what amounted to a theory of bondage and freedom, here she establishes an opposing theory of civic sacrifice that racializes protection and exposure and ties them both to an ethic of tenderheartedness.

As the conversation continues, Sybil comments that the "conduct of the colored troops [at Fort Wagner] has done much to turn public opinion in their favor," adding that "any white soldier would rather have his black substitute receive the bullets than himself"—precisely, as the two men are about to learn, the circumstances of Tom's death (49). Thus is the stage set for the tragic disclosure by imagining self-protection as the sacrifice of black bodies for the protection of white selves. White selves are protected, in other words, by the "substitution" of black bodies for white bodies—a substitution that can be carried out only in the absence of any sympathy for black suffering, and thus demands a hardening of the heart. Protection—meaning both bodily protection and emotional callousness—is the defining characteristic of whiteness in a racist society. But this particular ideal of self-protection will invariably unravel for the very reason that it relies on something other than itself. The white selfhood that it imagines is neither self-contained nor autonomous; it is, on the contrary, deeply vulnerable, and the stories that are clustered around the scene of Tom's death make that vulnerability clearly visible. Robert's last story before hearing of Tom's fatal injury is especially telling: an officer who had been imprisoned by the Confederate forces escaped and was aided by an aged colored man and his wife. "As he was going away" from their little cabin, Robert says, "the [colored] man took some shingles and nailed them on his shoes to throw the bloodhounds off his track" (52). The white officer's "kindly [feeling] towards colored people," then, stems directly from his realization that *he cannot protect himself,* that his own self-protection depends upon the knowledge of this couple, knowledge gained, we can imagine, from their own experience of such terror (52).

This version of sympathy, it is worth emphasizing, is quite different from Captain Sybil's sympathy for Robert's apparent whiteness. Unlike Sybil's compassion for Robert, the other officer's "kindly" feeling toward his helpers is self-interested. It originates within himself and is grounded in his own visceral experience of exactly the kind of vulnerability that Americans of color—slave and free—face routinely. Indeed, we might say that whereas Sybil's version of sympathy imagines whiteness as the common denominator, the other version grounds sympathy in a common experience of blackness. Furthermore, just as in the case of the white soldiers who send black substitutes into battle, the source of this officer's protection is society's most vulnerable members. As I noted earlier, this odd figure of a vulnerable thing being used as a protective shield appears with some frequency in Harper's writings. In the 1869 poem "Moses: A Story of the Nile," for example, the Egyptian princess Charmian saves the infant Moses from her father's decree by declaring, "The pathway to his life is through my own; / Around that life I throw my heart, a wall / Of living, loving clay" (*Brighter Coming Day* 142). The heart that becomes a body is the complement to the body that, in its sacrifice, becomes the heart of the nation: both figures reveal the underlying interdependency of vulnerability and protection. And, moreover, both figures demonstrate, in their radical instability, the inevitable tendency of protection to collapse into its apparent opposite. The civic model that would protect white selves at the expense of black selves becomes insupportable the moment that white selves look within and recognize their own true vulnerability, because the hardness of heart on which that model depends can no longer be sustained.

When Tom's bleeding body is brought into camp it is, significantly, one of the young white soldiers who tells Tom's story.[18] Their boat, stuck on a mud bank, had come under Rebel fire; after trying for a while to lie low and wait out the attack, the men began to realize the hopelessness of their situation. As the soldier tells Robert and Captain Sybil, "Tom took in the whole situation, and said: 'Some one must die to get us out of this. I mought's well be him as any. You are soldiers and can fight. If they kill me, it is nuthin.' So Tom leaped out to shove the boat into the water. Just then the Rebel bullets began to rain around him" (52–53). Tom was severely—fatally, as it will turn out—wounded, and the "soldiers" were saved. Just as in the story of the officer aided by the elderly black couple, the key here is in the white soldiers' recognition of their vulnerability, their experience of being someone's prey. Like the white men who send black "substitutes" into battle, they allow Tom to take the bullets that would otherwise be for them. But for these soldiers there is no illusion of safety, and no reasonable ground for supposing that they are protecting themselves. On the contrary, the overwhelming message is of their utter dependency on Tom's sacrifice of himself. Self-protection, independence, and autonomy are all exposed as fictions, and in their place are relations of vulnerability and dependency, and heartfelt emotions of sorrow and gratitude.

The Christian implications are, of course, inescapable: the blood "streaming from [Tom's] wounds," the water and the "rain[ing]" bullets, and the sacrificial death so that others may live, all carry powerful Christian significance. But Harper repeatedly imbues those Christian symbols with significance in the American civic mythology: Tom's "blood," as she wrote regarding John Brown's death, is—for the white soldiers and, indeed, the nation—"a new baptism of Liberty" (*Brighter Coming Day* 117). In her 1885 essay "A Factor in Human Progress" she tells the same story of the black soldier who offered up his life for his white compatriots, identifying it as a factual account from "among the annals of the civil war" (*Brighter Coming Day* 279–80). There she situates it in a long line of religious and patriotic examples of "self-sacrifice and self-surrender," including Curtius of ancient Rome and "the fathers of this republic." Clearly this is not a vision of radical political change: Tom's self-abasing refusal to consider himself a "soldier," and his apparent capitulation to racist assumptions about his expendability, make that painfully obvious.[19] Rather, it is a vision of a racist politics of protection that will end up dismantling itself—a process for which Tom's self-sacrifice operates as the catalyst. Tom, in other words, operates within a system of signification that he does not have to challenge because it will unravel of its own accord, from the force of its own internal contradictions.

The incident was also put into verse by Harper in "A Story of the Rebellion" and, just as in *Iola Leroy*, the poem tells the story in the voice of one of the presumably white soldiers who was saved (*Brighter Coming Day* 365–66). And once again, the vision of speech that emerges is both unsettlingly complicit with a racist configuration and also finally disruptive of that configuration. Here, first of all, is a black story being told by a white speaker, reminiscent of a long line of white appropriations of black stories and voices, from William Lloyd Garrison to Elvis Presley.[20] Such appropriations function to suffuse white speakers with "heart," thereby enabling them to arouse the sentiments of their audiences and rely on the racist association of blackness with emotion and whiteness with the capacity to put that emotion into intelligible language. And so, in contrast to the soldier's coherent account of Tom's story in *Iola Leroy*—which includes a reiteration of Tom's precise words, in Tom's own dialect—Tom himself "attempt[s] to speak, but the words [die] upon his lips" (53). As with Tom's assertion of his expendability, Harper's choices in this scene would appear to reinforce racist distinctions. But, problematic as they are, those distinctions enable Harper to envision the exclusive version of protected white citizenship collapsing under the weight of its own internal contradictions. What begins as a white self protected by a black body turns into a white body finding its black "heart": the protective shield becomes the vulnerable interior, which is then turned into speech to move the hearts of nations. It is the radical instability of these figures, which collapse from inside out and outside in and turn self-protection into tenderheartedness, that makes them work so powerfully for Harper. True protection against injury, in Harper's vision of citizenship, is achieved not by building fortifications and making selves impermeable but, on the contrary, by exposing their true vulnerability—a paradoxical project that she represents in her paradoxical figures of selves enveloped in tenderness, and hearts that are wrapped around bodies. And so often, for Harper, that project is accomplished through speech: as she vows in her poem "Songs for the People," her "music" will continue "Till . . . the hearts of men grown tender / Girdle the world with peace" (*Brighter Coming Day* 371).

Liberty, Security, and Passing

Although Iola Leroy is first introduced to readers through a conversation between Tom and Robert in chapter 5, Tom's deathbed scene marks her real entrance into the novel, and in some respects she takes Tom's place as the novel's representative of the ethic of self-sacrifice. Raised to identify as white, Iola learns about her "Negro blood" only as she is being sold into slavery. But after emancipation, Iola must choose whether to pass back into the white community by marrying a white doctor, thereby accepting a life of apparent privilege and protection from racism. It is a dilemma in which Frances Harper had particular interest: she also explored it in her portrayal of Moses, who is raised to believe he is Egyptian but when made aware of his origins chooses to identify as Jewish, and in the title character of her 1869 serial novel *Minnie's Sacrifice.* In each case the decision not to pass is represented as self-exposure—exposure *of* a legally subordinated status as well as *to* injury and derision—and thus as self-sacrifice for the sake of an oppressed people. Like Tom's death, Iola's claim to blackness both stands in opposition to a white ethic of self-protection and, in the end, exposes the fallacy upon which that ethic depends: the liberty that passing appears to secure turns out to be a false liberty, gained at the expense of ties to family, and dependent for its advantages upon a system of discrimination.

Much of the recent critical attention to passing has focused on the conflict between essentialist and constructionist versions of racial difference, generally regarding the act of passing—as opposed to the decision not to pass—as the more subversive choice, disruptive of the rigid categories of race that constitute the oppressive system of "caste," to use Harper's term. Such readings tend to leave no way of understanding Harper's insistence on Iola's blackness other than as a kind of strategic essentialism.[21] A notable exception is Julie Cary Nerad's reading of what she calls narratives of "unintentional passing"—that is, narratives of characters raised to identify with one race, only later to be denied that racial identity. Nerad argues that it is misleading to read such characters as having to choose whether to "return" to an essentialized racial identity that they never knew existed. Rather, "the passer's choice to claim a black identity constitutes a turn, not a return," and the moments of revelation are represented less as an exposure of some underlying racial truth than as an exposure of race itself as "a legal construct predicated on problematic biological evidence" (818). That a character like Iola Leroy can, as Nerad puts it, "renounce" one racial identity for another clearly figures race as something other than essence (832). I would argue that Harper figures Iola's choice of racial identity as a choice between protected self-abstraction and legally enforced vulnerability. To marry Gresham and reclaim the white identity of her childhood would be to accept a life of privilege and protection at the expense of her bonds to her mother, brother, and uncle. Harper does figure it as a kind of misrepresentation, but it is not racial misrepresentation so much as self-misrepresentation: the "happily ever after" fantasy of being rescued from a life of hardship is the fantasy that selfhood can be detached from family and protected by a system of legal discrimination. It is the fantasy of a public realm that is free by virtue of its abstraction from the private. Yet to choose a black identity is to renounce the fantasy of protected self-abstraction, to acknowledge being bound to family and community, and to imagine public selfhood as grounded in, rather than abstracted from, private selfhood. At issue for Harper is not whether racial boundaries can be crossed, but how best to secure the confidence and trust upon which public life depends, and how to live a virtuous life in accordance with one's heart.

Indeed, at times race seems metaphoric for Harper—a convenient vehicle through which she can examine the nature of civic virtue, or a figure for the truth of everyone's tenderheartedness. Her poems "The Contrast" and "A Double

Standard" can be read as raising issues similar to those raised in her treatment of racial passing, with gender rather than race as the vehicle.[22] Protesting the unequal treatment of men and women who have had sexual relations outside of marriage, the poems depict men who can be seen as passing into polite society while the women they "sullied" are shunned. "A Double Standard," written in the voice of the fallen woman, asks why "I wear the brand of shame; / Whilst he amid the gay and proud / Still bears an honored name" (345). The rhyme draws a parallel between the woman's "shame" and the man's "honored name," a parallel where society can see only stark opposition, effectively hollowing out both the stigma and the honor. To claim such an "honored name," the poem suggests, is to assume a public position that is based in a false discrimination. Moreover, it is to assume that public selfhood and social status exist independently of how one conducts one's private life. If we see the man in this case as having a kind of freedom that the woman is denied, then it is a freedom that issues from the possibility of self-abstraction, and from the separation of public selfhood from private virtue. Such a system protects his libertine behavior at the same time that it ensures his social acceptance. The previous stanza describes him as being offered "a civic crown," suggesting that his privilege extends not only to the drawing room but also to the halls of government, and the "double standard" is about civic exclusion as well as social exclusion. The language Harper uses here echoes the language she uses elsewhere to describe how racial discrimination enables a corruption of civic life.[23] Later in the poem, Harper uses the biblical image of "whited sepulchers" to describe such men, associating the color white explicitly with a clean surface that masks interior decay (346). It is a trope that invites a comparison between racial passing and this account of what we might call social and civic passing: like the person who chooses to identify as white, these men buy into a fantasy of privilege, autonomy, and security; they confuse the false status ascribed to them by a discriminatory social order with true self-worth. And it is upon this sense that passing is deceptive and entails somehow being untrue to oneself—precisely the sense that Elaine K. Ginsberg (8) argues operates in service of the repressive regime of racial essentialism—that Harper builds her critique of the white, male delusion of autonomy.[24]

A conversation between Iola and Robert Johnson, who has turned out to be her uncle, clearly lays out the terms in which Harper wants us to understand racial passing. The two are discussing Dr. Latimer, another light-skinned Negro, whose white grandmother had offered to receive him as her heir if he would deny his Negro heritage. His refusal of the offer leads Iola to compare him to Moses and Nehemiah—"characters," as Iola says, who also "were willing to put aside their own advantages for their race and country" (265). Robert reminds her of the "doors" that would be "open to him as a white man which are forever closed to a colored man." "To be born white in this country," says Robert, "is to be born to an inheritance of privileges, to hold in your hands the keys that open before you the doors of every occupation, advantage, opportunity, and achievement" (265–66). Iola's response is that Dr. Latimer "could not have retained [his honor, true manliness, and self respect] had he ignored his mother and lived under a veil of concealment, constantly haunted by a dread of detection" (266). This conversation establishes a choice between reliance on one's inheritance and reliance on oneself, between looking outside oneself for the "key" and looking within, between manipulating surfaces and embracing depths. Here we can see why the concept of essentialism falls short as an explanation of what is at stake for Harper. If the essence—of race, self, or whatever—is, as Harper imagines it, always beneath the surfaces, then its public manifestation will always be a matter of representation, and its professed exposure, always a matter of credit and confidence.

Iola's insistence on defining Dr. Latimer's honorable and manly acknowledgment of his "colored blood" against the false claim to whiteness, then, can be seen as a strategy to secure the credibility of something that is necessarily elusive. But, more than that, it shows that the protection of being "born white in this country," as Robert puts it, is illusory; the shield against injury that it seems to provide, actually nothing more than a "veil of concealment." Robert's conflation of passing into the white community with being "born white" is, I would argue, more than just exaggeration or careless phrasing. It requires us to read being "born white" figuratively, as a paradoxical kind of birth that, as Iola points out, arises from *ignoring* one's mother. Thus it recalls Robert's own figurative birth from slavery into freedom, a birth that required him to break "all the ties which bound him to his home"—a break facilitated by his master's heartless sale of his mother and sister when he was a child (35). It also recalls the terms in which Ben Tunnel explains his decision to reject that particular kind of freedom: "while I love freedom more than a child loves its mother's milk," he tells Robert, "I've made up my mind to stay on the plantation" (31). The irony, of course, is that Ben's decision reveals that he does, after all, love mother more than freedom. But the very fact that the decision is framed in those terms suggests that there is a kind of freedom that entails rejection of one's mother—exactly the freedom that, later in the novel, is associated with passing and thus racialized white.[25]

Iola's own childhood, too, can be read as advancing a particular vision of liberty and protection, and racializing the choices along similar lines. Her white father makes the decision to raise Iola and her brother Harry in ignorance of their Negro ancestry, wishing his children "to grow up without having their self-respect crushed in the bud" (84). "We will have our children educated," he declares to his wife, "without being subjected to the depressing influences of caste feeling" (85). Much later in the novel Dr. Latimer and Iola reflect on the path that Leroy had chosen for his children:

> "Was it not a mistake to have kept you ignorant of your colored blood?"
> "It was the great mistake of my father's life, but dear papa knew something of the cruel, crushing power of caste; and he tried to shield us from it."
> "Yes, yes," replied Dr. Latimer, thoughtfully, "in trying to shield you from pain he plunged you into deeper suffering." (274)

Here, again, something that is imagined to be a "shield" turns out to be quite the opposite: the apparent protection of growing up white in America is nothing more than an illusion, vanishing at the moment of the white father's death. And Leroy's notion of self-respect turns out to be similarly mistaken. Indeed, the false "self-respect" that he imagines his children developing by being treated as though they are white contrasts directly with Iola's view that Dr. Latimer's "self-respect" lies in acknowledging his blackness. While the former imagines self as the surface that one sees reflected back in the mirror of society, the latter posits an invisible, interior self that is independent of society's judgment. And while the former attributes self-respect to protection from injury, the latter attributes it to suffering and rising above injury.

Although Iola resembles Tom in her self-sacrifice, there are two key respects in which her journey of self-discovery parallels that of the white soldiers in the Civil War chapters. First, just as the soldiers believe themselves to be invulnerable ("those boys are too venturesome," says Captain Sybil), Iola is raised to think of herself as white and protected (50). And just as the soldiers are humbled by the sudden, traumatic recognition of their vulnerability, Iola awakens from her "dream" of domestic security to the "terrible reality" that she is a slave (103, 105). Moreover, it is the very system of laws that Iola had always believed would protect property and persons and secure the private realm from plunder that forces the devastating change upon Iola's family, "robbing us of our inheritance," as Iola says, "and reducing us to slavery" (107). She is forced to realize that all along she had unconsciously been passing—not just passing as white, but passing as secure and protected by law. Furthermore, just as the white soldiers' experience of insecurity generates a new, empathetic understanding of the plight of slaves, Iola and her brother Harry learn from the revelation of their blackness to see things in a new way. "Although I was born and raised in the midst of slavery," Iola tells Robert, "I had not the least idea of its barbarous selfishness till I was forced to pass through it" (149). Likewise, Harry comes to understand the "difference between looking on a man as an object of pity and protecting him as such, and being identified with him and forced to share his lot" (126). In both cases their "Negro blood" signifies that they have moved beyond an abstract capacity for sympathy to a shared experience of injury: while whiteness is associated with purely rational knowledge and "pity," blackness generates an epistemology of identification.

The second way in which Iola resembles the white soldiers—both the young soldier in the scene of Tom's death and the speaker in "A Story of the Rebellion"—is in the source of her eloquence. As the white soldiers move their listeners by telling black stories, so Iola has a black story to tell, a story that comes out of her experience of vulnerability and suffering, and that gives her voice its peculiar power to touch her listeners. Near the end of the novel, at a *conversazione* in Mr. Stillman's parlor, Iola joins other "earnest men and women deeply interested in the welfare of the race" for an exchange of ideas.[26] There she delivers a paper on the "Education of Mothers," and in the discussion that follows she enthralls the others with a heartfelt avowal that the present suffering of the race would give rise to a hopeful future, even as Christ's "cross of shame" was turned into a "throne of power." "As Iola finished," the narrator explains, "there was a ring of triumph in her voice, as if she were reviewing a path she had trodden with bleeding feet, and seen it change to lines of living light. Her soul seemed to be flashing through the rare loveliness of her face and etherealizing its beauty" (257). The company is "spell-bound," calling her "angelic" and "strangely beautiful," and likening "the tones of her voice" to "benedictions of peace." It is a typical moment of self-exposure: rhetoric that imagines itself not as rhetoric at all but as the unmediated outward expression of private suffering. The narrative at this point focuses not on her words but on her "etherealized" beauty and the "tones of her voice" because the power she has over her audience lies in her ability to convince them that she is not speaking in abstractions, but reliving the pain of her own "bleeding feet."[27] Thus is her own Christlike journey transformed into persuasive power. Moreover, it is a moment of transparency in which Iola's "face" seems to disappear, exposing the "soul" beneath: the body is imagined as "strangely" immaterial, while the soul takes on an "angelic" visibility.

In such moments it is easy to see why Harper has been criticized for hollow or flat characterizations, because the assumptions that such criticism makes about the nature of character are in significant respects antithetical to Harper's project. Deborah McDowell has described the character of Iola as "disembodied," "a static symbol rather than a dynamic character," an "exemplary type" about whom "nothing . . . is individualized," whom Harper "approaches . . . largely from the outside" rather than "from the inside" (284, 286, 288–89). According to McDowell, Harper's lack of emphasis on the "psychological, personal, and intimate" can be attributed in part to the "polemical and public role that she expected her novel to play" (289, 287). Reacting against the widespread stereotype of black women as immoral, Harper wanted to present black women in a positive light, as genteel, chaste, and spiritual—a project, McDowell argues, that ended up creating not "black women's reality," but instead a "countermyth," no less "homogenized" than the stereotype Harper was working to denounce. McDowell correctly identifies a tension between the creation of "individualized" characters and the "polemical . . . role" Harper envisioned for her novel. But that tension warrants closer analysis: it is not between approaching character from the inside and approaching it from the outside, for it is the exterior that creates the interior. Rather, the tension originates in how outside and inside are imagined in relation to each other—it is the tension between an opaque outside that protects and obscures the inside, and a transparent one that reveals it.

Character, then, becomes a matter of emphasis. Depth of character is created not when the surfaces are impenetrable, but when there are gaps and fissures, affording glimpses of the interior without permitting actual entry. As Henry James famously described it, the "apertures" in the "house of fiction . . . are but windows at the best, mere holes in a dead wall, disconnected, perched aloft; they are not hinged doors opening straight upon life."[28] Character for James, speaking here of Isabel Archer, is above all to be treated delicately, "preserve[d]" and "protect[ed]," kept "locked up indefinitely rather than commit[ted] . . . to vulgar hands" (47, 48). But to write at all, following James's metaphor, would be to unlock the protective enclosure, however delicately; it is not so much a matter of protection as of tactful and measured exposure, sufficiently discreet to preserve the illusion of delicacy. Nevertheless, if James's version of character inevitably belies its claim to modesty, Harper's emphasis on transparency, paradoxically, ends up constructing characters whose interior is inaccessible, characters that appear to the reader opaque and impenetrable. As McDowell notes, "we learn very little about [Iola Leroy's] thoughts, her inner life" (286). And it is precisely because, as McDowell puts it, "*Iola Leroy* is on trial before the world"— because, in other words, there is no place for Harper's novel to hide—that it must be, as it were, on its best behavior, always conscious of how it is being judged. P. Gabrielle Foreman identifies a similar predicament in Harper's own circumstances, and attributes it, significantly, to the burden she carried of representing her race. According to Foreman, writers like Harper engage in "literary veiling," creating a veil "more opaque than the Du Boisian one, . . . for

they are women." "This multi-tiered covering," Foreman continues, "acts both
to protect them and to mute their voices, which are as rich and complex as they
are difficult to gauge" (655). And to those who would claim that the popularity
of such writers afforded them a degree of security, Foreman argues just the reverse: "in fact," she maintains, "their visibility placed them in still more liminal
positions, with their lives and works exposed to particularly careful scrutiny"
(656). In Foreman's reading of Harper, representational status necessarily com-
promises one's privacy and security, and thus requires ever more intricate "veiling." And in yet another reminder of exactly how unstable this opposition of
protected self-abstraction and vulnerable embodiment turns out in practice to
be, Foreman identifies Harper's veil as "sentimental discourse" itself, the discourse of vulnerability, transparency, sincerity—the discourse characterized by
what Harper herself refers to as the "lifting of the veil."[29]

If George W. Cable's fantasy of civic abstraction draws an impermeable boundary between personal social relations and impersonal civic relations, and preserves racial prejudice by socializing it, Harper's citizenship of the heart entails a
radical reformation of the relation between the personal and the civic. In terms
of the freedman's participation in representative politics, Harper imagines self-
representation and civic representation as inextricably intertwined. The relation between constituent and representative is neither abstract nor impersonal;
on the contrary, it is grounded in personal identification and dependent upon
what Harper figures as the representative's vulnerable embodiment. In terms of
the novel's plot, it is Iola's personal integrity—figured as her decision to identify
as black, and thereby to subject herself to what Harper calls "the proud world's
social scorn"—that makes her eventual dedication to the civic life of her community possible (125). For Harper, there is a seamless progression from transparency of character to good citizenship and national renewal: her "Note" at
the end of *Iola Leroy* expresses her hope that her readers will "rise in the scale of
character and condition, and . . . add their quota of good citizenship to the best
welfare of the nation" (282). Joining "character," "citizenship," and "nation" together in a single, sweeping gesture, she represents her project of racial uplift as
a project of individual integrity and national unity. Instead of positing a civic
realm of protected abstraction that can accommodate the freedmen, Harper
presents self-abstraction as the problem that must be overcome if America's racial divisions are to be healed. To the extent that a civic self like the one Cable
envisions is necessarily cut off from the social self, Harper's reattachment of the
civic to the social amounts to a sort of communitarian critique of liberal individualism. But it is also her way of denying racial prejudice and racial violence a

hiding place. As long as what she calls the "spirit of caste" is ascribed to the private realm of personal choice, Harper's reasoning suggests, it will enjoy the nation's tacit approval.

More fundamentally, though, Harper can be seen as both capitalizing on and responding to the fraught narratives of protection that underlay official segregationist discourse, as exemplified in the exchange between Cable and Grady—above all, the glaring contradiction between the implicit idea that white women need protection from the sexual aggression of black men, and the alarming rise in incidences of racial violence and lynching.[30] Harper's younger colleague and fellow activist Ida B. Wells, whose *Southern Horrors* was published in 1892, the same year as *Iola Leroy,* approached the contradiction powerfully and directly. Identifying Henry W. Grady by name, she derided the call for Northerners to keep "Hands off!" Southern race relations, pointing out instead the ways in which the South had been "brutalized . . . by its own inhabitants" (66). Responding to Bishop Fitzgerald's charge that "those 'who condemn lynching express no sympathy for the *white* woman in the case,'" she documented cases of white women lying under oath to "save [their] reputations," and accused the South of "shielding itself behind the plausible screen of defending the honor of its women" (59, 54, 61). And in *A Red Record,* published three years later, she recounted a horrific lynching in Nashville in which a black man charged with raping a white woman was dragged out of prison, mutilated, and murdered, adding that "a white man, [serving time] in the same jail for raping eight-year-old Maggie Reese, a colored girl," was left unharmed, and calling it "a naked, bloody example of the nineteenth century civilization of the Athens of the South!" (129). Wells's stark juxtapositions—the South injuring itself in secret while broadcasting cries of Northern aggression, "shielding itself" behind imagined threats to its women's honor, and inflicting unspeakable violence to avenge a white woman presumably violated, while an "outrage upon helpless childhood need[s] no avenging" because of her race (129)—expose the utter hypocrisy of the white South's rhetoric of protection. Neutralizing both the claim that white interests are vulnerable and the charge that the black population needs to be restricted and kept under control, Wells denies her opponents the factual basis for their claims of injury. But more than that, her descriptions radically disrupt the metaphors. To imagine women's honor as a "shield" behind which white men hide, for example, is to invert the chivalrous idea that men protect the honor of women; it is to figure what is normally thought vulnerable as instead the instrument of protection. Moreover, to figure women's honor as a "screen" is to change it from an essence into a performance—recalling the woman who lied to protect her reputation—and thus to reconceive protection itself as a vice rather than a virtue.

Although *Iola Leroy* treats this volatile matrix of Jim Crow laws, fears of racial contamination, and fantasies of imperiled female honor less directly and
without the piercing irony of either *Southern Horrors* or *A Red Record,* Harper
similarly depicts a white ideology of self-protection collapsing under the weight
of its own hypocrisy and voiding its own metaphors. In one of the many conversations about race relations that dominate the last third of the novel, Harper
introduces a minor character named Dr. Latrobe, who represents a prosegre-
gationist, states' rights position akin to that of Henry W. Grady. Challenging
Dr. Latrobe's claim of white supremacy, Dr. Latimer points to the generations
of miscegenation carried out by whites and asks whether it is not hypocritical
to "consort" with blacks intimately while refusing to associate with them socially. But his examples of interracial intimacy—"your children nestle in their
bosoms; they are around you as body servants"—both cast blacks in the role
of protectors of whites (227). The rejection of blacks, his examples suggest,
amounts to a rejection of one's own defenses, and white racism turns out to be
self-destructive. That Dr. Latrobe is unknowingly socializing with a mixed-race
man—after having boasted that he "can always tell them"—simply underscores
his self-delusion and his misplaced confidence in his own supremacy (229). Earlier in the same conversation, it is Dr. Gresham who unwittingly exposes the
fallacy of a civic realm that holds self-protection as its primary value above the
promotion of decent and principled interpersonal relations, for example. Elsewhere Dr. Gresham seems to be a spokesman for a Cablesque republican fantasy of self-abstraction and its implicit logic of civic protection. But here, when
Robert Johnson brings up the issue of lynching—asking "what protection does
the colored man receive from the hands of the Government?"—Dr. Gresham
"compassionately" explains that "it is impossible to have a policeman at the back
of each colored man's chair, and a squad of soldiers at each crossroad, to de-
tect with certainty, and punish with celerity, each invasion of his rights" (224).
Surely we are intended to hear Gresham's tone deafness here, his trivialization of
lynching as a minor "invasion of . . . rights." But, despite their being spoken by a
character who is to a large extent oblivious to their real significance, these lines
ultimately express the vision of the novel as a whole: self-protection, taken to its
extreme, cannot create the sort of civic community we desire. In fact, that they
are spoken by a white character who elsewhere seems to represent an ideology of
self-protection highlights what for Harper is the inherent instability of such ideologies, their inevitable tendency to unravel in a jumble of self-contradiction.

　　A few moments later, Gresham is back to criticizing the South's failure to
"have placed protection to [the rights of life and liberty] at its base, not in theory
but in fact" (225). He imagines those whose rights have been violated—like the
signers of the Declaration of Independence—as "stat[ing] their . . . grievances

and appeal[ing] to the conscience of the nation [and the world]." But the trope he uses is subtly at odds with an ideal of protected self-abstraction and, once again, illuminates an apparent contradiction at the heart of Gresham's worldview. "'The world,' said Dr. Gresham, 'is fast becoming a vast whispering gallery, and lips once sealed can now state their own grievances and appeal to the conscience of the nation, and, as long as a sense of justice and mercy retains a hold upon the heart of our nation, you cannot practice violence and injustice without rousing a spirit of remonstrance. And if it were not so I would be ashamed of my country and of my race'" (225). The gist of Gresham's argument is that the freedmen must be protected by law from racist violence and thereby permitted fully to participate in the civic life of the nation, and that a "spirit of remonstrance" will be aimed at the South to the extent that it fails. However, drawing on the familiar trope of giving voice to what had previously been voiceless, he depicts this exposure of "grievances" to the world not as an open court of public opinion, but as a difficult and possibly painful confession of things that have only been "whisper[ed]." It is less a picture of bold declarations than of reticence, perhaps due to the delicacy of the grievances, perhaps due to a history of enforced silence. This way of imagining speech draws its emotional impact less from the content of the speech than from the conditions out of which speech arises—in particular, from the sense that this speech has had to overcome powerful barriers that would have prevented the matters from being made public. To the extent that the barriers are those that would have protected a delicate privacy from the harsh light of public exposure, then, this figure dismantles the conditions for protected self-abstraction as much as it depends upon them.

As we have seen, this conception of speech that struggles against powerful forces of repression so as to make itself heard is a favored trope of both Cable and Grady in their debate over segregation, both of whom claimed to be speaking for a feminized "Silent South." I argued above that, by evoking the victimized white woman, such a figure raises the specter of the black rapist and the threat of racial contamination without having to make that argument explicit. More generally, though, it confers upon the speaker a chivalrous regard for feminine delicacy. It is a fantasy of rescue that both aligns itself with liberty's struggle against tyranny and reassuringly affirms the speaker's virtue and his (often white, male) authority. For the character Gresham—as for Cable—the trope offers a way of identifying his vision of moderate, civic inclusiveness as the enlightened and civilized position, the one most respectful of "justice and mercy," and closest to "the heart of the nation." But it is equally applicable to an ardent defender of Jim Crow like Grady. At a crucial moment in his article replying to Cable, he describes a failed effort by Northerners to integrate the Methodist Episcopal Church in the South, and diagnoses the failure thus: "It was the race instinct that spoke there. It spoke not with prejudice, but against it. It spoke there as it speaks always and everywhere—as it has spoken for two thousand years. And it spoke to the reason of each race" (911). This impressive reiteration of various forms of the verb "to speak," six times in four short sentences, spreading itself out over both time and space, not only gives the impression of speech multiplied, but also takes on the quality of the imperative. Moreover, having begun his article by asserting that "where [the South] has been silent, it should now speak," and drawn it to a close with his description of the South saying, "Thus far and no farther," here Grady explicitly identifies the South's speech as "the race instinct" (909, 916). It is a remarkable application of the trope of repressed speech, figuring the forces of repression not only as the opponents of segregation but also as those who would "silence" the race instinct. And it is the race instinct, by contrast, that both stands in need of protection from the tyranny of enforced racial mixing and must resist the forces that would deny it a public voice.

The previous chapter examined how Angelina Grimké applied this configuration of speech as overcoming forces of repression, and as the salutary exposure of things that had been silenced, to a progressive feminist and abolitionist politics. Here we see the same configuration applied to a moderate, antisegregationist argument and to a reactionary defense of Jim Crow. As I argued previously, there is an important distinction to make between one who claims to speak for the disenfranchised or silenced, and one who speaks authentically from a position of disenfranchisement. But it is also important to note that claims of injury are routinely challenged with the charge of inauthenticity, and that the pressure to authenticate can itself be seen as a manifestation of the tensions inherent in rhetorics of protection.[31] More broadly, the trope of repressed, female speech thrives on the tension between the ideal of protected privacy and the healing that is promised through the public airing of grievances; between the anxiety that the private realm harbors brutal secrets, and the fear that public exposure is tantamount to surveillance and an invasion of privacy. In other words, the trope of repressed speech manages the apparent conflict between private experience that is created in the process of its public expression and a private realm that must continually be reinscribed as pre-public. Grady fits the trope to his political agenda by identifying the "race instinct" as the thing that must be expressed publicly (that is, codified into law) and at the same time figured as irrevocably private. But the trope is equally useful to someone like Cable, who also claims to be on the side of a silenced, feminine "South." It enables him to fantasize a fixed realm of private preference and consent that is separate from civic relations, while at the same time imagining it as endangered and in need of rescue, a Southern damsel in distress. And it allows both men to adopt a tone of moral outrage, implying that their own position is not just correct, but honorable, and suggesting—as Dr. Gresham makes explicit—that a victory for their opponents would bring "shame" to their "country and [their] race."

Iola Leroy, by contrast, is remarkable for the extent to which Harper avoids such configurations: for all the talking that goes on in the novel, very little of it can productively be understood as speech that resists repression or gives voice to the voiceless. On the contrary, even the intimate conversations among characters have a public-speaking quality to them, and perhaps the most powerfully emotional moment in the novel—Robert's reunion with his mother—takes place in a public prayer meeting. I do not wish to suggest that Harper somehow escapes the dynamic of vulnerability and protection that characterizes the liberal imagination. Rather, at a time when the dominant white discourse of race relations had appropriated a highly charged language of protection, Harper reconfigures the elements and redirects the emphasis. If the dominant discourse professes a chivalrous defense of a vulnerable femininity, Harper's heroine rejects Dr. Gresham's chivalrous proposal; and when she chides Dr. Latimer for "belong[ing] to the days of chivalry" he "smiles and says, 'he only belongs to the days of hard-pan service'" (265). With the exception of Gracie, Harper's female characters are anything but delicate. Iola is decidedly not a "tragic mulatta," and Lucille Delany thinks that men who shirk their burdens and put them on the shoulders of their wives "ought to be drummed out of town!" (253). Yet the white characters who represent the dominant racial discourse—both the ostensibly progressive argument for greater inclusion, and the overtly racist defense of Jim Crow—ultimately betray the flawed assumptions on which their positions rest. Their logic of protection, successful inasmuch as it controls the definition of privacy and manages its conflicted emergence into public, is also liable to unravel in contradiction when its hold on the slippery terms loosens.

I would like to conclude this chapter by briefly examining an image that neatly complements Harper's representation of a well-meaning white ideology of protection collapsing from within. In "A Fairer Hope, A Brighter Morn," which dates to around the same time as *Iola Leroy,* Harper addresses the "demon" of racism and racial violence, envisioning "A fate that shall crisp and curl your hair / And darken your faces now as fair" (*Brighter Coming Day* 327–30). Reimagining the ritualized burning of the black body as the burning of white bodies in hell, this figure follows Harper's pattern of turning acts of destruction into acts of self-destruction. But the impact of the image—an impact she borrows from the horrific spectacle of lynching—is in its materiality; it doesn't render the violence of lynching figurative so much as it literalizes the fires of hell. Moreover, that this transformation of violence by whites into violence against white bodies is also figured as racial transformation—the darkening of the skin and the curling of the hair—raises the issue of the materiality of race. To believe in white superiority is to believe that race exists empirically, and so this blackened white "demon" is condemned not only by his own racism but also by his insistence that the visible, material markers of race have a single, fixed significance. The following two lines of the poem highlight exactly this conundrum: "fate" will not only "darken your faces," the poem predicts, but also "send through your veins like a poisoned flood / The hated stream of the Negro's blood" (329). Again, it is these white supremacists' own ideology of "blood"—their construction of race as a biological certainty, and their codification of it into the law of the land—that seals their fate. They are the ones who established the equivalence of black skin and "Negro blood" and thus condemned themselves to what Harper depicts as a nightmarish sort of transfusion once hell's fires have blackened their skin. The brilliance of her poem is that the horror lies not in the racist fictions themselves, but in their being misrecognized as empirical fact, and in their being inescapably established as such by law and by custom.

White supremacy—whether attached to a moderate political agenda like Cable's or to a reactionary agenda like Grady's, whether imagined benignly as a matter of preference and consent or more virulently as "instinct"—insists on the privacy of race precisely so that it can be produced publicly and authenticated. At the same time, however, such ideologies depend upon the conviction that public and private (or civil and social, as Cable puts it) represent fixed realms of life that can be clearly delineated. By reattaching public and private, Harper paradoxically disables the mechanism by which race is made fundamental to the organization of society and the constitution of citizenship. Moreover, if the 1860 "Declaration of the Immediate Causes Which Induce and Justify the Secession of South Carolina from the Federal Union" based its appeal on having been denied "the power of . . . self-protection," thus identifying the preservation of slavery with the protection of the Southern "self," Harper reimagines regimes of racial oppression as instruments of white self-destruction. Her radical revisions to the dynamic of protection and vulnerability characteristic of liberalism both undermine a racially exclusive fantasy of civic abstraction and propose an alternative vision of African American citizenship after Reconstruction.

4

The Eloquent Girl

Liberal Publicity and Unprotected Privacy in Henry James's *The Bostonians*

[Until Rousseau discovered intimacy, the] innermost region in man . . . had needed no special protection.

  —Hannah Arendt, *The Human Condition*

In her speech to Mrs. Burrage's gathering of the Wednesday Club, Verena Tarrant likens the oppression of women to imprisonment in what her "gentlemen" listeners would argue is "a very comfortable, cosy, convenient box, with nice glass sides, so that we can see out." "All that's wanted," she declares, gently mocking the gentlemen's line of reasoning, "is to give another quiet turn to the key" (James, *The Bostonians* 232). Depicting a space that is simultaneously protected and exposed, the glass box is a concise figure for the sort of selfhood that is available to women under the protection of men, and highlights the primary fallacy in the logic of chivalry. Women, it is assumed, are delicate and precious, and the greater their delicacy, the more precious they are. The more in need of protection women are, then, the more they are worth protecting: their value, in other words, is directly proportional to their defenselessness and fragility. Thus is the gallant protection of women by men an inherently unstable ideal, an ideal that claims as its goal the safety of women, while at the same time working to enhance their value by ensuring their vulnerability. The glass box is a figure for just such a contradictory security device. Glass makes an improbable fortress; it doesn't protect so much as it preserves and displays; its virtue lies not in its strength, but rather in its fragility and transparency. In Verena's figure women are restricted, we imagine, not by force, but out of fear of breaking the "nice glass sides" of their box. Its transparency gives the illusion of openness and freedom of movement, exactly the opposite of its actual effect, and the last "quiet turn to the key" merely confirms it as an image of "quiet," invisible confinement.[1]

The day after Verena's speech to the Wednesday Club, Basil Ransom, having realized the previous evening that he is in love with her, arrives at the boardinghouse where she and Olive Chancellor are staying. In his conversation with Verena he brings up the same figure: "He kept talking about the box; he seemed as if he wouldn't let go that simile. He said that he had come to look at her through the glass sides, and if he wasn't afraid of hurting her he would smash them in. He was determined to find the key that would open it, if he had to look for it all over the world; it was tantalizing only to be able to talk to her through the keyhole. If he didn't want to take up the subject [of women's emancipation], he at least wanted to take her up—to keep his hand upon her as long as he could" (276). With intriguing consequences, Ransom transforms the figure from something that keeps women in to something that keeps men out, a "tantalizing" space to which men are denied access. Like Verena's use of the image, Ransom's conveys the collapse of the ideal of protection: no device that creates so strong a desire to violate it can truly be said to be protective. But unlike Verena, Ransom chooses to stress the capacity of glass to place whatever is behind it on display. He imagines the figure, in other words, from the point of view of an audience, giving it an exterior face, and public—rather than merely private—significance. In public, Ransom suggests, the glass box creates a dynamic of desire, defining an inviting space that is visible from the outside but accessible only through violence. And so, not only is the box's ultimate effect at cross purposes with its protective function; it also creates contradictory impulses in its viewers, who wish to "smash in" the glass sides at the same time that they wish to treat the delicate thing inside with tenderness and care. And the more successfully the box creates its illusion of tantalizing delicacy, the more powerful are both the impulse to violate and the impulse to refrain from violating.

This chapter traces the complex dynamic of liberal privacy in *The Bostonians,* focusing primarily on its entanglement in the machinery of publicity. Like the glass box, liberal privacy gains its hold on our collective imagination as a thing always at imminent risk of violation, as well as a thing we are always tempted to violate. We build an elaborate legal and constitutional apparatus designed to protect it at the same time that we harbor suspicions about anyone who erects too impenetrable a barrier of privacy, and the stronger the barrier of protection, the greater our anxiety that it will be used to hide wrongdoing.[2] We cherish our belief in a region of privacy that innocently and modestly shuns the light of publicity, while at the same time fostering an insatiable appetite for its shameful and shattering public exposure. It is at once an essential American value and a cover under which iniquity is allowed to flourish, and its breach—or anticipated breach—is a powerful means of attracting public attention and eliciting public outcry. From the inside, privacy can function as a prison, keeping such issues as slavery, child abuse, and domestic violence out of the public discourse.[3] But from the outside, privacy appears as a promise, often sexualized—the promise of an ideal intimacy that we do not have, the desire for a glimpse into an inviting region of life that we see only dimly, a richly fulfilling source, of which there will always be more to reveal.[4] Furthermore, as something that controls the movements and desires of individuals while itself remaining invisible, the glass box also evokes the ideological force of liberal privacy. In both of its guises—as the vulnerable thing in need of protection and as the hidden, inaccessible thing begging to be exposed—liberal privacy has a powerful emotional appeal. It is profoundly persuasive, unmatched in its ability to hold an audience's rapt attention and move them to tears and outrage, and thus of inestimable value to particular political agendas.

In the classical republican paradigm, civic discourse is free because it is abstracted from the private realm. But liberalism—and, in particular, the liberal revaluation of privacy—imparts a powerful allure to those voices that can convincingly portray themselves as issuing from outside the realm of civic protection, those voices that can, in other words, invoke an unprotected privacy.[5] Verena Tarrant has just such a voice. Indeed, it is illuminating to read Verena as a figure for liberal privacy: she is described as having the same sort of "hollowness" that both Jürgen Habermas and Ann Douglas observe when privacy is put to public uses,[6] and yet the other characters—the narrator included—persist in trying to pin down her "essence" (54, 328). She is, as Judith Wilt has written, "compellingly 'empty,' . . . [remaining] everywhere in the narrative . . . an object of interpretation, first to Basil, then to Olive, finally, mysteriously, to herself"; her "emptiness," Brook Thomas observes, "allows her to be both vulnerable and seductive" (Wilt 293, 298; Thomas 740). Moreover, for both Olive and Ransom, Verena's public performances give rise to the same contradictory impulses as the spectacle of privacy: they respond intensely to her vulnerability, entertaining fantasies of rescue and even vicariously experiencing the violation of which Verena herself is unaware, while at the same time fantasizing her possession, in imagery both violent and sexual. Olive imagines herself as Verena's "protectress," "rescu[ing] the girl from the danger of vulgar exploitation"; Ransom sees Verena as "a touching, ingenuous victim, unconscious of the pernicious forces which were hurrying her to her ruin," and himself as her "rescue[r]" (*The Bostonians* 73, 215). Olive "suffer[s] . . . from the idea that [Selah Tarrant lays] his hands upon her to make her speak"; Ransom resents "Tarrant's grotesque manipulations . . . as much as if he himself had felt their touch," deeming them "a dishonour to the passive maiden" (101, 52). And yet Verena also provokes impulses in both Olive and Ransom that would seem to contradict these protective instincts. Olive's own version of the glass box whose sides Ransom imagines "smashing in" comes in Marmion, when she senses Verena slipping away from her: tracing her reaction to Verena's shameful apostasy so soon after Miss Birdseye's death, the narrative reads, "Olive would have liked . . . to see the locked door which *she* would not have managed to force open!" (353). Although the precise tenor is unclear, the metaphor nevertheless provides an image of invasion, a violent incursion into a space that had been locked and presumed safe—an image that coexists uneasily with all the rhetoric of protection and rescue. Like Ransom's version of the glass box, it suggests that Verena generates a complex and volatile mix of emotions in her admirers, at once tender and violent, suffering at the spectacle of Verena's victimization, but, as Ransom puts it, "suffer[ing] deliciously" (215).

Finally, just as privacy beckons to its beholders from a region of promise, a region against which our own impoverishment stands out with particular clarity, so Verena's inviting voice continually elicits extravagant metaphors of richness and promise.[7] The language of wealth reaches a peak in the chapters that narrate Verena's Wednesday Club performance, which we get from the point of view of Ransom, whose own financial prospects are then at their lowest ebb. At Monadnoc Place, Ransom had attributed Verena's "added luster" to her "success"; in the Burrages' music room, with its "white and gold" decor, its "polished floor and marble busts of composers," as Verena reduces "the fashionable world" of New York society to "unanimity," Ransom can feel "success . . . in the air" (193, 216, 229). And, in a series of puns and metaphors from the language of finance and exchange, we come to see that the "success" Verena represents for Ransom is above all monetary success, precisely the success that is eluding him in his own legal career. Verena's "golden voice," we read, "solicit[s]" Ransom's ear; she lectures "like a singer spinning vocal sounds to a silver thread" (227, 228). Calling to mind the biblical parable, Ransom imagines the "tone" of Verena's voice, "so pure and rich, and yet so young, so natural," as "a talent," presumably to be invested and multiplied rather than buried (228). A "glimpse," the narrator explains, "was all that was wanted to prove to him that she was a person for whom he might open an unlimited credit of tender compassion" (215). Ransom figures Verena's richness, then, not simply in monetary terms, with the pun on "tender," but as unrealized wealth, as the promise of future returns; it consists not in her actual, independent condition so much as in the "unlimited credit" she can garner from her admirers.

Olive, too, uses a financial metaphor to describe Verena's "qualities," but unlike Ransom she uses it so as to distinguish Verena's gift from the merely monetary: "her qualities had not been bought and paid for," reasons Olive; "they were like some brilliant birthday-present, left at the door by an unknown messenger, to be delightful forever as an inexhaustible legacy" (101). Money has value because its supply is limited: from that condition arises the system of exchange and equivalencies that constitute the monetary economy. Verena's richness, by contrast, is not fungible, nor can it be depleted; it is an endless source, mysterious in its origins and unlimited in its bounty.[8] The difference in emphasis between Ransom's and Olive's metaphors, I would suggest, stems from the difference in their own financial solvency: while Ransom wants entrance into the monetary economy, Olive wants to escape it, and in each case Verena represents the sort of riches they do not have. It is not surprising, then, that both Ransom and Olive have a tendency to slip into the optative mood when reflecting on Verena's gift, Ransom imagining the future intimacy that he now only "glimpses," and Olive extravagantly projecting it into eternity.

We can, then, begin to construct an anatomy of Verena's extraordinary power to move her audiences, the quality of voice that can "shake" Olive "from head to foot," and "tantalize [Ransom's] ear" and "fix his attention" even though he considers "the matter of her speech . . . ridiculous" (70, 227, 230, 229). She is, above all, precious and vulnerable, but neither her value nor her vulnerability is simple. Her value is not in what she is but in what she promises to be; it exists not as hard currency, so to speak, but as credit. As such it is not subject to the limits of the immediate, tangible world, but is limited instead only by the dreams and desires her audience is willing to place in her. Furthermore, because Verena is perceived as utterly without protection—exposed to all manner of exploitation for the very reason that her innocence renders her unaware of the danger—her value is enhanced by a sense of urgency, a sense that without immediate action all will be lost. She is both immeasurably precious and in imminent danger of ruin, and that combination of attributes creates a powerful emotional response in her audience. Ransom, as he puts it, "watch[es] her in very much the same excited way as if she had been performing, high above his head, on the trapeze" (228). Clearly, just as a trapeze artist would lose a certain appeal if there were no danger of falling, Verena would be less capable of holding her audience's rapt attention were she not at risk of injury: her extraordinary power as a speaker is a direct consequence of her perceived exclusion from the zone of civic protection. But I would argue that Verena's odd promissory value also stems from the sense that she speaks from outside the civic realm—from the realm of private life—and that the dynamic of desire initiated by her voice replicates that of liberal privacy when it is put to public use.⁹ For it is precisely when the private is brought into the public realm—when speech becomes, as Ransom describes Verena's performance at Miss Birdseye's, "an intensely personal exhibition"—that audiences are drawn beyond the surfaces to imagine the underlying source (54). And that imagining, like the desire simultaneously to violate and to refrain from violating, is a conflicted process, wanting to bring the depths of private selfhood into public view, and at the same time to preserve the illusion that there are still more depths to be exposed.

In "Archimedes and the Paradox of Feminist Criticism," Myra Jehlen argues that the novel—the genre most profoundly concerned with charting the interior life—envisions that interior life as female. More than simply an account of gender and literary form, however, Jehlen's essay also offers insight into how privacy functions as ideology. Using Richardson's epistolary novels as a case study, Jehlen contends that characters like Clarissa represent the private self, and that such characters are interesting because they are thwarted in their efforts to realize themselves. Privacy, then, is most richly and pleasurably evoked as something violated, as something that is at odds with the world in which it exists, coming poignantly into being to the extent that it is inhibited, suppressed, confined. Moreover, Jehlen observes, privacy and autonomy function inversely: the novel's production of selfhood requires that female characters be defined in such as way as "effectively [to] preclude their becoming autonomous" (142). In other words, liberal individualism can successfully be achieved only when the interior life is conceived as a vulnerable and violated thing.

Jehlen's analysis sheds light on what I see as a recurring problem in *Bostonians* criticism, much of which has considered James's treatment of privacy and publicity.¹⁰ Often *The Bostonians* is read as depicting an older public ideal under siege by the spread of an insidious new publicity, "a shift," to use Ian F. A. Bell's terms, "from the civic to the advertisable" ("The Personal" 241). For Bell, such a transition threatens the integrity of the self, rendering it no more than "a cluster of attributes, effects, performances," and permitting it no existence "outside the relationships established by the manipulations of desire" (241). Bell admits that regimes of publicity are capable of co-opting the very terms that they have debased: "under such conditions," he argues "the 'private' and the 'personal' are revealed as the most sustaining fictions for the self's return to substantiality," becoming "resources for the 'real'" (251). But his argument nevertheless relies on what he refers to as an "earlier autonomy," an integral version of selfhood that the mechanisms of publicity have "impoverished" and "distorted" (251, 249; "Language" 237). I see a different configuration of elements: rather than an autonomous selfhood that requires an integral privacy, I propose that liberal individualism requires a protected privacy—one that, in order to be worthy of protection, must be ever at risk of violation. From this view, the mechanisms of publicity that Bell identifies do not debase privacy; on the contrary, they create it, and the notion that there was once a pure and unsullied privacy to be debased is one of their foundational assumptions. As Jehlen shows, private life is never so compellingly drawn as when its dreams of self-fulfillment have been thwarted, when it has been confined and fettered and violated.

This sense of dreams that have been disappointed, that have remained un-realized, could also describe the end of *The Bostonians,* Verena having been wrenched away from her performance at the Music Hall into what the narrator coolly suggests will be an unhappy marriage. But to a much greater extent than Richardson, James invites us to wonder exactly what self-fulfillment would have meant in Verena's case, what sort of self was ever there to be fulfilled. It is James's critical triumph, I would argue, to have created in Verena a character whose appeal—for her readers as well as her fellow characters—stems solely from our desire to see her as having an essence that her father, and then Olive, and then Ransom violate.[11] Just such a desire motivates, for example, Michael Kearns's morally charged call for a sympathetic reading of Verena. Despite what he sees as the narrator's persistent tendency to "depreciate Verena as a human being," to "trivialize" and "ignore" her, to render her exclusively from the perspective of other characters, refusing us direct access to her inner life, Kearns resists ascrib-ing her the shallowness that such treatment would seem to warrant (163, 173, 166). On the contrary, he sees in such treatment an incitement to the reader to "criticize the narrator for lacking sympathy, and develop a heightened attach-ment to Verena" (168–69). According to Kearns, we cannot know whether Verena "really" is as shallow as she at times appears to be, simply because "we [don't] know enough about her to make such a judgment" (172). But that, for Kearns, is beside the point: "even if she is shallow," he submits, "surely she de-serves a more loving and sympathetic response from someone, narrator or char-acter or, if neither of those, then reader" (172). Kearns's Verena, in other words, gains her hold on the reader not because of who she is, but solely by virtue of having been mistreated and maligned, prevented from developing as an indi-vidual. Her single most salient characteristic is that she has been violated—and "violated," Kearns stresses, "by more persons than Olive and Basil" (180). Yet still Kearns persists in personalizing her, in reading her not as "that girl," but as "this person," a "human being" who has a "real" existence apart from her flawed and inadequate representation in the text, because thence arises the moral im-perative of sympathy (180, 163, 172). Such logic, it is worth emphasizing, rep-licates the contradictions inherent in the production of liberal privacy: as the

thing of supreme value that must be protected, privacy is defined by its suscepti-
bility to violation; at the same time, however, we must believe it to have a deeper
essence, a reality beyond what is immediately visible, because only then is our
protective concern for it justified.

While unlike Kearns in his insistence on taking Verena at face value, Alfred
Habegger nevertheless offers an analysis of *The Bostonians* that illuminates a related aspect of liberal privacy's peculiar nature. He writes,

> Regardless of James's nervous and disarming beguilements, the novel, on
> [the issue of women's proper role in society], stands directly behind Basil.
> He may be brutal and opinionated about some things, but he knows women.
> He is right about Verena's nature and he is right in opposing women's entry
> into public life. The novel's central event is Verena's final cave-in, where
> her affective nature cancels her commitment to freedom. It's a mistake
> to assume she capitulates because of some sort of individual weakness.
> Rather, she yields because a generic femininity has come into operation.
> Pretty, graceful, easy to please, Verena is constituted by the familiar femi-
> nine traits, and the commenting author insists that this vulnerable femi-
> ninity is her greatest triumph. ("*The Bostonians*" 338)

If instead of "women" and "Verena" we read "privacy," this passage describes exactly the paradox generated by the liberal protection of privacy. Privacy unhap-
pily recedes from public display—chooses, that is, confinement and suppression over "freedom"—not because of particular circumstances, but because it is
in its very "nature" to do so. It cannot do otherwise and still maintain the qualities that make it what it is. It is condemned always to yearn for liberation and
self-fulfillment, but always to be frustrated in that desire, and both the yearning
and the frustration are essential to its being. As much as we would like to see in
protected privacy a space of freedom, its own nature—like that of a "vulnerable
femininity"—is to triumph, pathetically, in its own "final cave-in."[12]

Habegger's reading suggests, too, that Ransom somewhat cynically uses his
knowledge of Verena's inherently self-defeating nature to his advantage. But Habegger doesn't go far enough, in my view, in critically examining Ransom's own
rhetoric of endangered privacy. Repeatedly the novel shows the muddled logic
and internal contradictions of his philosophy—contradictions, I will argue, that
arise not from his conservatism, but from his adherence to a specifically liberal
notion of privacy. Such privacy, it turns out, despite its claim modestly to es-
chew publicity, does not exist apart from its public display. Moreover, Ransom's
commitment to Verena's safety is belied by the brutality with which he mounts

his campaign to extract her from public life, not to mention his arousal at the spectacle of her vulnerability. Several scholars—Habegger included—have recently noted James's own vehement denunciation, in an 1887 notebook entry, of the "invasion, the impudence and shamelessness, of the newspaper and the interviewer, the *devouring* publicity of life" (qtd. in Salmon 3).[13] Such rhetoric bears a clear affinity to Ransom's worldview, and will provide a useful window into its contradictions. I turn, therefore, to a *Harper's Magazine* editorial that appeared in print during *The Bostonians'* thirteen-month serialization in the *Century,* in which the *Harper's* editor, Henry Mills Alden, very like James in his notebook entry, assumes the posture of defending an outraged privacy. Ultimately, however, the real danger for Alden comes not from those who would violate privacy, but from those who would forget that privacy is a thing always at risk of violation. Like the glass box, the privacy that emerges in the *Harper's* editorial is not a safe place, nor is it hidden from public view; rather, it is fragile and transparent, its fragility and transparency both restrictive and tantalizing.

The Popular Press and the Rhetoric of Shame

In the June 1885 issue of *Harper's New Monthly Magazine,* the "Editor's Easy Chair" lamented the scurrilous new abuses that had begun to taint the journalistic practice of interviewing. Relating a "striking tale . . . told recently and privately [by] a distinguished authoress," in which a young reporter takes advantage of her good nature to gain access to her personal opinions, the editorial covers the familiar territory of outrage over "gross" violations of privacy by the popular press. This section will examine the editorial's rhetoric in some detail, focusing primarily on two things. First, I am interested in its need both to exploit the very privacy it purports to defend, and to assume a posture of anonymity, while at the same time denouncing the "fatal facility of print." Its remarkable capacity to say one thing at the very moment it is doing the opposite suggests that it is functioning as ideology, obscuring the contradictions inherent in the production of privacy in late nineteenth-century America, and an analysis of its persuasive force can provide some insight into that process. Second, I will examine the complicated interplay of dignity and indignation, shaming and being ashamed, in the editorial's rhetorical strategy. The powerful tactic of shaming one's opponent—or, more precisely, charging one's opponent with shamelessness—merits closer attention here not only because it exploits the volatile opposition of self-protection and self-exposure, but also because it is, I will show, Ransom's primary strategy for ending Verena's career in public speaking.

In the incident Henry Mills Alden recounts in his editorial column, the young female reporter introduces herself to the established authoress as an aspiring writer, engaging her "attention and sympathy" through her "earnest" manner, her "modesty," and the "pathetic note" of her introduction. A "pleasant and discursive chat" ensues, in which the authoress "criticize[s] and suggest[s] and cheer[s]," and which "naturally" touches upon other authors of the day. Finally, "with a touching effusion of gratitude and regard, the literary aspirant depart[s]," only to "repair . . . straightway to her hotel and [write] a letter to a newspaper distorting and caricaturing the conversation, falsifying and vulgarizing and parodying all that had been said, reporting opinions of persons that had never been expressed, and perpetrating the outrage with a recklessness and audacity which would have seemed very comical if it had not been necessarily infinitely mischievous." Here the abstraction of print is a danger to free and open expression because of the protection it affords libelers. Contrasting it with face-to-face relations, which are at the very least constrained by politeness, Alden represents print as "reckless" and impudent, and exposes the cowardice and hypocrisy of journalists who present themselves in person as fawning "admirers," but publish criticism that is both malicious and personal. What Alden calls "the fatal facility of print" could very well refer to its lack of accountability, and the loss of public credibility that must necessarily ensue.

Moreover, Alden entangles himself in a series of contradictions by making use of the very aspects of the print medium that he denounces. The "Editor's Easy Chair" situates itself clearly in the tradition of genial, reasoned criticism that gestures back to *The Spectator:* the column's very title evokes the same air of armchair amateurism and easy spectatorship that Addison and Steele so successfully created. And, as Richard Steele wrote in *The Spectator*'s final issue, there is inevitably a certain "Licence allowable" in anonymous or pseudonymous publication that is not permitted "a Writer who sets his Name to his Work"—a "Licence" that is more generally a function of print's abstraction from face-to-face relations. But it is precisely such "Licence" to which Alden so strenuously objects in the female reporter's account of her conversation with the authoress. One might argue, of course, that it is not the license itself that the editor objects to, but its "unscrupulous abuse"; the female reporter, after all, not only names her source but also misrepresents the conversation in her letter to the newspaper. But the very charge of misrepresentation makes epistemological assumptions that run counter to the public ideal of abstraction established in the tradition of print discourse epitomized by *The Spectator.* There are, in effect, two competing sets of assumptions about authority in the *Harper's* editorial: that implicit in the column itself, which assumes the legitimacy of public discourse to be a function of the persuasive force of its ideas, as abstracted from their author's person, and that implicit in the charge of misrepresentation, which clings to an ideal of authorial integrity. Perhaps nowhere is that conflict clearer than in Alden's ambivalence toward politeness. On the one hand, journalistic rhetoric such as that of Addison and Steele is characterized by its politeness, and the relative politeness of the female reporter's conversation with the authoress is clearly the standard against which the rudeness and vulgarity of her letter is judged. But on the other hand, politeness will always fall short against a standard of integrity, and the false note in the reporter's politeness is evident in her "pathetic" introduction and her "touching effusion of gratitude." We read her "modest" demeanor as insincere, and her "earnest desire for literary advice" as a mere performance, and the "audacity" and opportunism of her letter only confirm what we had suspected all along. In short, Alden manages to convict the reporter of a hypocritical politeness without letting on that politeness can only be hypocritical once the standard of judgment is personal integrity.

Significantly, the *Harper's* editorial depicts a public sphere that is clearly feminized and identifies the reporter's crime as a violation of privacy—the "gross offense" that Alden calls "making free with private life to gratify at any cost a morbid public curiosity." Alden establishes himself as the defender of "personal privacy" and "decency," which is manifested in the editorial as his gallant defense of the victimized authoress. It is a conventionally gendered scheme, much like Catharine Beecher's critique of the Grimkés, in which a feminized privacy is threatened by an aggressive and prying publicity that is also feminized. The only defense appears to be the interposition of a masculine voice of reason, both as protection for the endangered privacy and for the requisite chastisement of its persecutor, and the end result is a femininity that is privatized for its own good. The distinguished authoress herself, Alden assures his readers, "was sorely tempted to declare that under no pretense would she ever again admit a stranger, or mention an author to any one whom she did not intimately know"—closing her doors upon the world, as it were, restricting literary discourse to private conversation with intimates, and thereby excluding herself from the kind of abstract, impersonal relations that characterize the neoclassical public sphere. It is a powerful argument, pitting, as it does, not man against woman, but a corrupt against a virtuous femininity. Indeed, in the *Harper's* editorial masculine public discourse does not appear to be at issue at all. Alden can convincingly distance his own version of abstract, critical discussion of the literary scene from that of the female reporter, casting the charge of misrepresentation as an internal contradiction in her particular version of publicity that has no bearing on his own, masculine logic. Superimposed on an otherwise self-contradictory argument, then, gender difference provides the ultimate explanation, beyond which one tends to question no further.

Nevertheless, if the "Editor's Easy Chair" obscures the contradictions inherent in its own presumption of a neoclassical publicity, it unwittingly exposes those inherent in liberal privacy. Alden's defense of the offended authoress's privacy, after all, takes the form of yet another publication of a tale "privately" told, a tale that in both cases exposes the backbiting world of professional writing. Its primary difference from the reporter's letter is that Alden makes a show of *not* naming names, referring to the authors in her letter as "Timotheus," "Althæa," and "Diogenes," and gallantly refusing to name even the reporter. The abstraction of print—for the female reporter simply an invitation to "recklessly" irresponsible misrepresentation—is for Alden a means of protecting a vulnerable privacy. But Alden is also deeply engaged in generating a vulnerable privacy: the shameful finger he points at the female reporter—referring to her, with cutting irony, as "modest" three times in the space of a short column—is but one facet of his investment in the dynamics of shame and indignation. Another, more subtle use of that dynamic can be seen in the posture of indignation Alden fashions for his readers.

Although Alden and the female reporter both offer accounts of private conversations with the authoress, they conceive their ideal reader quite differently. While the reporter fosters curiosity in her readers, Alden fosters indignation— indignation that must extend not simply to the reporter's "offense of making free with private life" but also to the "impertinent and unhealthy curiosity" that underwrites and enables it. And so, although the *Harper's* readers are given a glimpse into the private life of a distinguished authoress, they must take no pleasure in it; they must deny the allure, fashioning themselves as observers, but not voyeurs. Sylvan Tomkins's account of the affect he refers to as "shame-humiliation" is particularly illuminating here, because it is precisely such anxiety over looking that he identifies as its origin. The child's first experience of shame, Tomkins explains, occurs when he looks into a face expecting to see his mother, but realizes that it is the face of a stranger—the moment that gives rise to "the taboo on unashamed looking and being looked at" (141). The child's shame response is reinforced by the parent's embarrassment at his desire to stare and, obversely, at his shyness: he is, as Tomkins writes, "caught between the shame of looking and the shame of being ashamed to do so" (146). A similar dynamic is at work in the *Harper's* editor's cultivation of his readers' indignation. They, too, are caught in a bind of wanting to look and at the same time having to distinguish themselves from those who want shamelessly to look—a bind that mirrors the ambiguity of Alden's own position. And they, too, must guard against the voyeuristic pleasure that they might otherwise have derived from "unashamed looking," convincing themselves that in the authoress's private affairs they see not an inviting space of intimacy (the face of the mother), but rather an outrage from which they would prefer to turn away. They must, in short, imagine themselves as looking out of duty rather than pleasure, their looking as contrary to their inclination.

Tomkins's account of shame, moreover, entails a compelling vision of self-hood—a vision that will ultimately provide insight into the contradictions inherent in the "Editor's Easy Chair's" claim to be defending "personal privacy." According to Tomkins, the shame response—dropping one's eyes and head—signifies not only the desire to hide one's face from scrutiny, but also a turning inward of the gaze, making the self that so desperately wishes to avoid observation into its own observer. As Tomkins explains, "shame is the most reflexive of affects in that the phenomenological distinction between the subject and object of shame is lost" (136). Unlike fear, which can be relieved by escaping its object, shame cannot be protected against; indeed, the more profoundly one retreats inside oneself, the more intensely one experiences shame. The perversely self-defeating nature of shame is demonstrated by nothing quite so clearly as the blush that, as Tomkins points out, only heightens the painful self-consciousness that gave rise to it in the first place. The self that wishes only to hide its face from the world has "unwittingly become more visible"; in the blush shame calls attention to itself, thereby compounding its effects. As Tomkins puts it, "one is as ashamed of being ashamed as of anything else" (137). The image that emerges from Tomkins's discussion is of a self incapable of self-protection, a self betrayed by its own face—a betrayal made all the more poignant by Tomkins's claim that "the self *lives* in the face" (136, emphasis added). Shame is depicted as the unraveling of self-protection, as an impulse to hide away and seek shelter in the self, an impulse whose inevitable result is greater and greater self-exposure.

Significantly, shame is the affect that Tomkins associates with democratically organized societies, and his logic is illuminating. As a model not just of selfhood but also of intersubjective relations, shame is a powerful means of marking distinctions between citizens without abandoning the principle of equality. This is because, unlike contempt, shame "does not renounce the object permanently": shame always holds out the possibility that, at some future point, the breach can be healed and shame can be supplanted by identification (139). In one respect, that possibility can be understood as performing a normative function, stigmatizing certain behaviors and individuals as shameful so as to reform them.[14] But Tomkins also points to another way in which democracy is what he calls the "political counterpart" of shame. Contempt, which promotes a hierarchical social organization by maintaining distance between individuals, must "be used sparingly in a democratic society lest it undermine solidarity." In its place, he argues, we find "empathic shame, in which the critic hangs his head in shame at what the other has done" (139). In other words, public shame works on a principle similar to that of private shame, blurring rather than heightening the distinction between shaming subject and shamed object. A public humiliation does not situate the public at a comfortable distance from the humiliated object of its attention; on the contrary, its experience mirrors that of its target. First, as I have shown, public shame reproduces exactly the conflicted dynamic of looking that comprises the child's initiation into a culture of shame. And second, in the other's shame we recognize our own past or potential shame: as Tomkins writes, "the nature of the experience of shame guarantees a perpetual sensitivity to any violation of the dignity of man" (136).

Tomkins's comment suggests that this mechanism is bound up with the concept of dignity—a concept that is fundamental to democratically organized societies.[15] But by focusing on how it comes to be cherished as a social value, Tomkins brings an unusual perspective to bear on the concept of human dignity. For Tomkins, it is our own personal experience of shame that "guarantees" our commitment to protecting the dignity of others; without that experience, he suggests, we would not be sensitive to "any violation of the dignity of man." The implication is that we do not really know what dignity is—or, at least, how valuable it is—until our own dignity is violated. And so, while dignity is often associated with autonomy and self-determination, Tomkins suggests that dignity cannot be a social value unless there is a culture of shame already in place, and the more widespread the experience of shame, the greater the esteem in which we hold human dignity. Shame and dignity, in other words, are mutually constitutive rather than opposite: like privacy, dignity is figured by Tomkins as something in perpetual danger of violation—something, indeed, whose value is directly related to our capacity to see it as in perpetual danger of violation. Moreover, our capacity to see dignity in that way is figured as a function of our own experience of its violation. And the more vulnerable we imagine dignity to be—the more imminent the possibility of its undoing in shame—the more precious it will be to us, and the greater the effort we will put into protecting it.

To see Alden as "the critic [who] hangs his head in shame at what the other has done," then, is to begin to see his investment in a much larger culture of indignation—one that promotes the idea of personal privacy as a vulnerable thing even as it claims to be protecting it from violation. He ends the column, tellingly, with this rhetorical question: "Is not this, asks the authoress who has suffered so severely from the betrayal of her confidence, a burning disgrace of journalism?" The authoress whose "confidence" has been "betrayed"—who has, in other words, let down her guard and admitted another into a privileged relation of intimacy, only to have that intimacy violated—is the very picture of anguished self-exposure. She stands as an emblem of exactly how vulnerable our private lives are to the harsh and unforgiving light of publicity, her gentle and trusting nature cruelly betrayed. But the most revealing aspect of the column's final word is that it foregrounds not the authoress's injury, but the interviewer's "burning disgrace," phrasing it, moreover, in the interrogative. The rhetorical question allows Alden to leave no doubt about the answer in the minds of his readers, and at the same time to suggest, inconceivable as it may be, that there may be doubt in the minds of some. The real threat is not that privacy is vulnerable to exposure, but that there are some—the interviewer, of course, foremost among them—who could fail to see the shame involved in such a betrayal of confidence. Had the interviewer seen her actions for the "burning disgrace" they so clearly are, the gentle and trusting authoress would have been safe. And so shame—the failure of self-protection—comes paradoxically to serve the editor's cause of protecting a vulnerable privacy. A world in which our actions are governed by our awareness of the ever-present possibility of shame, our capacity for self-protection ever at risk of collapsing, is a world in which privacy is both defenseless and safe.

RANSOM AND THE SHAMING OF VERENA

Public speaking has often been associated in the popular imagination with overcoming shame, but that association was never more explicit than in the case of women who took the lecture platform in the first half of the nineteenth century. Those who opposed the public participation of women routinely cited the Apostle Paul, who wrote in his first epistle to the Corinthians that "it is a shame for women to speak in the church" (14:35). Similarly, an 1837 pastoral letter criticizing the antislavery advocacy of Sarah and Angelina Grimké reflected the popular outrage against women who lectured publicly, predicting that they would "fall in shame and dishonor into the dust" (Ceplair 211). Moreover, we know from Angelina Grimké's letters that such ideas had considerable influence on her own experience of speaking publicly: in a December 1836 letter to her friend, Jane Smith, she described her mental turmoil before an address to an antislavery meeting, and marveled that when the time came she "spoke for about 40 minutes, . . . feeling perfectly unembarrassed" (89). Eight months later, in a letter to Theodore Dwight Weld and John Greenleaf Whittier responding to their misgivings about her increasingly public role in the movement, she was more defiant: "What *then* can *woman* do for the slave," she asked, "when she is herself under the feet of man & shamed into *silence?*" (284, emphasis in original). For Ralph Waldo Emerson, too, the forces of convention and social decorum functioned by shaming the individual into silence, making him "ashamed" to "speak the utmost syllable of his confession." "We but half express ourselves," he admonished in "Self-Reliance," "and are ashamed of that divine idea which each of us represents" (*Essays and Lectures* 260). But Emerson saw shame as more than just an obstacle to be overcome; its suppression was in fact the very essence of eloquence. The moment the orator loses his self-consciousness as a public performer and grounds himself entirely in "interior truth" *was,* for him, the moment of eloquence (756).[16]

The Bostonians also attributes Verena's eloquence, at least in part, to an absence of self-consciousness, but in Verena's case it is figured as innocence—specifically, sexual innocence. Furthermore, because we are given so much of Verena's performances from Ransom's point of view, we gain a very different insight into the nature of her appeal. Verena's immunity to shame—her ability to speak "without a flush in her whiteness"—is attractive to Ransom not because it suggests unimpeded self-expression, but because it confirms her innocence and thus places her in a completely different category from Ransom himself. His appreciation of her, then, stems not from his absorption in her performance, but—on the contrary—from his greater knowingness, his ability to see the entire picture, as Verena herself is incapable of seeing it. At Miss Birdseye's, for example, Ransom is struck by "the sweet grotesqueness of this virginal creature's standing up before a company of middle-aged people to talk to them about 'love.'" "It was the most charming touch in the whole thing," he decides, "and the most vivid proof of her innocence" (*The Bostonians* 56). If she were conscious of the suggestive nature of her performance—in the way that Ransom is—modesty would forbid her from doing it. But Verena's innocence doesn't simply make her immune to shame and enable her to do something a more knowing woman could not; it transforms something vulgar and indecorous into something "charming." That she says coquettish things "without the least supposable intention of coquetry" (207) merely intensifies her attractiveness.

Verena's "talent" is described in a series of oxymorons that highlight the question of self-consciousness: she is "artlessly artful" (328) and "naturally theatrical" (46); her "costume" is her "condition" (194); she is "apparently flirtatious" yet "not in the smallest degree a flirt" (280, 105). An actress is most splendid, such phrases suggest, when she is not acting at all; she is most charming not when she is consciously and creatively producing her art, but rather when she is unconsciously reproducing a delusion. But if the ideal actress is characterized by her inability to differentiate fantasy from reality, then the ideal audience must occupy a contrasting position of rationality in order to appreciate the performance. Ransom (who writes for the *Rational Review*) is vehement about separating the aesthetic and erotic appeal of Verena's "exhibition" from the content of her argument: "The effect was not in what she said, . . . but in the picture and figure of the half-bedizened damsel (playing, now again, with her red fan), the visible freshness and purity of the little effort." Her words "made no difference; she didn't mean it, she didn't know what she meant, she had been stuffed with this trash by her father" (53–54). Indeed, not only is Verena's "little effort" charming *despite* the nonsense of her argument; it is charming *because* it is nonsense, and because Ransom's own highly developed critical faculty can appreciate it as such. At Mrs. Burrage's gathering, Ransom "found himself rejoicing that she was so weak in argument, so inevitably verbose. The idea that she was brilliant, that she counted as a factor, only because the public mind was in a muddle, was not an humiliation but a delight to him; it was a proof that her apostleship was all nonsense, the most passing of fashions, the veriest of delusions, and that she was meant for something divinely different—for privacy, for him, for love" (233). The dizzying circularity of Ransom's logic in this passage notwithstanding, its point is clear enough: it is Ransom's ability to see through Verena's delusion that allows him truly to appreciate her "talent." If Verena is the ideal actress, the "half-bedizened damsel" playing with her red fan and not knowing what it means, then Ransom is the ideal audience, the connoisseur, whose privileged position of rationality enables him to recognize Verena's true aesthetic and erotic value.

Ransom's civic humanist assumptions about the nature of the public sphere are familiar—it is a place of reasoned argument, debased by the personal, the sentimental, the sexual—and he grounds his opposition to Verena's public aspirations in those assumptions.[17] From the beginning he dismisses her ideas by personalizing her speech. "The argument, the doctrine," he decides at Miss Birdseye's, "had absolutely nothing to do with it. It was simply an intensely personal exhibition, and the person making it happened to be fascinating" (54). At the Burrages' his response to Verena is quite similar: "her meaning faded again into the agreeable vague, and he simply felt her presence, tasted her voice" (233). Verena is not an intellectual pleasure; she is a sensual pleasure: "I don't listen to your ideas," he tells her in Central Park; "I listen to your voice" (288). By personalizing and eroticizing her lectures—by giving her a voice without words— he effectually denies her a place in the public sphere as he defines it. She cannot participate in civic discourse because she is incapable of self-abstraction, without which such discourse would be neither legitimate nor free. But, as with so much of Ransom's logic, there is a willfulness and a circularity to his reasoning here. Even Olive, after all, admits that Verena is "not abstract"; indeed, Olive criticizes Mrs. Farrinder's style of oratory for being "too abstract," "not personal enough" (75). For Olive a lack of abstraction is no reason to exclude Verena from public discourse; on the contrary, it is precisely Verena's air of "hav-[ing] lived in imagination through all the ages" that so particularly suits her for advancing the cause of women's rights (75). Ransom's logic for excluding Verena from public debate simply has no force behind it unless the public buys into it and, like Ransom, refuses to pay any heed to Verena's argument—an outcome that seems unlikely, given Verena's considerable eloquence.

And so Ransom's strategy for extracting Verena from public life goes beyond—and, in certain significant ways, conflicts with—his civic humanist reasoning. First, he teases Verena with an idea of a private, secret self. The lecturing self "isn't *you*," he tells her, "but an inflated little figure (very remarkable in its way too), whom you have invented and set on its feet, pulling strings, behind it, to make it move and speak, while you try to conceal and efface yourself there" (293). Here, in fashioning the public self as artificial and the private self as real, Ransom is imagining selfhood within a fundamentally liberal paradigm. He seems to be offering Verena a stable and integral selfhood that does not depend for its existence on an observing audience, a selfhood that comes into being, to use Philip Fisher's apt phrase, by "disappearing" from public.[18] But—again typical of liberalism—no sooner does Ransom propose the existence of an invisible self than he undermines that idea of selfhood by bringing it into visibility. "Ah, Miss Tarrant," he continues, "if it's a question of pleasing, how much you might please some one else by tipping your preposterous puppet over and standing forth in your freedom as well as in your loveliness!" (293). Thus is the disappearance immediately followed by a reappearance; Ransom wants Verena to disappear from her audience of thousands only to reappear to an audience of one. The difference between what Ransom fashions as Verena's public and private selves, then, is a difference only of degree—a point that is made with even more emphasis in one of the conversations at Marmion. Verena asks Ransom why she should be prevented from using her talent to bring pleasure to large audiences, suggesting that it would be "a great waste, a great violation of nature." "It is all very well to be charming to you," she says, "but there are people who have told me that once I get on a platform I am charming to all the world" (336). Being "charming to all the world," in Verena's construction, is essentially no different from being "charming to [Ransom]," except that the one would seem to make better use of her charm, her talent, by giving it a larger platform. The implication is that, despite Ransom's promise, she will have no more of a private self—no more, that is, of a secret, solitary, invisible self—if she marries Ransom than if she continues in her public career. And indeed, though Ransom can be very persuasive when speaking of Verena's "freedom" from the demands of the public, or when urging her to keep secrets from Olive, we can assume that he would be less enthusiastic were Verena to keep secrets from him.

Ransom's reply to Verena's comment is once again noticeably short on logic (or, in the charitable view of the narrator, "appreciat[ive] of a very considerable mystery"): "Charming to me, charming to all the world? What will become of your charm?—is that what you want to know? It will be about five thousand times greater than it is now; that's what will become of it. We shall find plenty of room for your facility; it will lubricate our whole existence. Believe me, Miss Tarrant, these things will take care of themselves" (337). Ransom's bind, I would argue, is indicative of the inherently contradictory nature of liberal privacy. From the opening scene in *The Bostonians* Ransom is established as one who is sensitive to the rich lure of privacy, in his appreciation of the "organized privacy" of Olive Chancellor's drawing room, her "cushioned feminine nest" with its array of "objects that spoke of habits and tastes"—an appreciation so strong that he momentarily considers "becoming a partner in so flourishing a firm" (15, 16). Ransom's attraction to Verena, his belief that she is "meant . . . for privacy, for him, for love," arises from the same liberal conviction that one's true life is the interior life, and one lives it in the private, not the public sphere (233).[19] But the notion that privacy is most "charming" when it retreats from public entails a contradiction: to admit that Verena is charming is necessarily to imagine her from the perspective of an audience, because charm is a quality that does not inhere in the object. A thing cannot be charming without an observing public that it can charm, and its charm is measured by the intensity of feeling it arouses in its observers. Verena's concern that her charm will be diminished when it is hidden away in Ransom's parlor, then, is quite reasonable, and Ransom's floundering assurance that it "will be about five thousand times greater than it is now" is manifestly unconvincing. Ransom, in short, wants to have it both ways, believing that privacy can thrive only when it is protected from public exposure at the same time that he holds on to a liberal version of privacy as a charming and desirable thing—a thing that must appear before the public and exhibit itself for popular consumption in order to have charm and desirability. Ransom's muddle, however, is not the result of a lapse in his logic, but arises from the nature of liberal privacy: just as he must believe that Verena's true calling is to grace his parlor rather than publicly to espouse the cause of women's rights, our fervent attachment to privacy is bound up with our belief that its essence is modestly to shun the light of publicity. And just as Ransom's desire for Verena plays out in fantasies of rescue, and is thus intensified by her utter vulnerability to exploitation, our attraction to privacy is inseparable from our sense of it as a thing always at risk of violation and public exposure.

As James represents it, Ransom's belief system—his conviction that privacy can flourish only when it is protected from the prying eyes of the public—appears as a matter of will and necessity rather than logic. His response to Verena's legitimate concern about the future of her gift shows as much; indeed, it is difficult to imagine a more unconvincing response, and the truly remarkable thing, as the narrator points out, is that Verena appears to be convinced by it. But a closer look at Ransom's success reveals that it is, in the end, not by logic that he wins, not by metaphysical arguments about selfhood or reasoned claims about the nature of privacy, but by shaming her. He succeeds in incapacitating Verena for public speaking not by persuading her of the rightness of his position, but by awakening her sexually and making her ashamed. Notably, if Verena's walk with Ransom in Cambridge doesn't signify the birth of a private self, it does engender her first feelings of embarrassment.[20]

One of Verena's most remarkable qualities in public, as we have seen, is her perfect lack of self-consciousness, her ability to speak without embarrassment. At Miss Birdseye's, for example, she begins "perfectly undisturbed by the public discussion of her mystic faculty" and finishes "without a flush in her whiteness, or the need of drawing a longer breath"; and at Mrs. Burrage's we see her "delightful eyes wandering over the 'fashionable audience' (before which she was so perfectly unabashed)" (50, 56, 229). However, tiny "sign[s] of embarrassment" begin to appear later that same day: when Olive asks her how Ransom came to be at the Burrages', the narrator tells us that Verena "spoke without a single instant's hesitation, and the only sign of embarrassment she gave was that she got up from her chair, passing in this manner a little out of Olive's scrutiny" (249). Similarly, when Ransom appears in Marmion, Verena, we are told, "blushed crimson; but she did not, like Olive, stand voiceless." Instead, she issues Ransom a "gay challenge . . . as promptly as if she had had no cause for embarrassment" (314). While acknowledging Verena's embarrassment in both instances, the narrator makes it clear that it did not interfere with her ability to speak, a circumstance that "may perhaps be explained by the habit of public speaking" (314). But something very different happens after Verena returns from the boat ride with Ransom.[21] Olive discovers her

> in the room, motionless, in a corner . . . , looking at [Olive] with a silent face which seemed strange, unnatural, in the dusk. . . . She was unwilling to speak; . . . it was a kind of shame, shame for her weakness, her swift sur-

render, her insane gyration, in the morning. Verena expressed it by no protest and no explanation; she appeared not even to wish to hear the sound
of her own voice. Her silence itself was an appeal. . . . Distinctly, it was a
kind of shame. After a while the parlour-maid, very casual, in the manner of the servants at Marmion, appeared on the threshold with a lamp;
but Olive motioned her frantically away. She wished to keep the darkness.
It was a kind of shame. (356–57)

Here certainly is no triumphant emergence of an individual will, no celebration of privacy, silence, invisibility. Verena returns to the house unannounced
and hides herself "motionless, in a corner" of the darkening parlor, the unspoken events of the boat ride—unspoken not only by Verena but also by the narrative itself—looming large by virtue of their very unspeakablility. This, then, is
the novel's vision of the private: the unspeakable, the secret that cannot be told,
not just to Olive but to the reader as well. It has little to do with anything the
novel might call a "self," which we could argue is as much a public creation for
James as it is a private fact.[22] Rather, it has to do with Verena's sexual awakening, of which we see only the violent beginning—Ransom "seiz[ing] her hand,
[drawing] it into his arm, forcing her to walk with him along the road" (351)—
and the bleak aftermath.

Significantly, Verena attributes her inability to speak at the Music Hall to
the shame that Ransom's presence induces in her: "I didn't know, till I saw you,"
she says, "that if I attempted to speak—with you sitting there—I should make
the most shameful failure" (386). It is Ransom's gaze that, as Verena says, has
"paralysed" her—or rather, it is Verena's consciousness of the true nature of
that gaze, her consciousness of herself as an object of his sexual desire (387).
No longer can she stand innocently "before a company of middle-aged people
to talk to them about 'love' " as she did at Miss Birdseye's, for she has seen herself through Ransom's eyes and glimpsed the sexual component of her "charm"
(56). Her own modesty—which, earlier, was immaterial because of her sexual
innocence—is now preventing her from speaking. As I argued above, regimes
of shame give rise less to a protected privacy than to a privacy that is in imminent danger of exposure, and it is our painful awareness of that danger, rather
than the soundness of privacy's protective shell, upon which its safety depends.
And so Ransom's claim to be defending privacy from an invasive and exploit-
ative publicity is belied by his ultimate reliance on shame to win Verena over to
his side. He is, in the end, interested not in seeing Verena safe and secure, but in
making her more vulnerable, and in making her conscious of her own vulnerability.

That interest is evident in the language the narrator uses to describe Ransom's campaign to get Verena away from Olive. It is his "brutality"—not his protective instincts or gentle chivalry—that surfaces virtually every time he is alone with her, from his consciousness of "a man's brutality" when he pushes her to keep their Cambridge meeting secret from Olive; to the "throb in his heart" in Marmion when he realizes that "she [is] afraid of him, . . . tremendously open to attack" and his ensuing decision "to press, to press, always to press"; to his "perception" at the Music Hall, "which brushed aside remorse, . . . that he could do what he wanted, that she begged him, with all her being to spare her, but that so long as he should protest she was submissive, helpless" (212, 316, 334, 382). All these elements—Verena's intensifying shame and reluctance to speak, Ransom's titillation at his power to wound her, and her desperate wish that he "spare her"— come together in a moment at Marmion during Miss Birdseye's final hours. Convinced that Verena has won Ransom over to the cause, Miss Birdseye asks to see him one last time, and Verena silently begs him not to disillusion her. "The wish touched him immensely; she was dreadfully afraid he would betray her to Miss Birdseye—let her know how she had cooled off. Verena was ashamed of that now, and trembled at the danger of exposure; her eyes adjured him to be careful of what he said. Her tremor made him glow a little in return, for it seemed to him the fullest confession of his influence she had yet made" (344). Ransom's "glow" in this passage is quite different from his arousal at Mrs. Burrage's home, when he indulged in fantasies of rescue and saw Verena as "a touching, ingenuous victim, unconscious of the pernicious forces which were hurrying her to her ruin" (215). Here Ransom is the one with the power to wound her—his excitement is more sadistic than sympathetic—and Verena is neither ingenuous nor unconscious of her precarious position. Indeed, we might read the earlier scene as representing Ransom's ideological stance—his image of himself as protector of a vulnerable and innocent privacy, and all its attendant, necessary beliefs about the nature of that privacy—while the later scene exposes the relations of power that that ideology masks. Henry Mills Alden provides a useful comparison: like Ransom, he assumes a righteous posture of defending a weak, feminine thing against the vulgar forces of publicity. And, like Ransom, he "saves" that delicate thing not by working to make it invulnerable, but by fostering a culture of shame—a culture that produces and promotes vulnerability, inducing women's withdrawal from public life by exposing or threatening to expose feminine guilt and duplicity. Just as Verena "confess[es]" Ransom's "influence" and seals his victory by silently acknowledging his power to wound her, the female reporter, in Alden's ideal scheme, will have to admit defeat, retiring in "burning disgrace" from her once honorable profession of journalism. Moreover, the authoress too learns the wisdom of never again "admit[ting] a stranger, or mention[ing] an author to any one whom she did not intimately know": Alden is able to position himself gallantly on the side of women, while at the same time working to ensure their exclusion from public life.

In *The Bostonians,* the ideal that Ransom opposes to what he famously calls "the most damnable feminization," the "hysterical, chattering, canting" machinery of publicity and the Northern marketplace that supports it, is nowhere articulated so clearly as when he is asked to speak to Miss Birdseye's group about the South (290):

> To talk to those people about the South—if they could have guessed how little he cared to do it! He had a passionate tenderness for his own country, and a sense of intimate connexion with it which would have made it as impossible for him to take a roomful of Northern fanatics into his confidence as to read aloud his mother's or his mistress's letters. To be quiet about the Southern land, not to touch her with vulgar hands, to leave her alone with her wounds and her memories, not prating in the market-place either of her troubles or her hopes, but waiting as a man should wait, for the slow process, the sensible beneficence, of time—this was the desire of Ransom's heart. (44)

Conflating physical injury with emotional trauma, feminizing the wounded party, and associating the scene of injury with making intimate confessions to a "roomful of Northern fanatics," Ransom unfolds what amounts to a theory of speech and protection. On the surface, Ransom's theory appears to be precisely opposite that of Angelina Grimké, who imagined that healing would come through the public exposure of wounds, through the letting in of sunlight. Ransom, by contrast, imagines public exposure as itself a kind of violation— as "touching . . . with vulgar hands"—and healing as a matter of protecting the vulnerable thing from the indignity of having to indulge the public's curiosity. But I have been arguing in this book that exposure and protection are mutually constitutive rather than opposite, and a closer look at Ransom's image of the South as a fragile woman in need of protection reveals the contradictions such reasoning entails. First, what Ransom imagines as his noble and heartfelt desire to protect his "mother's or his mistress's" dignity is actually his reluctance to humiliate himself by speaking about the South's military defeat: the metaphor disguises Ransom's self-interest as virtuous self-sacrifice and restraint. Second, the figure's emotional impact, as well as its tone of moral righteousness, derives from the spectacle of wounded innocence; Ransom's silence is justified, in other words, by the feminized South's enduring state of injury. The injunction to "wait" for healing to come is problematic, then, when its coming will diminish the moral authority of Ransom's vision. Waiting, too, turns out to be in his interest, and the longer the better.

Finally, Ransom uses gender in much the same way as Alden does, feminizing not only the vulnerable thing in need of protection but also the vulgar and prying publicity that poses the threat. What he later dubs "the most damnable feminization" of American public life is represented in the scene at Miss Birdseye's as Ransom's "conscious[ness] of all these middle-aged feminine eyes, . . . of curls, rather limp, that depended from dusky bonnets, of heads poked forward, as if with a waiting, listening, familiar habit" (44). The suggestion of repulsive, depleted female sexuality that is nevertheless pushy, "pok[ing]" its way forward, is echoed later in the novel, in Ransom's nightmarish visions of the grand Female Convention, its "overheated hall," and the "flushed women, with loosened bonnet-strings, forcing thin voices into ineffectual shrillness" (205). Like Alden, Ransom imagines himself as saving a virtuous femininity from a corrupt one—and, incidentally, a nubile femininity from a withered and "shrill" one—as though masculine selfhood were not in any way at issue. But clearly Southern masculinity is at issue in the ever-present fact of the Civil War, and so—again, as for Alden—the idea that a modest and vulnerable femininity needs to be protected against an aggressive one obscures the contradictions inherent in Ransom's own troubled masculinity.[23] His rationale for not speaking about the South to this audience of Northerners recalls Henry W. Grady's indignation at what he pronounces George W. Cable's "false witness against her," as well as the passage from Catharine Beecher's *Essay on Slavery and Abolitionism* that envisions the threat to "husbands and fathers" when a female agent "retails" their "sins and neglects" to a reading public hungry for such exposures. By turning the tables and asking Northerners to imagine such scrutiny of themselves, Beecher makes it clear that at stake is not feminine decency and delicacy, not the secrets of mothers and mistresses, but rather the authority of husbands and fathers.

Interestingly, Alden exhibits a related anxiety in a two-paragraph digression in the "Editor's Easy Chair" on the media coverage of General Grant's terminal illness. Outraged by the press's scandalous violation of "the sacred privacy of the sick chamber," the editor goes so far as to suggest that a man "insult[s] his country" when he "desires to listen to a cough of distress or to hear the death rattle of a hero." Although he claims merely to be defending "decency," it is clear that what really disturbs him is the degrading exposure of "weakness" in an "illustrious soldier" and former president. To give a detailed account of Grant's "expectorations, and what one paper has called his 'shambling' from room to room in his extreme agony," is to undermine his image as the embodiment of military and political strength; it is to diminish his status as a representative American man by reminding us of the limits of his corporeality, the inevitability of bodily suffering, and the weakness of the flesh. Significantly, Alden objects to such reporting "whether accurate or false": at issue is not the truth of the account, but its transgression into a region that should be kept out of the light of publicity. That region—feminized and sentimentalized in the story of the offended authoress—appears, in the discussion of Grant, more akin to the classical realm of necessity, the harsh realm of work, survival, and the biological life processes. We could, then, see Alden as defending the boundary upon which the republican fantasy of civic liberty depends, enforcing the abstraction of public discourse from the world of physicality and violence. But the very idea that that boundary is in need of defense from what the editor refers to as "morbid public curiosity" indicates the conditions of modernity, and the fact that the passage is embedded in the story of the offended authoress suggests its complicity with the liberal project of constructing a vulnerable privacy. In short, just as Ransom seems to be advocating a classical republican notion of public discourse while at the same time adhering to a liberal sense of privacy, so Alden espouses a sort of classicism of convenience, denouncing the indecent exposure of the public man's vulnerability, while at the same time making a spectacle of the authoress's injury and adopting for himself a strategy of exposure, shaming his opponents into silence. For both Ransom and Alden, the classical ideal of autonomy slips into the liberal ideal of protection—and its corollary of a vulnerable privacy—with remarkable ease.

Olive and the Politics of Self-Exposure

The figure of Selah Tarrant—who is forever violating some social or cultural boundary—provides an amusing counterpart to Alden's indignation at published accounts of General Grant's "expectorations," if only because the *Bostonians* narrator imagines the violation literally, as Tarrant's bodily penetration into newsprint. I have been arguing that, of all the boundaries that structure our understanding of public life, the most crucial is the one between language and bodily existence—precisely the boundary that is blurred in strategies of self-exposure. Tarrant offers an extreme version of that blurring: he is fascinated by the "*penetralia* of the daily press," and its inaccessibility "only add[s] to the zest of forcing an entrance" (91–92). He is described as "persistent and penetrating," known to the journalists and typesetters and newsboys as "the irrepressible Tarrant." And, the narrator continues, "he was always trying to find out what was 'going in': he would have liked to go in himself, bodily, and, failing in this, he hoped to get advertisements inserted gratis" (92). If, prior to this passage, a figurative connection had been established between Tarrant's efforts to force his way physically into the newsrooms and presses and his efforts to introduce his name into print, here even that nicety is abandoned. The image of Tarrant forcing his way "bodily" into print not only offends our understanding of print as a specifically disembodied medium; it also makes Tarrant's body into a kind of publicity, one that "get[ting] advertisements inserted gratis" can, albeit imperfectly, substitute for. This is because getting advertised without having to pay also blurs the boundary between the sort of publicity whose appeal is personal and whose intent is interested, and a public ideal whose legitimacy stems from its abstraction from the personal, its disinterestedness. Tarrant's "vision of . . . publicity," his "ideal of bliss" (89), is not self-abstraction; on the contrary, it is a kind of corporealization of print, a "state of intimacy with the newspapers" (107).

Moreover, the narrator envisions Tarrant's wish to "force an entrance" into the newspapers as a "penetration" or invasion, thereby establishing an inside and an outside that corresponds in interesting ways to the zone of liberty envisioned by Mill. Inside is the abstraction of print and its promise of a free, public selfhood; outside is the grotesquely and inescapably embodied existence of Tarrant. Inside are the twin ideals of disinterested virtue and the common good; outside are self-interested deception, humbuggery and confidence, and the new publicity of advertising. And so, in what seems to be a reversal of rhetorical strategies of exposure, the zone of liberty appears threatened by—and in need of protection from—the areas of life it excludes. This section examines the relation between these two apparently contradictory figures: the vulnerable thing that is excluded from citizenship and therefore in need of its protections, represented for Olive Chancellor by Verena Tarrant, and the idea that citizenship is itself in need of protection from a debased and debasing publicity, represented most strikingly by Selah Tarrant. Because Olive is so deeply invested in both figures—as moved by and attracted to Verena as she is repulsed by her father—her politics warrant closer consideration here. Furthermore, the idea that Verena is antithetical to and yet also descended from Selah takes on an added resonance if, as I have been suggesting, we read Verena as a figure for liberal privacy. The suggestion is not simply that privacy has sordid antecedents—a mother who degraded the family tradition of public speaking by corporealizing it, marrying a mesmeric healer, a charlatan notable for his "eloquence of the hand"—but also that its persuasive force depends upon its ability to distinguish itself from those antecedents (65). As Olive puts it, "Miss Tarrant might wear gilt buttons from head to foot, [but] her soul could not be vulgar" (70).

Olive's conviction that Verena's "soul [cannot] be vulgar" is clearly bound up with her feminist politics. But it is also indicative of her conflicted attitude toward things bodily, an attitude that manifests itself in her frequent recourse to the religious imagery of bodily suffering. The "dreadful image that was always before her," the narrator tells us, was "the image of the unhappiness of women. The unhappiness of women! The voice of their silent suffering was always in her ears, the ocean of tears that they had shed from the beginning of time seemed to pour through her own eyes. Ages of oppression had rolled over them; uncounted millions had lived only to be tortured, to be crucified. They were her sisters, they were her own, and the day of their delivery had dawned. This was the only sacred cause; this was the great, the just revolution" (33–34). With both an epic, biblical scope, and corporeal imagery—"ears" and "eyes," torture and crucifixion—this passage is expansive without being disembodied. It depicts the blurring of individual boundaries, the dissolution of particular bodies into a giant, universal female body, a body that transcends time and space, that unites by shared suffering. The image of the "tears" of historical women "pour[ing] through [Olive's] own eyes" is a fiction of identification, of a shared but purely subjective knowledge, unmediated by language, and her project involves translating that "silent" knowledge into speech, into what Olive thinks of as "the history of feminine anguish" (158). Verena is the perfect vessel for that history, for the very reason that she "seem[s] to have lived in imagination through all the ages": her "prophetic impulse," Olive is convinced, "had not been stirred by the chatter of women . . . ; it had proceeded rather out of their silence" (75).

Olive's fantasy of martyrdom is presented to readers of *The Bostonians* with a similar melodramatic extravagance. Early on we are told that "the most secret, the most sacred hope of her nature was . . . that she might be a martyr and die for something" (13). Her first clash with Matthias Pardon leaves her with "the glow of dawning success . . . , and something of the ecstasy of the martyr"; and Miss Birdseye's appeal is summed up, for Olive, in her "aroma of martyrdom" (127, 156). When Verena visits her Charles Street home for the first time, Olive presents what the narrator calls her "scheme of renunciation" thus: "[She] drew in her breath for an instant, like a creature in pain; then, with her quavering voice, touched with a vibration of anguish, she said: 'Oh, how can I ask you to give up? *I* will give up—I will give up everything!'" (71, emphasis in original). And much later, when Olive confronts Verena about inviting Ransom to her lecture at the Burrages,' Olive, we are told, "lay there, white and weak, like a wounded creature" (252). The "creature" that Olive becomes in these scenes, "wounded" and "in pain," is her embodiment of "feminine anguish," the somatic expression of a simultaneously generalized and personalized trauma. "You have such a fearful power of suffering," says Verena, in which the word "power" suggests both Olive's capacity for suffering and its impact on her beholder (252). Figured as private, her suffering is nonetheless also imagined as public, as a visibly wounded body; her own martyrdom part and parcel of "the long martyrdom of women" (153).

Like the claim of injury, the spectacle of suffering works as an argument for reform by challenging the protective boundaries of civic liberty from the outside. Everything about Olive's vision of womanhood identifies it as existing outside the zone of civic protection—its exposure to oppression and torture, its utter vulnerability, its silence, its physicality. The unprotected voice is granted a peculiar power in liberalism: it can claim self-protection as its cause, which trumps those causes advocated from within the civic realm because self-protection is a value that precedes liberty.[24] To make private suffering into public spectacle is to transform vulnerability into influence, or, to borrow from Frances Harper, the "cross of shame" into the "throne of power." But Olive's personal suffering is more problematic: for one thing, it comes not only from the systemic oppression of the patriarchy but also from the very reformers who resist that oppression. She "loathed" the streetcar, we are told, but took it regularly "by reason of a theory she devotedly nursed, a theory which bade her put off individual differences and mingle in the common life" (21). Similarly, she "mortally disliked" Miss Birdseye's "long, bald" apartment which, with its borrowed chairs ranged along the walls in preparation for Mrs. Farrinder's lecture, "produc[ed] the similitude of an enormous street-car" (27, 28). In both cases, Olive's antipathy is explained as arising from her "exposure," as if what James elsewhere calls the "items of high civilization" that comprise the "texture" of society (James, "Nathaniel Hawthorne" 351)—precisely those "objects" and "accessories" that give Olive's own "cushioned feminine nest" its richness (*The Bostonians* 15)— actually form a kind of protective coating that can prevent such "exposure." Nevertheless, despite her instinctive recoil from vulgarity and commonness, she continually places herself in its proximity: the "injury of her taste," indeed, occasions Olive's "most poignant suffering," and "the prospect of suffering [is] always, spiritually speaking, so much cash in her pocket" (27, 97). These offenses to Olive's taste persist despite her diligent efforts "to kill that nerve, to persuade herself that taste was only frivolity in the disguise of knowledge" (27). And so she suffers silently from the "absence of nice arrangements" at Miss Birdseye's;

she resists being associated with Beacon Hill "society"; and, when Ransom mentions her "elegant home," she responds with embarrassment, "dislik[ing] to be reminded of certain things which, for her, were mitigations of the hard feminine lot" (22).

Perhaps nowhere are Olive's contradictions as evident as in her scheme for Verena's education. On the one hand, Verena's attraction—her "value for Olive"— is inextricably bound up with her impoverished background, her upbringing in "the social dusk of that mysterious democracy which Miss Chancellor held that the fortunate classes know so little about" (97, 70). Just as for Ransom, Verena's innocence is confirmed by "the sweet grotesqueness of [her] standing up before a company of middle-aged people to talk to them about 'love'" (56), for Olive her "artless" purity is assured by her unconscious vulgarity—her innocent declaration that she "prefer[s] free unions," for example, or her "jacket with the gilt buttons" (74, 69). The Tarrants' interior, Olive happily discovers on her first and only visit, is "as bad as she could have desired" (97). On the other hand, Olive's plan for Verena's improvement is aimed at "rescuing" Verena from that vulgar "*milieu*," at instilling in her precisely that sense of taste that Olive has been unsuccessfully attempting to "kill" in herself. With Verena there, the Charles Street residence, according to the narrative, "shone with superfluous friction, with punctuality, with winter roses" (151). Olive, we are told, cultivates only "the best" music; she and Verena read the classics and study German and discuss history in their "little island of lamplight" on "nights of deep snowfall, when Charles Street [is] white and muffled and the door-bell foredoomed to silence" (153).

But Olive's instinctive desire to distinguish between "high" and "low" pleasures is always being undermined by a sentimental ideal whose standard is figured as subjective experience rather than abstract, intersubjective agreement. When Olive takes Verena to the "superior programmes" in "that high, dim, dignified Music Hall," and they find that "Bach and Beethoven only [repeat], in a myriad forms, the idea that [is] always with them" (155), her assumption is that pure sentiment always elevates. She believes, in other words, that the sentimental is distinct from the vulgar and the bodily, the self-serving and the commercial. But when Verena is due to perform the same idea in the same Music Hall, vulgarity and commercialism are everywhere: in the "itinerant boys" selling "Photographs of Miss Tarrant—sketch of her life!" that give a "catch-penny effect [to] the whole thing" (372, 373), as well as in Pardon's offer to "work up these last hours for her" with "any little personal items—the sort of thing the people like" (366). In such vignettes, sentiment becomes a type of publicity— one that figures itself as an exposure of the "personal," and thereby appeals not to an audience's "taste," but rather to its curiosity, to its appetite for intimate details, even to its prurience. A related moment occurs in the scene at the Tarrants' home, when Mr. Burrage and Mr. Gracie are pressing Verena to speak for them, and Olive decides to urge Verena to resist their entreaties. Their "discussion had brought the blood to Olive's face," explains the narrator;

> everything that had been said was benighted and vulgar; the place seemed thick with the very atmosphere out of which she wished to lift Verena. They were treating her as a show, as a social resource, and the two young men from the College were laughing at her shamelessly. She was not meant for that, and Olive would save her. . . .
>
> "I want you to address audiences that are worth addressing—to convince people who are serious and sincere." Olive herself, as she spoke, heard the great shake in her voice. "Your mission is not to exhibit yourself as a pastime for individuals, but to touch the heart of communities, of nations." (114)

The distinction Olive makes here—between being "a pastime for individuals" and "touch[ing] the heart of . . . nations"—is precisely the distinction Ransom makes between Verena's (true) domestic self and her (false) lecturing self: the difference is simply that while Ransom ascribes a reality or solidity to the former, Olive elevates the latter. The distinction itself, then, appears to be misleading: in either case—whether she is "a show" for the two Harvard men in the Tarrants' parlor, or "address[ing] audiences" of thousands at, say, the Music Hall—Verena is public and visible, intended, as Ransom says, "to please." Olive also, of course, makes a distinction about the nature of that pleasure, between audiences who "laugh at her shamelessly" and audiences who are "serious and sincere." But that distinction too is spurious. Mr. Burrage's rejoinder to Olive's tremulous speech is his conviction that "Miss Tarrant will touch [his] heart!"— a declaration of sincerity that can only be judged, not disproved. Moreover, the very indeterminacy of the phrase "touching the heart"—suggesting at once a virtuous sympathy for the suffering of women and an interested, perhaps even sexual, love for the speaker—reveals Olive's notion of sentiment to be slippery indeed. For even though she may want Verena's message to be impersonal, her appeal—for Olive just as for Ransom and Mr. Burrage—is distinctly personal.

Olive's feminist politics rely on the distinction between personal and impersonal interest: she challenges Matthias Pardon, for example, by asking him whether his "sympathy [is] a sympathy with our sex, or a particular interest in Miss Tarrant?" (112). But the distinction, again, is a specious one, because it is precisely Verena's personal appeal that makes her an attractive representative; it is her personal charm, her "subtle feminine desire to please," that makes her a valuable vessel for "embodying [the] cause" of women's rights (105). Her public success is not distinct from, but dependent on—and representative of—her personal fascination. And, once the audience's attraction is figured as private and sentimental—once it is situated in "the heart"—then the means of distinguishing between virtuous and vulgar motives, high-minded and crude interests, evaporates. The pleasure of watching Verena perform is the pleasure of seeing privacy exposed, whether it is the righteous exposure of centuries of "feminine anguish" for public consideration, or the "touching" exposure of a vulnerable girl to a presumably more knowing audience, or the prurient exposure of innocent girlhood for the entertainment of "shameless" men. Moreover, Olive's willful insistence on distinguishing between personal and impersonal interest mirrors her conflicted aesthetics: her attribution of "vulgar" interests to Mr. Burrage, for example, calls not only his sincerity into question, but also—if we take "sincere" sentiment as an aesthetic standard—his taste. But if anyone in the novel shares Olive's appreciation for fine things and excellent music, it is Mr. Burrage, whose superior taste attracts him to Verena in the first place. "He liked her," we are told, "for the same reason that he liked old enamels and old embroideries"— he "collected beautiful things"; "he prized Verena for her rarity" (129, 267).

In depicting Olive's commitment to reform as a violation of her taste, the central figures are clearly Miss Birdseye and the Tarrants. The society of Miss Birdseye is said to be always a "pleasure" for Olive, comparable in one passage to the "joys" of Bach and Beethoven (24, 155). But there is also, as I have already discussed, a sense in which Miss Birdseye—or at least Miss Birdseye's apartment—is an offense to Olive's taste, the occasion not of her pleasure, but of her suffering. That is, in one respect, because the "pleasure of seeing [Miss Birdseye]" is a sentimental pleasure, a pleasure of the sort that is intimately bound up with suffering.[25] Here, however, I would like to examine another aspect of the contradiction, one that is rooted in Miss Birdseye's being the quintessential representative of the great moral reforms of the nineteenth century—abolition, temperance, and women's rights. Emerson was fond of punning on the word "reform," conceiving it as an attack on the old "forms" in order to "form" anew, and Miss Birdseye's "formlessness"—she is described as an "essentially formless old woman, who had no more outline than a bundle of hay"—is just such a pun (27, also 316). Her lack of "outline" is in fact the first thing we are induced to notice about her: the novel introduces her as having "a sad, soft, pale face, which (and it was the effect of her whole head) looked as if it had been soaked, blurred, and made vague by exposure to some slow dissolvent. The long practice of philanthropy had not given accent to her features; it had rubbed out their transitions, their meanings. The waves of sympathy, of enthusiasm, had wrought upon them in the same way in which the waves of time finally modify the surface of old marble busts, gradually washing away their sharpness, their details" (24). It is notable, first of all, that Miss Birdseye's "formlessness" is from the beginning attributed to her "long practice of philanthropy," the "waves of sympathy, of enthusiasm," that characterize her particular sort of reform. In other words, it is not simply that any reform effort must necessarily target the structures and conventions of the status quo, that Miss Birdseye's "testi[mony] against the iniquity of most arrangements" means, as Olive fears, that "an absence of nice arrangements [is] a necessary part of the enthusiasm of humanity" (25, 27). Rather, Miss Birdseye's "formlessness" attests to her theory of reform, to the assumptions upon which her vision of reform is based—"formlessness," in short, is a quality not simply of the society she envisions but of the reformed self as well.

This reformed self is defined first and foremost by its capacity for sympathy, its ability to identify with the suffering masses: "all [Miss Birdseye's] history," the narrator explains, "had been that of her sympathies" (27). The "vagueness of boundary" that characterizes Miss Birdseye's life should be understood in light of this ideal of sympathy, an ideal in which there are no boundaries, no walls that protect a private self and, in so doing, keep other private selves out; it is an ideal in which everything—especially the most intimate and heartfelt sentiment—is shared (26). The "mysterious articles of clothing" that are "always hooked to something in [Miss Birdseye's] hall" signify precisely that—once-personal items that have become a sort of public property. Thus Miss Birdseye's selflessness—her lifetime of "carrying the Bible to the slave," washing the "sore bodies" of filthy street children with her "slippery little hands," "smoothing the pillow of exile for banished conspirators" (156, 157, 26)—necessarily manifests itself as formlessness, as "vagueness of boundary," as "features" whose "meanings" and "transitions" have been "rubbed out." And, obversely, a lack of form means a lack of self. The image of the dissolving face, its features being slowly eroded away by the relentless "waves of sympathy," is also an image of disintegration, of the loss of identity and individuality. It is the image of a self "consumed by the passion of sympathy," a self that can have no interior for the simple reason that it has no exterior (34). The ideal of universal sympathy also means for Miss Birdseye a perfect lack of discrimination: she treats her guests "kindly, . . . but without the smallest discrimination," "wander[ing]

about among them with repetitions of inquiry and friendly absences of attention"; the narrator accounts for her tolerance of the "odour of india-rubber"
emanating from their overshoes by explaining that she "neither knew what she
smelled nor tasted what she ate" (25, 29). She accounts Ransom, Verena, and
Selah Tarrant all "geniuses"; indeed, "there [is] a genius for Miss Birdseye in every bush" (30). Her conscious disregard for differences of race and social class
and nationality manifests itself as a disregard for differences of all kinds; she replaces the old aristocracy of birth not with an aristocracy of talent or beauty or
intelligence, but with an aristocracy of everyone.

If Miss Birdseye's "vagueness of boundary" and indiscriminate trust are ultimately endearing, however, the Tarrants take the same qualities to their repulsive extreme. Selah Tarrant's bodily penetration into the abstract medium of
print, as I have already pointed out, is a transgression of the boundary between
a private sphere of violence and physical necessity and a public sphere of linguistic abstraction. But penetration also has sexual connotations—suggesting
that extreme case of print's venture into the realm of the bodily, pornography—
and so it is not surprising that Tarrant's sexualized body should haunt the pages
of *The Bostonians.* By far his most striking physical features are his "long, lean
hands" and a smile that suggests sexual arousal, a "strange and silent lateral
movement of his jaws," "as noiseless as a patent hinge" (51, 144, 88). When his
"eloquent" hands aren't "strok[ing] and smooth[ing] his daughter," executing
the "grotesque manipulations" that initiate her speech (and deeply offend both
Ransom and Olive), they are performing "gratifying cures" on his mostly female
patients (52, 65). That there is a sexual component to Tarrant's spiritualism is
suggested in his "associa[tion]" with Mrs. Ada T. P. Foat at the Cayuga community ("that was Selah's expression," the narrator explains parenthetically, "in
referring to such episodes"), in Mrs. Tarrant's "private conviction that he par-
took, at the houses of his lady patients, of little lunches," and, generally, in the
admission that his "poor" wife "matrimonially, had a great deal to put up with"
(63, 91). And, when Olive gives him the check intended to appease him for
Olive's appropriation of Verena, Tarrant's hands seem to be doing something
more masturbatory: "Selah looked at the cheque, at Miss Chancellor, at the
cheque again, at the ceiling, at the floor, at the clock, and once more at his host-
ess; then the document disappeared beneath the folds of his waterproof, and
she saw that he was putting it into some queer place on his queer person. 'Well,
if I didn't believe you were going to help her to develop,' he remarked; and he
stopped, while his hands continued to fumble, out of sight, and he treated Olive
to his large joyless smile" (144). Even Tarrant's "eternal waterproof" is somehow

lecherous: like the garment of a flasher, it always implies the possibility of an appalling exposure; it both renders the unspecified "queer place on his queer person" perversely fascinating and keeps it thankfully "out of sight."

The constant threat of the sexual that attends "the irrepressible Tarrant" is only the crudest manifestation of a publicity that figures itself as an exposure of the private. The uncomfortable fact of Verena's conception is, I would argue, more deeply menacing to the world of *The Bostonians.* Ransom finds it "annoying" and "disconcerting" that Tarrant should be her father, and "shame[ful]" that Mrs. Tarrant should "have mated with such a varlet" (51). For Olive it is a "perpetual enigma"—a "mystery" that she "turn[s] over in her mind for hours together"—that "such people" should be "Verena's progenitors at all" (100), and she decides that Verena's "precious faculty" must have "dropped straight from heaven, without filtering through her parents" (73). Even the narrator can't help but "wonder immensely how she came to issue from such a pair" (68). The odd persistence with which the novel revisits the fact of Verena's parentage, combined with its fervent insistence upon the inexplicability of it all, indicates an underlying anxiety about Verena's origins and nature. That Verena should have descended from so repulsive a father—that she should be the product of the respected Greenstreet family's "descent" into the "social swamp" of Tarrant's quackery, the "disten[sion] and demoraliz[ation]" of Mrs. Tarrant's "conscience"— seems to cast doubt upon exactly what both Olive and Ransom so cherish in Verena: her purity (63, 65). One of the central arguments of this book, however, is that innocence, transparency, and purity are never unproblematic qualities in public life: such qualities *must* distinguish themselves from deception and duplicity precisely because they are so closely related. The genealogy of American reform that emerges in *The Bostonians* moves from the "heroic age of New England life—the age of plain living and high thinking, of pure ideals and earnest effort, of moral passion and noble experiment"—to a kind of tactless and tasteless public life that the Greenstreets never intended, and finally to their eloquent progeny (157). Ironically, it is the very "earnestness" of that heroic age of abolitionism—represented in the novel by the Greenstreets and Miss Birdseye, with their rejection of dissimulation and pretense and false social "forms"— that paves the way for a publicity like Tarrant's that triumphs as a vulgar spectacle of exposure. The Greenstreets disapproved of their daughter's marriage: "much as they desired to remove the shackles from the slave," the narrator explains, "there were kinds of behavior which struck them as too unfettered" (62). But the monstrous and "irrepressible" Tarrant turns out to be both the inescapable consequence of a vision of publicity that grounds itself in fictions of sympathy and sincerity and the forebear of a powerful eloquence that can touch the heart of the nation.

I will conclude this chapter with a brief consideration of safety, a concept with peculiar resonance in rhetorics of protection, which must maintain a commitment to safety as an ideal, and at the same time convincingly demonstrate an ever-present risk of injury. Safety, in short, is most persuasive as a desire, as an unattained but attainable and enviable state, because the argumentative edge is lost the moment safety is perceived to have been established. And so the purveyors of such arguments often face the dilemma of both wanting and strangely not wanting safety, fostering a sense of outrage at their subjects' vulnerability and yet also tending to overemphasize and even revel in that vulnerability. We can see just such a dilemma in the familiar injunction to "keep our children [or streets, homes, neighborhood, highways, food supply, blood supply, citizens, etc.] safe," which loses its urgency when the children, or whatever, are perceived to be no longer in danger. The politician elected on a platform of public safety benefits from the feeling of vulnerability generated by news reports of abducted children, terrorism, tainted meat, and the like, and public life comes to be characterized by a self-perpetuating cycle of moving pleas to protect the public safety and repeated reminders of public vulnerability.

In this chapter I have been arguing that both Olive Chancellor and Basil Ransom entangle themselves in some crucial contradictions in their efforts to secure Verena's eloquent voice to their cause, and I will conclude by examining how, especially in Olive's case, those contradictions get expressed in figures of safety. One way to frame the difference between Ransom's and Olive's projects is that Ransom's rhetoric of protection promises Verena a safe place, whereas Olive's rhetoric of exposure equates that version of safety with bondage and confinement. But both parties end up depending upon exactly the thing they claim to abhor: Olive, upon a payment that several critics have likened to the purchase of a slave, as well as—quite literally—upon walls and locks and security guards; Ransom, upon Verena's openness to attack. Olive's dilemma arises the evening she meets Mr. Burrage and Mr. Gracie at the Tarrants' home and tries to extract a promise from Verena not to marry. By the time she sees Verena again she has reconsidered: she had panicked, she explains to Verena, "seeing . . . how exposed you are." Although she wants her to be "safe," she continues, "your safety must not come from your having tied your hands" (120). It is a key moment. Olive has chosen to cling to the ideal that Verena can be safe—safe, that is, from the insidious allure of men—without being bound or confined, despite her intuitive sense to the contrary. But Olive's intuition, of course, turns out to be correct. When Ransom arrives at her cottage in Marmion, Olive desperately reminds herself that Verena "was safe, that . . . in New York [she] had repudiated, denounced her pursuer" (315); days later she "repent[s] . . . with bitterness and rage" her refusal to accept Verena's "vow of eternal maidenhood" (329); and finally, at the Music Hall, having "hidden her away" for the previous ten weeks, Olive is reduced to locking Verena and herself in a room backstage and "appl[ying] for the protection of [a policeman]" (362, 374). Olive's bind could not be more starkly drawn: Verena's safety requires her confinement, and her confinement prevents her from appearing in public.

Olive herself represents a different sort of unraveling of the ideal of safety, an unraveling that begins humorously. "She had erected it into a sort of rule of conduct," the narrative reads, "that whenever she saw a risk she was to take it; and she had frequent humiliations at finding herself safe after all" (14). Olive's own privileged safety—her wealth, her security, her "cushioned feminine nest"—is an embarrassment rather than a comfort to her; she is the archetypal bleeding-heart liberal, who responds to the social injustice of which she is a beneficiary with a fruitless and self-indulgent sense of guilt (16). Moreover, Olive's "rule of conduct" generates a paradox reminiscent of Henry Mills Alden's deployment of shame as a guardian of public conduct. On the one hand, the "rule"— something generally "erected" for our protection—is in Olive's version allied with "risk"; on the other hand, "humiliation" comes not from self-exposure, but from "safety." In fact, safety is, for Olive, an embarrassing exposure of privilege. The world in which Olive lives is not simply a world in which one is always in imminent danger of injury, a "sea of risk," to apply Sylvan Tomkins's useful description of negative affect; it is a world in which the very effort to find a spot of safety is futile, because safety is itself a shameful spot to occupy (38, 174). As in Alden's exposé of the vicious world of popular journalism, self-protection turns out to be an inherently self-defeating endeavor, an endeavor that, for Olive, is bound to unravel in shame. Notably, of all the characters in *The Bostonians,* Olive is the most susceptible to shyness and shame: she is, the narrator confides very early in the novel, "subject to tragic fits of shyness, during which she [is] unable to meet even her own eyes in the mirror" (10). It is not surprising: shame, too, is a defensive and self-protective impulse that results only in greater and greater self-exposure.[26]

If in the novel's earlier scenes Olive's suffering is amusingly theoretical, however, by the scene at the Music Hall it has become brutally real. We get only glimpses of Olive's "sightless, soundless shame" and her "scared, haggard face," for much of it is hidden from our view by the locked door of the backstage room in which she is trying to protect Verena from Ransom (382, 383). In fact, since the final scenes at Marmion, the narrator has been increasingly reluctant to give us Olive's interior directly, declaring that Olive's darkest thoughts are "mysteries into which I shall not enter, speculations with which I have no concern" (354). At the same time, however, we get Olive's final humiliation with excruciating realism, down to the brutal detail of the insult from Mrs. Farrinder that strikes Olive as if it were a "lash" (388). In two crucial ways, then, fundamental elements of the rhetoric of protection—precisely those elements that make Verena's lectures touching and engaging and pleasurable—have been turned around to constitute Olive's torment. First, such rhetorical strategies are always poised to cross the boundary between literal and figurative violence, between the actual "lash" and the description so vivid that we can imagine that we feel it. In Olive's case, however, the shift over the course of the novel from imaginative suffering— her identification with the "historic unhappiness of women"—to the actual pain and humiliation of the Music Hall scene represents the undoing of sentimental pleasure, the collapse of the detachment upon which the sentimental response, after all, depends. When Olive experiences pain of an intensity that she had hitherto only imagined, we are reminded that, as much as rhetorics of protection encourage us to imagine the boundary between speech and action as ever at risk of breaking down, they are in the end dependent upon the very abstraction they yearn to have overcome.

Even more fundamentally, rhetorical strategies like Verena's are effective because the voice seems to issue from outside the zone of civic protection, from some outlaw place where nothing is safe and speech has bodily consequences. Listeners sense a tender thing in imminent danger of ruin, of being brutalized or shamefully exploited, and respond to it with instincts both protective and predatory. Notably, those conditions, in their melodramatic extreme, precisely describe the scene at the end of *The Bostonians* where Olive appears before the Music Hall crowd: rushing toward the stage, she strikes the narrator as one who seeks "expiation . . . in exposure to the thousands she had disappointed and deceived, in offering herself to be trampled to death and torn to pieces" (388). And, in imagery that evokes Olive's own fantasies of martyrdom, she is likened to "some feminine firebrand of Paris revolutions, erect on a barricade, or even the sacrificial figure of Hypatia, whirled through the furious mob of Alexandria" (388). There is, then, something doubly cruel about Olive's final public humiliation. Not only is her devastating personal failure held up for all of Boston to see, she is also, in effect, forced into a public appearance that resembles, in all its particulars, the publicity that she had developed and capitalized on for Verena's success and for her own sense of mission. But while Verena is "a touching, ingenuous victim, unconscious of the pernicious forces which were hurrying her to her ruin" (215), Olive is agonizingly aware of her own exposure. And what in Verena's case elicits her audiences' tender compassion, in Olive's case, she fears, will draw only "hiss[es] and hoot[s] and insult[s]" (389).

Throughout the entire novel, Olive longs to escape her spot of safety. In the end she is granted her wish, and it is not a happy moment. By ending the novel as he does, James exposes the contradictions entailed in claims of injury and rhetorics of protection. In order for such strategies to be effective, the audience must buy into the premise that the protective structures of the bourgeois public sphere have failed; they must envision themselves in one of those "moments of crisis" Lauren Berlant describes, when "persons violate the zones of privacy that give them privilege and protection in order to fix something social that feels threatening. They become public on behalf of privacy and imagine that their rupture of individuality by collective action is temporary and will be reversed once the national world is safe, once again, for a return to personal life" (*Female Complaint* 22). These are the conditions that establish the priority of such arguments over mere logic and trigger the desire to protect that constitutes their persuasive force. Listeners are drawn both to empathize with the vulnerable and to experience their own self-protection as a barrier to their tenderness, as an obstacle that must be overcome. Nevertheless, rhetorics of protection must maintain their productive tension between security and insecurity; they cannot allow their subject position to become fixed at either pole. By making Olive's wish for martyrdom perversely come true at the end of *The Bostonians,* and by forcing her reformist project into public view without the medium of Verena's beguiling voice, James envisions the collapse of such mechanisms of publicity in their own disingenuous rejection of safety in abstraction. What Olive had envisioned as a triumphant victory over detached masculine logic has become something else entirely, and James leaves us to imagine what sort of reception she will get from the disappointed Boston audience—an audience, Ransom thinks with relief, that appears unlikely "to hurl the benches at her" (*The Bostonians* 389). Verena is whisked away, helpless to resist, and what we come to realize is that rhetorics of protection are not only interested in breaking down the structures of civility but also, in the end, reliant on the very structures of civility that they claim have broken down.

Epilogue

Civility, Incivility

Civility is liberating. It frees us from slavery to self-absorption, impulse, and mood.

—P. M. Forni, *Choosing Civility*

The liberal public sphere makes great promises: the dissemination and expansion of knowledge, tolerance, individual growth and self-realization, enlightened critical thinking, and civility. However, the liberal public sphere is structured in such a way that it also generates another, very different model of public exchange. John Stuart Mill famously wrote that *On Liberty* "assert[s] one very simple principle. . . . That principle is, that the sole end for which mankind are warranted, individually or collectively, in interfering with the liberty of action of any of their number, is self-protection" (13). Mill intends this principle to establish the widest possible zone of liberty, a zone that can be breached for only this one, single reason. But the unintended consequence of Mill's principle has been to elevate the cause of self-protection above all other causes, to imbue the cause of self-protection with such importance and urgency that it alone can justify compromising the liberty of others. Moreover, if liberty of speech and action requires that persons be protected against injury, then to elevate the cause of self-protection is to amplify the voices of those who are excluded from the zone of liberty—those who can convincingly portray themselves as unprotected, at risk of injury, and therefore incapable of the self-abstraction into language characteristic of free exchange and free public participation.

This book has examined how this paradoxical structure of the liberal public sphere has influenced and enabled arguments about citizenship in different historical conditions. In the three decades before the Civil War, I see its most profound impact in antislavery rhetoric: although causes as diverse as women's rights, temperance, proslavery, and nativism all associated themselves with the cause of self-protection, it was abolitionism that most successfully capitalized on the contradictions that arise from the liberal public sphere and harnessed the morally charged energy those contradictions generate. After the Civil War, we can see comparable opportunism and comparable energy in the rhetoric that figured the South as a violated white woman. Like Grady's and Cable's "silent South," Basil Ransom's desire "to be quiet about the Southern land, not to touch her with vulgar hands, to leave her alone with her wounds and her memories" evokes a volatile mixture of reticence and outrage, tenderness and self-righteousness. Because such figures direct our attention to someplace outside the zone of civic protection and the free exchange of ideas, their logic also necessarily tends toward violence, and directly fueled the extreme violence of lynching. And because such figures capitalize on women's disenfranchisement, they can—and in these cases do—function not to remedy women's exclusion but to reinforce it. The rhetoric of protection comes into being within a dynamic field, and there is nothing inevitable about these particular outcomes; nevertheless, the same paradox that gives the rhetoric of protection its persuasive power can also propel the debate toward incivility, division, and violence—toward an undoing, in other words, of all that the liberal public sphere promises. It is this latter possibility that interests Henry James in *The Bostonians,* which I read as depicting the undercurrent of incivility that is generated when various political interests compete to claim and profit from the cause of a vulnerable privacy.

Henry's brother William was also deeply interested in the character of American public discourse, and his lecture "What Makes a Life Significant" offers a useful complement to the picture that emerges from *The Bostonians.* He describes a "happy week" he had spent at Chautauqua in the summer of 1896 as precisely the sort of orderly and enlightened public exchange of ideas that liberalism envisions, the figurative space of the public sphere literalized in the "sacred enclosure" of the Assembly Grounds.[1] "Sobriety and industry, intelligence and goodness, orderliness and ideality, prosperity and cheerfulness, pervade the air," writes James (646). "You have culture, you have kindness, you have cheapness, you have equality, you have the best fruits of what mankind has fought and bled and striven for under the name of civilization for centuries. You have, in short, a foretaste of what human society might be, were it all in the light, with no suffering and no dark corners" (647). What James envisions here is Mill's zone of liberty expanded and spread out to include the whole of human society, Mill's zone of liberty with no outside. If *The Bostonians* imagines a public sphere with nothing but competing claims of injury and fantasies of rescue, William James's Chautauqua is a place where there can be no such claims or fantasies because everyone is protected. However, no sooner does he leave this "middle-class paradise" than his "lawless fancy," in his account, perversely breathes a sigh of relief: "Now for something primordial and savage," he finds himself "quite unexpectedly and involuntarily saying." "This human drama without a villain or a pang, . . . this atrocious harmlessness of all things—I cannot abide with them" (647). What was "lacking in the Sabbatical city," James continues, was "the element of precipitousness, so to call it, of strength and strenuousness, intensity and danger. . . . [What] the grim civic monuments remind us of, is the everlasting battle of the powers of light with those of darkness; with heroism, reduced to its bare chance. . . . But in this unspeakable Chautauqua . . . the ideal was so completely victorious already that no sign of any previous battle remained" (647–48).

We might be tempted to hear in James's "lawless fancy" something akin to Ransom's rant against the "damnable feminization" of American society—both of which hover somewhere between seriousness and hyperbole—mourning the loss of "strength and strenuousness" and imagining it on the masculine field of battle, lamenting the decline of "heroism" and the rise, as both Ransom and James say, of "mediocrity." But while Ransom's frustration seems to be with the proliferation of injury claims, James stresses the absence of adversity, the disappearance of the conditions out of which stories of suffering arise. For Ransom the public sphere is debased by emotional accounts of "historic unhappiness"; for James such accounts are the very stuff of our "grim civic monuments." Always conscious of the paradox, James doesn't dispute "the ideals for which our civilization has been striving: security, intelligence, humanity, and order" (647). But the attainment of those ideals turns out to degrade the quality of our public life and impoverish our public discourse. James's pun on "unspeakable" plays on Chautauqua's association with lecturing, but also suggests that public speech itself is somehow diminished when speakers are perfectly safe, when there is, as he says of Chautauqua, "no suffering and no dark corners." It suggests that speech flourishes in circumstances of adversity and danger, and possibly even requires "dark corners" from which to emerge. James goes on in the lecture to chide those who would romanticize suffering and poverty. But his point serves mostly just to highlight the fine line he is drawing in his lecture: between rejecting middle-class security and romanticizing hardship, between cries of victimization and challenges to injustice, between believing in an ideal and yet not wanting to attain it.

These are the tensions that constitute the liberal public sphere. I have tried to show in this book how remarkably malleable and productive they were, how not only liberalism's claims but also its denials and even the critical exposure of its fictions have given structure to a wide variety of arguments about citizenship in the nineteenth century, and have supported progressive as well as conservative and reactionary political agendas. At the heart of many of liberalism's most productive denials is privacy, the thing that modestly shuns public exposure and yet must continually be produced in public, the site of our most cherished beliefs and emotions and yet also the site where we are most vulnerable to manipulation and subjugation. To the extent that privacy has been gendered female, it has generated both the possibility and the scandal that women can appear in public, and has endowed their public appearance with charm, suspense, shame, and vulnerability. The contradictory nature of privacy has functioned both to protect domestic relations from public oversight and to provide domestic relations with a public platform. Privacy's close cousin, negative liberty, establishes its own matrix of claims and denials, above all its avowed opposition to tyranny at the same time that it depends upon the ever-present possibility of invasion and injury by a tyrannical power. Thus has the slave's declaration of independence assumed an iconic status in liberal accounts of American liberty, generating the principle of "a more perfect union," our faith in an ever-expanding zone of liberty that at the same time guarantees the continued presence of the forces of tyranny. The association of free civic participation with protected abstraction—the fantasy, that is, of a civic realm that is separate from the personal—has given rise to the complementary fantasy of embodied vulnerability and the enduring risk of injury. While embodiment can and has functioned to exclude racialized and gendered subjects from full citizenship, it can also serve as a marker of sincerity and passionate devotion and an inducement to sympathetic identification, promising an escape from callousness and isolation. And if the normative belief in civic abstraction and privatized domesticity—their establishment as valuable, separate and fixed states of being—erects barriers to enfranchisement and reinforces discriminatory practices, it also, as we can see in the example of Frances E. W. Harper, is liable to being exposed as fiction and thereby opened up to critique.

William James ends "What Makes a Life Significant" with a quote from Fitz-James Stephen, a London barrister and a critic of John Stuart Mill. Describing past progress and anticipating future advances in ocean liner technology, Stephen marvels that passengers will one day "cross the seas without . . . [ever feeling] that they have left firm land. . . . They will have a pleasant passage and plenty of brilliant conversation. They will wonder that men ever believed at all in clanging fights and blazing towns and sinking ships and praying hands; and, when they come to the end of their course, they will go their way" (659–60). Like James's Chautauqua, however, Stephen's transatlantic crossing is ultimately a diminished affair, leaving the passengers safe and secure but without any real knowledge of "the great ocean on which they sail, with its storms and wrecks, its currents and icebergs, its huge waves and mighty winds," and therefore without ever having been brought "full into the presence of time and eternity, their maker and themselves" (660). Although Stephen's primary concern here is the "praying hands" and the knowledge of one's "maker," we might also read this passage as challenging Mill's assertion of self-protection as the fundamental social value. Stephen suggests, on the contrary, that having as our ultimate goal the protection of selves from violence, from the elements, from injury and loss, condemns us to a life of a certain kind of ignorance, to a life of "brilliant conversation" but without the struggle and experience necessary to real knowledge. Notably, Isaiah Berlin cites Stephen's "formidable attack on Mill" in his "Two Concepts of Liberty," saying that if it is true "that integrity, love of truth and fiery individualism grow at least as often in severely disciplined communities . . . as in more tolerant or indifferent societies, . . . Mill's argument for liberty as a necessary condition for the growth of human genius falls to the ground" (200). To the extent that Mill himself had bought into the fictions of liberalism—in particular the fiction that liberty and tyranny are mutually exclusive rather than mutually constitutive—this stands as a valid critique. But I would argue that it only serves to validate the powerful system of claims and denials that I have been describing as liberalism in this book. Liberalism has no way of imagining absolute self-protection, no way of imagining self-protection without the ongoing presence of a threat, and so the idea that "integrity, love of truth and fiery individualism" grow out of resistance to tyranny only confirms liberalism's deepest convictions. That liberalism can generate such critique and impassioned debate without any challenge to its broader contours only highlights its remarkable capacity to endure.

Notes

Preface

Qtd. in Lyric Wallwork Winik, "'We Need to Pay More Attention to Boys,' An Interview With Laura Bush," *Parade Magazine, The Philadelphia Inquirer* 16 Jan. 2005: 5.

1. A note on terminology: among other connotations, the word *liberal* has been used to refer both to a broad tradition of political philosophy and to a cluster of political aims associated, in the United States, with the modern Democratic Party. To avoid confusion, I will used the word *liberal* to refer to the former, and the word *progressive* to refer to the latter.

2. See also Julie Ellison's discussion of what she calls "Cato discourse," which, she argues, should be understood "as a cluster of narrative or dramatic relationships rather than as a stable republican ideology" (72–73).

3. I am treating these as general political tendencies here; I do not wish to suggest that either conservatism or progressivism in the United States is monolithic.

4. Katharine Q. Seelye, "Over the Airwaves and on Cable TV, Health Care Dominates," *The Caucus: The Politics and Government Blog of the* Times, 6 August 2009, Web, 22 August 2009.

5. Ian Urbina, "Beyond Beltway, Health Debate Turns Hostile," *New York Times,* 8 August 2009, Web, 22 August 2009.

6. Calvin Woodward, Associated Press, "FACT CHECK: Poll finds health overhaul myths gaining traction, fabled 'death panels' included," *Newser,* 19 August 2009, Web, 22 August 2009. Woodward reports on an NBC News poll that found, among other things, "45 percent said it's likely the government will decide when to stop care for the elderly; 50 percent said it's not likely."

7. Favorite quotes of the protesters included Thomas Jefferson's "The tree of liberty must be refreshed from time to time with the blood of patriots and tyrants," and "It is the duty of every patriot to protect his country from its government," attributed to Thomas Paine.

8. "Online NewsHour Debate: Mayors Fight Gun Legislation," *PBS Online,* 11 July 2007, Web, 12 July 2007.

9. See, for example, Rodin and Steinberg.

INTRODUCTION

1. See Pocock.

2. Arendt, *The Human Condition*. For a summary of recent challenges to Arendt's paradigm, see McKeon 7–9.

3. Warner, *The Letters of the Republic*.

4. Feminist critics who have argued that the republican model of the public sphere was structured in such a way as to exclude women include Fraser, Landes, and Ryan.

5. In *Women in Public*, for example, Mary Ryan's initial questions—"How did public man characterize the women who were banned from his lofty domain?" and "How can women lay claim to and make use of the public citadels that continue to elude their sex?" (9)—establish a revealing metaphor. The public sphere is figured as a bounded space that excludes women, and its mechanisms of exclusion are figured as the walls or fences that mark its boundaries. In order to "lay claim" to public attention, then, women must breach the "citadel's" walls and, as Ryan writes, "trespass . . . across the border of the private realm" (8). Her metaphor entails two key assumptions: that the exclusive, white male version of public selfhood is the only version available, and that women must necessarily rupture or dismantle the mechanisms by which they are excluded. By contrast, I understand the public sphere as a contested space, therefore shifting the focus of inquiry from the means by which women were excluded from public life to the frames within which they reconciled their femininity with their public speech. In other words, instead of seeing a woman's development of a public voice as hindered by her construction as a private being who is denied civic protections, I wish to see that construction as itself a way of figuring publicity.

More recently, Nancy Isenberg's excellent history of women's participation in antebellum American civic life demonstrates both the variety and the theoretical sophistication of their efforts. But despite Isenberg's claim that antebellum supporters of "women's rights . . . developed a coherent feminist critique," her account seems to me to depict a movement that is less coherent than it is pragmatic, at times using republican civic structures and assumptions about gender difference to its advantage, at times challenging them (xiii). My readings will, I hope, add another analytical dimension to certain of Isenberg's accounts. For example, to her description of a series of judicial rulings and polemics that link citizenship to what she calls "the theme of self-protection," I would add that the case for self-protection is always joined at the hip with claims of injury or vulnerability to injury (28–39). Elsewhere Isenberg correctly analyzes the spectacle of slave women on the auction block thus: "unable to defend their bodies from a hostile invasion and captivity, [they] failed to disclose themselves as persons, appearing instead as mere bodies incapable of displaying the marks of citizenship or personhood" (113). At the same time, however, it is important to note the absolute centrality of the spectacle of the slave auction—and in particular the auctioning of girls and women—to antislavery discourse. Nevertheless, I would attribute what sometimes appear to be inconsistencies in the way antebellum reform movements positioned themselves in relation to the dominant constructions of citizenship and gender less to theoretical incoherence than to their strategy of capitalizing on the internal contradictions inherent in the dominant constructions of citizenship and gender.

6. I do not wish to suggest that there were not simultaneously challenges being made to the mechanisms of civic exclusion; on the contrary, I see my work as a supplement to the already extensive scholarship that examines those challenges. In his introduction to *National Identities and Post-Americanist Narratives,* Donald Pease proposes a theoretical framework for examining the complex relation between an exclusive American national identity and the various emancipatory social movements that have emerged to challenge those exclusions. "These postnational forces for social change," Pease argues, "are neither wholly intrinsic to the previously subjugated social categories of race, class, and gender nor reducible to a capability external to them. Idealized stereotypes of race and gender were often reaction formations designed to combat negative stereotypes but which in fact corroborated the same impulse to universalize social norms. Postnational forces understand every social category as the ongoing antagonism between internalized models and external forces" (5). Similarly, Pease argues that nationalist mechanisms of exclusion never function simply to stabilize racialized and gendered social hierarchies. The readings in this book can productively be seen to reside, to appropriate Pease's phrase, "at the intersection between interpellation and exclusion" (9). For another examination of how exclusionary categories can also function to threaten or unsettle the cohesiveness of national identity, see Bhabha.

7. David Leverenz summarizes the vast scholarship on paternalism in *Paternalism Incorporated.* Leverenz himself wishes to recover progressive possibility—especially the possibility of upward mobility—in the paternalistic social structures of what he calls the "early corporate era." Like Leverenz, I see conflicting consequences, both for white, male authority and for the inclusion of marginalized groups, in ideologies of civic paternalism, but whereas Leverenz focuses on successful paternalistic relations, I focus on the internal contradictions generated by paternalistic ideologies that paradoxically open white, male authority up to criticism. More generally, Isaiah Berlin and others have seen a commitment to negative liberty as antipaternalistic. I argue, on the contrary, that negative liberty is always imagined as vulnerable to tyranny and therefore in need of paternalistic protection. To conceive the authority of the state as limited is not to conceive it as antipaternalistic; it is merely to figure it as a good parent rather than a meddling or overbearing one.

8. The "Declaration of Sentiments" is reprinted in Rossi 416–20. The description of Weld is attributed to Henry Brewster Stanton, from an unpublished manuscript in Sarah Grimké's hand, dated 1838, in the Grimké-Weld Collection at the William Clements Library, University of Michigan, Ann Arbor.

9. See Halttunen, "Humanitarianism and the Pornography of Pain in Anglo-American Culture." Halttunen examines not only the sense that pain is unacceptable but also the related representation of pain "as obscenely titillating precisely because the humanitarian sensibility deemed it unacceptable, taboo" (304).

10. See Bailyn and Pocock. For a summary of the contours of the larger scholarly debate over the comparative influences of liberalism and civic humanism in eighteenth-century American political thought, see Fruchtman.

11. Fanuzzi summarizes the scholarship in *Abolition's Public Sphere:* "Many scholars of the antebellum era have rightly concluded that the conventional Americanist linear model of ideological succession—first republicanism, then liberalism—needs to be replaced with a model of synchronism and dialectical interdependence" (xviii).

12. Berlin goes so far as to attribute the degree of a society's freedom to the "barriers" that prevent such trespassing: asserting the "moral validity . . . of some absolute barriers to the imposition of one man's will on another," he argues that "the freedom of a society . . . is measured by the strength of these barriers" (237).

13. For discussions of the mechanics of sentimental detachment, see Noble, and Davidson 319. The political implications of the sentimental appeal, its prominent role in antislavery arguments, and the extent to which it produces an uncritical public of consumers rather than a critically engaged citizenry, are issues that have been debated since Ann Douglas's 1977 *The Feminization of American Culture* and Jane Tompkins's *Sensational Designs.* Subsequent considerations of such issues are collected in Samuels's *The Culture of Sentiment.* In addition to Ellison's *Cato's Tears,* other significant contributions to the literature on sentiment and American citizenship include Jehlen, "The Family Militant," Stern, Burgett, Burstein, and Hendler.

14. My own readings draw heavily on Berlant's keen description in *The Female Complaint* of what she calls "liberal national sentimentality":

> So, in the nineteenth-century history and legacy of liberal national sentimentality we see that at moments of crisis persons violate the zones of privacy that give them privilege and protection in order to fix something social that feels threatening. They become public on behalf of privacy and imagine that their rupture of individuality by collective action is temporary and will be reversed once the national world is safe, once again, for a return to personal life. Sentimental politics in that idiom works on behalf of its eradication. This horizon of autoerasure constitutes the dream-work of sentiment and the culture industry that supports it, and in the heritage of sentimentality the nationally supported taxonomies—involving race, gender, class, and regional hierarchies in particular—still largely govern the horizon of failure and possibility sentimental authors and readers construct. (22–23)

I diverge from Berlant, however, in seeing this dynamic construction as a rhetoric that has no inherent political content, but can be appropriated by a variety of political agendas.

15. Notably, Arthur Riss proposes just the opposite: he contends that sentimentality has been associated not with embodied vulnerability, but with a "will toward disembodiment," claiming that "sentimentality posit[s] pain as a universal category that attests to our abstract equality" (94). Again, I would argue that this tells only half the story. The

sentimental imagination is drawn to spectacles of bodily injury not only because of the fantasy that we can feel one another's pain, but because pain is also fantasized as something irretrievably private and interior. As Elaine Scarry has written, "when one hears about another person's physical pain, the events happening within the interior of that person's body may seem to have the remote character of some deep subterranean fact, belonging to an invisible geography that, however portentous, has no reality because it has not yet manifested itself on the visible surface of the earth" (3). Hannah Arendt makes a similar point in *The Human Condition:* "the most intense feeling we know of, intense to the point of blotting out all other experiences, namely, the experience of great bodily pain, is at the same time the most private and least communicable of all. Not only is it perhaps the only experience which we are unable to transform into a shape fit for public appearance, it actually deprives us of our feeling for reality to such an extent that we can forget it more quickly and easily than anything else. There seems to be no bridge from the most radical subjectivity, in which I am no longer 'recognizable,' to the outer world of life" (50–51). Incapable of being abstracted from embodied experience into language, pain epitomizes that which cannot be admitted to public life without compromising its liberty. As Arendt reminds us, in classical Greece and Rome persons subject to physical violence were disqualified from public participation. "Nothing . . . ejects one more radically from the world," she writes, "than exclusive concentration upon the body's life, a concentration forced upon man in slavery or in the extremity of unbearable pain" (112). The fantasy of shared pain has such heightened significance in the sentimental imagination, I would argue, precisely because pain seems to come from someplace inescapably private. Models of self-abstraction and shared sentiment, in other words, are neither opposite nor unproblematically the same; rather, they form a mutually constitutive and dynamic opposition. On the fraught relation of violence and American public culture, see also Shklar, Seltzer, and also Dillon's association of spectacles of violence with what she calls "the widening of an intermediate space between public and private" (235).

16. A number of scholars have pointed out that to suggest that a reader can imaginatively experience slavery is to diminish the suffering of slaves; it is to assume that the vicarious, perhaps even self-indulgent anguish of a reader whose heart bleeds for the slave is somehow equivalent to what the slaves themselves endure. Hazel Carby, in *Reconstructing Womanhood,* and Frances Smith Foster, in *Witnessing Slavery,* both make this point about Jacobs's narrative. See also Sánchez-Eppler, *Touching Liberty,* and Hartman.

17. In *Public Sentiments,* Glenn Hendler discusses sympathy as a conflicted process: referring to Adam Smith's *Theory of Moral Sentiments,* he identifies "a mediating force between the sympathizer and the sufferer"—a mediating force, he argues, that "is always at risk of collapsing. . . . Put slightly differently, the risk of sympathy is that the idea that one can feel *like* another person feels can be overshadowed by the paradoxically self-negating desire to feel *with* that other, to share the other's experiences as if they were one's own" (4, 5, emphasis in original). Similarly, Jacobs can be seen as negotiating degrees of similarity and difference with her primarily white, female readership, many of whom chose to see their condition as analogous to the condition of slaves. The aboli-

tionist and feminist Sarah Grimké famously signed her *Letters on the Equality of the Sexes,* "thine in the bonds of womanhood." See Ceplair 204–72. Nancy F. Cott took the title of her classic study of the "woman's sphere" from Sarah Grimké, *The Bonds of Womanhood: "Woman's Sphere" in New England, 1780–1835.* Cott writes, "'Bonds' symbolized chattel slavery to [Grimké]. She must have composed her phrase with care, endowing it intentionally with the double meaning that womanhood bound together even as it bound them down" (1).

18. Although Orlando Patterson challenges the simplistic division of freedom into "positive" and "negative" liberty, his reading of its earliest expressions in classical Greece depicts it as something most profoundly understood by those most in danger of losing it. "While slavery was not of any structural significance," he writes, "its cultural and psychological impact was increasingly important. Indeed, there was one important category of persons to whom slavery and, antithetically, freedom were critical—namely, women. Freedom began its long journey in the Western consciousness as a woman's value. It was women who first lived in terror of enslavement, and hence it was women who first came to value its absence, both those who were never captured but lived in dread of it and, even more, those who were captured and lived in hope of being redeemed or, at the very least, being released from their social death and placed among their captors in that new condition which existentially their whole being had come to yearn for." Patterson, *Freedom, Volume One,* 51.

19. See also Juliet A. Williams's recent critique of what she calls the liberal "discourse of line-drawing" in *Liberalism and the Limits of Power.*

20. The idea of American progress as an ongoing series of efforts to realize the ideals laid out in the founding documents—what we might call the "more perfect union" model—is examined in Pauline Maier's *American Scripture.*

21. Here I would also point out that Taylor's description of a version of positive liberty—self-realization—imagines it negatively, as freedom from certain forces that would hinder it. Ronald Dworkin has characterized Catherine MacKinnon's argument for the censorship of pornography in similar terms: "Pornography, on this view, denies the positive liberty of women; it denies them the right to be their own masters by recreating them, for politics and society, in the shapes of male fantasy" (106). Dworkin is ultimately critical of such arguments (100–109).

22. Critics of liberalism also frequently misrecognize protection from invasion as autonomy. Citing liberal theorists from Isaiah Berlin to Bruce Ackerman, David Gauthier, and Gerald Dworkin, for example, John Kekes identifies autonomy as "the true core of liberalism, the inner citadel for whose protection all the liberal battles are waged. . . . Autonomy is what the basic political values of liberalism are intended to foster and protect." To "foster and protect" autonomy, however, is to imagine it as in some sense childlike, as something always at risk of being compromised, something that in the absence of the paternalistic forces marshaled to defend it would inevitably suffer and waste away. Such "autonomy" is neither independent nor self-sufficient; on the contrary, it is dependent for its very existence on the armies that do "battle" with those who would invade its "citadel" (15, 16).

23. As Lakoff observes, "what is one man's constraint on free movement is another man's protection against encroachment" (87).

24. See also Dillon's reading of Habermas, which distinguishes the work of the "political" public sphere and the "literary" public sphere (25–36).

25. Hamilton begins his argument, significantly, by suggesting that bills of rights—historically seen as cornerstones of English republican or Commonwealth thought—are central to republicanism only as it developed within and in opposition to monarchy. That sense of opposition is fundamental to bills of rights, Hamilton argues, which make sense only as long as rulers and ruled are perceived as having conflicting interests, only as long as liberty is understood as an endangered thing. Once government is established according to republican principles—once, that is, government is understood as representative and the people as sovereign—the underlying logic for a bill of rights begins to break down. Gordon S. Wood explains the reasoning thus: "The people under monarchy, of course, had possessed long-standing rights and privileges immune from tampering by the prerogative powers and privileges of the king. But under republicanism could such popular rights continue to be set against government? In the new republics, where there were no more crown powers and no more prerogative rights, it was questionable whether the people's personal rights could meaningfully exist apart from the people's sovereign power—the general will—expressed in their assemblies. In other words, did it any longer make sense to speak of negative liberty where the people's positive liberty was complete and supreme?" (*The Radicalism of the American Revolution,* 188–89). See also Wood's account of the Federalist opposition to a bill of rights, and his discussion of how the notion of government as a "contract" between rulers and ruled loses its logical foundation once rulers are seen as representative of the people, in *The Creation of the American Republic,* 536–43, and 282–83.

26. *The Human Condition* is Arendt's fullest account of this tradition.

27. In *The Human Condition,* Arendt reminds us that private life was not always perceived to be precious. In contrast to what she calls "the enormous enrichment of the private sphere through modern individualism," the ancient world saw private life as a state of deprivation. "A man who lived only a private life," she explains, "who like the slave was not permitted to enter the public realm, or like the barbarian had chosen not to establish such a realm, was not fully human" (38). In the modern age, our sense of where we become "fully human" has in large part shifted from the public sphere to the private sphere of family and personal relationships. In *Sources of the Self,* Charles Taylor describes this shift as "the rise of the ordinary," the idea that a fulfilling life is available not simply to the elite but to the ordinary masses of people as well. And Isaiah Berlin associates the idea that "the area of personal relationships [is] something sacred in its own right" not only with negative liberty but also with "an entire moral outlook" (201).

28. At its most basic, this hypocrisy stems from the fact that bourgeois privacy necessarily has what we might call a public face, but it cannot be acknowledged as such; it is fictional not only in its constructedness but also in its fundamental investment in our denial and our desires. In the nineteenth century, literary sentimentalism was a primary medium for generating the fiction of bourgeois privacy, and several critics, begin-

ning with Ann Douglas's astute account, have identified a certain hypocrisy at its core. Douglas describes the sentimental as a profoundly commercial, exhibitionist, and self-indulgent literary form that claims to promote an ethic of modesty and self-sacrifice. Similarly, bourgeois privacy must present itself as a region of life that modestly shuns publicity, but must nevertheless be manifested publicly in order to perform its constitutive function for the liberal subject. Milette Shamir frames her analysis of antebellum privacy by identifying precisely this apparent hypocrisy in contemporary U.S. society: "This book began with a moment of naïve but genuine perplexity," she explains. "When I first arrived in the United States to pursue my research, I was struck by what then seemed an inexplicable paradox. On the one hand, never had I felt so engulfed in privacy. The white, middle-class American socialscape—with its isolated, suburban homes and anonymous public spaces, with its codes of politeness and respect for what is none of anyone else's business—seemed very far removed from the crowded, meddlesome, Mediterranean setting I had left behind. On the other hand, never had I witnessed such compulsion to *expose.* This was the heyday of confessional talk shows on television, of political scandal in the public arena, and of identity politics in academia, and I was amazed by how smoothly private stories seemed to translate into public currency and marketable commodity in the United States" (1).

29. Locke states the distinction even more vehemently later in the *Second Treatise:* "But these two powers, political and paternal, are so perfectly distinct and separate; are built upon so different foundations, and given to so different ends, that every subject that is a father, has as much a paternal power over his children, as the prince has over his; and every prince that has parents owes them as much filial duty and obedience as the meanest of his subjects do to theirs; and can therefore contain not any part or degree of that kind of dominion, which a prince, or magistrate has over his subject" (150).

30. Other studies that have productively complicated the public-private binary and examined the implications for the status of women include Gillis and Levander.

31. If the feminine is burdened with representing a region of life that must deny an essential aspect of its nature, then, it is also at the very center of the work of the literary public sphere. Dillon writes that her analysis "cracks apart the rigid dualism of the public/private coupling that insists upon women's exclusion from the public sphere, and cracks it less by arguing that there is no such dualism than by arguing that the two sides of this dyad are mutually constituting at every moment, and thus that women figure on both sides of the divide" (36).

32. I have been blurring the distinction between private selfhood and the private or domestic sphere so as to emphasize the parallels between them, in particular the way they both function as the space out of which a critical public emerges, to use Habermas's terms. However, there are also significant differences between them, as Milette Shamir points out in *Inexpressible Privacy.* Shamir identifies a gendered division in nineteenth-century constructions of privacy that corresponds roughly to the difference between domesticity and interiority: Hawthorne, for example, "registers . . . a symmetrical layout whereby femininity is linked with intimacy, social compliance, and sociopetence, and

masculinity with isolation, invisibility, and sociofugality" (72). Shamir's analysis offers an important reminder that the feminine is often burdened with representing privacy's vulnerability to invasion and exposure; my analysis differs from hers only in emphasizing the mutually constitutive relation between these two gendered versions of privacy. Stacey Margolis and Christopher Castiglia have also recently made significant contributions to the study of private interiority in the nineteenth century. Margolis argues that private experience could be mediated through public forms and public effects in ways that were not necessarily disciplinary, and not necessarily in the service of a repressive social or state apparatus. Castiglia is interested in how social conflicts and divisions in the state are displaced into the human interior, not as a mechanism of ideological reproduction so much as a means of fostering techniques of self-management. He reads the drives and desires that are not successfully managed as "an archive of democratic aspirations that have been discredited or foreclosed, the visions of citizens who are socially dead yet living—often persistently and even ragefully so—in the interior state" (11). For both Margolis and Castiglia, then, the political implications of privacy are varied and complicated and go well beyond the Foucaludian model. My analysis contributes to that general project: by focusing on how privacy functions rhetorically, I am interested less in whether the construction of privacy as both deserving and in need of state protections has a certain political effect than in how that construction has been used historically to various political ends.

33. Saidiya Hartman's study of nineteenth-century racial subjugation examines how the power relations entrenched during slavery were perpetuated after the institution of slavery was officially abolished. Violence and domination did not simply require the slave's explicit dehumanization, she argues, but were also "enabled by the recognition of humanity, licensed by the invocation of rights, and justified on the grounds of liberty and freedom" (6). Like Hartman, I am interested in how the language of liberty and tyranny came to be a resource for white supremacists, particularly during and after Reconstruction. Unlike Hartman, however, I would argue that the same language can also be used to challenge white supremacy and advance a progressive political agenda.

Chapter 1

1. The poster is reproduced in Lowance 91.

2. For an alternative interpretation, see Fanuzzi, who reads the abolitionists' invocation of the American Revolution as part of their project "to create a deliberately anachronistic public sphere" (xv). He argues that the "historical analogy" functioned "to reverse the identities of citizen and noncitizen" and thereby enabled antislavery activists "to appropriate the historical narrative of the American republic for the struggle of the disenfranchised" (xxiii–xxiv). While I of course agree that the American revolutionaries were enfranchised citizens—in stark contrast to the disenfranchisement of women and slaves of the antebellum era—I will argue that the revolutionaries nevertheless *imagined* themselves as having been unjustly disenfranchised by the tyranny of George III. While

Fanuzzi sees the "comparisons between the disenfranchised and the enfranchised of another time" as "awkward," I would argue that the comparison makes perfect sense in light of the revolutionaries' insistent focus on the "injuries" done to them by George III (xxviii).

3. It was an argument Douglass likely picked up from the Senate debates over the bill in 1853, during which Salmon P. Chase and Benjamin Wade made similar arguments. See Maier 200.

4. Notable dissenters from this conventional reading of slavery as an anomaly in a state expressly founded on liberty include Morgan, Patterson (*Slavery and Social Death*), and Morrison, all of whom see the rise of the American republic and the American conception of free citizenship as dependent upon the existence of the institution of slavery. More recently, Waldstreicher's account of American freedom's entanglement in the institution of slavery focuses on the link between self-making and escaping from slavery or servitude. Waldstreicher argues that free citizenship in eighteenth-century America often turned on one's ability to manipulate appearances to one's advantage and, in particular, whether that manipulation is seen by others as resourceful self-making or deceit and criminality.

5. See also Armitage, whose primary purpose is to recover the Declaration's significance as an assertion of independent statehood—a significance he claims has been obscured by the emphasis on its assertion of individual rights and liberties. But Armitage agrees with Maier that it was when the Declaration came to be interpreted as emphasizing rights and liberties that it "became domesticated" and appropriated by reformers for "specifically national purposes" (96).

6. Shaffer identifies a similar dynamic at work in early American drama, citing Jefferson's conception of liberty as "a political ideal . . . that seems to be in perpetual retreat from the inevitable onset of corruption and the machinations of encroaching statesmen" (20). Using a similar vocabulary of protection and vulnerability, Pocock describes the American revolutionaries as attempting "to reconstitute that form of polity in which virtue would be both free and secure." Virtue was seen to be threatened by "corruption emanating from a source now alien, on which Americans had formerly believed themselves securely dependent. The language began to sound that paranoiac note which is heard when men are forced by the logic of mental restriction to conclude that malign agencies are conspiring against the inner citadels of their personalities" (507–8).

7. For Aristotle, it would have meant being master of a household in which women and slaves took care of the necessities.

8. In *Prodigals and Pilgrims*, Fliegelman discusses the relevance of *Clarissa* to the colonists' depiction of their revolution against British tyranny.

9. The Negro Convention movement, lasting from the early 1830s right up to the Civil War, produced many such documents. See Howard Holman Bell.

10. Isenberg reminds us that Elizabeth Cady Stanton drafted the Declaration of Sentiments "at a table resembling the desk at which Thomas Jefferson wrote the Declaration of Independence," and that it "was signed by the members of the convention much

as the celebrated founders did in Philadelphia in 1776" (4, 29). She also points out that the temperance movement also found inspiration in the Declaration of Independence (160, 165).

11. Reprinted in William Wells Brown, *Clotel* 497–99.

12. It is, to say the least, paradoxical that Thomas Jefferson, for whom the independent yeoman farmer represented the model citizen of a republic, should draft the document that would become the model for extending citizenship to the vulnerable and the dependent. As I stated in the introduction, I see republicanism and liberalism functioning—both in the revolutionary and in the antebellum eras—not as distinct political philosophies, but as clusters of ideas that often intersect.

13. See also Lampe, esp. 264–68.

14. I would emphasize that here I am examining the representation of Douglass by a white abolitionist, not Douglass's representation of himself. Douglass increasingly found himself at odds with the efforts of the antislavery leaders to fashion his public persona—differences I address in more detail later in this chapter. In 1847, when Douglass returned from a twenty-one-month trip to Great Britain, his disagreements with the Garrisonians intensified: his English friends had arranged for his freedom to be purchased, against the wishes of the Americans, who felt such a transaction conceded that human life could be ascribed a monetary value. But they also must have sensed that Douglass would never again be quite so dramatic a voice on the lecture platform, with the "halter" of the Fugitive Slave Law no longer "about his neck." See also Lampe, esp. 289.

15. In a footnote, Arendt maintains that slaves were prevented not only from speaking publicly, but even more fundamentally, also from *appearing* in public.

> An anecdote, reported by Seneca from imperial Rome, may illustrate how dangerous mere appearance in public was thought to be. At that time a proposition was laid before the senate to have slaves dress uniformly in public so that they could immediately be distinguished from free citizens. The proposition was turned down as too dangerous, since the slaves would now be able to recognize each other and become aware of their potential power. Modern interpreters were of course inclined to conclude from this incident that the number of slaves at the time must have been very great, yet this conclusion turned out to be quite erroneous. What the sound political instinct of the Romans judged to be dangerous was appearance as such, quite independent from the number of people involved. (*Human Condition* 218 n. 53)

16. Warner, *The Letters of the Republic,* and "The Mass Public and the Mass Subject." For a discussion of the gendering of individualism, see Gillian Brown.

17. A correspondent for the *Practical Christian,* describing a 25 June 1845 antislavery meeting, wrote that Douglass presented "himself as an outcast, without protection, living in the midst of monuments reared to *liberty,* and steeples towering to heaven, and yet a *slave*" (qtd. in Lampe 275, emphasis in original).

18. For analysis of the relation between a notion of embodied personhood and the discourses of abolition and women's rights, see Sánchez-Eppler, *Touching Liberty.*

19. For both Habermas and Arendt, the public sphere is intersubjective: the classical ideal of the polis, Arendt writes, "is the organization of the people as it arises out of acting and speaking together, and its true space lies between people living together for this purpose" (*Human Condition* 198). For Habermas, too, ideas in the public sphere are mediated through discussion, and the bourgeois public sphere depends upon such enabling structures as coffeehouses and, particularly, print culture and "traffic" in "news" (15).

20. "Frederick Douglass" is, of course, an assumed name, as we learn in the *Narrative.* Douglass both uses the pseudonym of Douglass and tells the story of how he acquired it, thus exposing it as a pseudonym and divesting it of its capacity to protect his identity.

21. There is a large body of critical literature on the relation of speech to writing. Derrida has theorized extensively on and in response to the idea that writing is a fallen form of speech. See *Of Grammatology, Writing and Difference,* and, specifically regarding the signature as a kind of absent presence, "Signature, Event, Context" in *Margins—of Philosophy.* Warner has argued that the greater abstraction of print particularly suited it as a medium for the development of a critical public in the eighteenth century: see *Letters of the Republic,* and also Fliegelman's response to Warner in *Declaring Independence.* For a discussion of the relation of speech to the body, see Kahane.

22. Garrison uses an intriguingly similar figure in an 1854 speech: "Convince me that one man may rightfully make another man his slave, and I will no longer subscribe to the Declaration of Independence. Convince me that liberty is not the inalienable birthright of every human being, of whatever complexion or clime, and I will give that instrument to the consuming fire" (Lowance 126).

23. Chapter 3 of this book examines in more depth the tendencies to inscribe white and black versions of publicity. For an analysis of how Douglass's relation to language differs from white speech and writing, see Stepto, "Storytelling in Early Afro-American Fiction" and "Distrust of the Reader in Afro-American Narratives." Douglass himself contrasted his speech about slavery to that of white abolitionists by referring to his bodily knowledge of it. As Lampe writes, "[Douglass] argued that although white abolitionists knew much about slavery, 'were acquainted with its deadly effects,' and could 'depict its horrors,' they could not speak, as he could, 'from *experience.*' White abolitionists, he said, 'cannot refer you to a back covered with scars, as I can; for I have felt these wounds; I have suffered under the lash without the power of resisting. Yes, my blood has sprung out as the lash embedded itself in my flesh'" (67).

24. For example, a correspondent for the *Liberator* described an address by Douglass thus: "He spoke calmly and deliberately at first; but as he went on, his soul kindling as the subject opened before him, his voice grew louder, clearer, and deeper—his whole frame seemed to expand, while he poured forth the feeling of 'mighty heart,' in a torrent of eloquence, loftier and more powerful than I have ever before listened to" (qtd. in Lampe 215). Similarly, the antislavery activist Angelina Grimké's eloquence "kindled,"

as William Lloyd Garrison described it, under the threat of mob violence. Chapter 2 of this book considers Grimké's public speech in more detail.

25. Judith Butler addresses this problematic and persistent association of speech with what she calls "burning acts," as in the application of First Amendment arguments to flag burning and cross burning. We might also think here of the classic example of *un*protected speech—shouting "fire" in a crowded theater.

26. See also duBois, *Torture and Truth.* In her excellent study of the uses of torture in classical Greece, duBois writes: "the slave's body is . . . constructed as [a] site of truth, like the *adyton,* the underworld, the interiority of the woman's body, the elsewhere toward which truth is always slipping, a utopian space allowing a less mediated, more direct access to truth, where the truth is no longer forgotten, slipping away. The *basanos* gives the torturer the power to exact from the other, seen as like an oracular space, like the woman's *hysteria,* like the inside of the earth, the realm of Hades, as other and as *therefore* in possession of the truth" (105). For duBois, this figuring of truth as hidden—and thus in need of extraction by breaking open the body—oppresses women and slaves by making them the objects of torture. I argue that, in the realm of liberal civics, women and slaves can also *capitalize* on this figuration of truth by figuring themselves as the injured vessels of truth. Such a move does not *escape* the oppressive nature of such beliefs; rather, it capitalizes on their own internal contradictions.

Wendy Brown describes just such a move in contemporary feminism's desire to "retain . . . women's experiences, feelings, and voices as sources and certifications of postfoundational political truth," a desire manifest in the centrality of consciousness-raising to second-wave feminism. Consciousness-raising, she explains, "operates as feminism's epistemologically positivist moment. The material excavated there, like the material uncovered in psychoanalysis or delivered in confession, is valued as the hidden truth of women's existence—true because it is hidden, and hidden because women's subordination functions in part through silencing, marginalization, and privatization." Such a configuration is further problematized, Brown argues, by its reliance on precisely the fiction of a unified and coherent subject that feminism denounces as masculinist, racist, and heterosexist. "Dispensing with the unified subject," she maintains, means "that our words cannot be legitimately deployed or construed as larger or longer than the moments of the lives they speak from; they cannot be anointed as 'authentic' or 'true' since the experience they announce is linguistically contained, socially constructed, discursively mediated, and never just individually 'had'" (40–41).

For another approach to terror and its entanglement with pleasure and sentiment, in particular as it relates to the North American institution of slavery, see Saidiya Hartman.

27. The circumstances by which George is convinced to speak to the court recall the "Dialogue between a Master and a Slave" in *The Columbian Orator,* in which the slave's account of the injustice he faces is held up as a model of eloquence and wins him his freedom. Douglass, of course, refers specifically to the "Dialogue" in his *Narrative* (Bingham 209–12).

28. Nat Turner originally planned his rebellion to begin on 4 July 1831.

29. This line of reasoning finds perhaps its fullest expression in George Fitzhugh's *Cannibals All!*, where the threat issues, as the subtitle explains, from "slaves without masters." Fitzhugh is well known for his depiction of slavery as a paternalistic institution that nurtures and protects the slaves, but he gives equal emphasis to its capacity to keep order, also describing it as "the best and most efficient police system" (29). Indeed, Fitzhugh makes no attempt to disguise control as paternalistic protection. On the contrary, he claims that the two functions are inseparably linked: " 'It is the duty of society to protect the weak,' " he writes; "but protection cannot be efficient without the power of control; therefore, 'It is the duty of society to enslave the weak' " (187).

30. In his history of antislavery litigation, Robert Cover identifies the appeal to the victim's helplessness as a fundamental strategy of antislavery attorneys. "Playing upon the potential for empathy," he writes, "the abolitionists always tried to personify the victims; to stress the personal, dire consequences of an impersonal rule; to relate the victim's life story; to introduce the familial and vocational context from which he was torn. In a certain sense, almost every slave is a sympathetic victim to a man morally opposed to the institution" (216). Fugitive slaves like Thomas Sims who were captured in a Northern state and denied a legal opportunity to challenge their capture were especially sympathetic and gave rise to appeals such as this one by a Mr. French of New Bedford: "We have been told that every citizen however humble, may come before our courts, and spread out his case and demand his rights," he told an 1853 constitutional convention. "I stand here and tell you, that a free citizen of Mass.—as free, Mr. Pres., as either you or I—has failed to be protected by the judiciary" (qtd. in Cover 178).

31. See also Geoffrey Hartman's account of what he calls the "Philomela project" (164–75).

32. In 1853 Stowe reprinted extended excerpts from Ruffin's opinion in *A Key to Uncle Tom's Cabin*, 77–79. See also Gregg Crane's excellent reading of Stowe's use of the Ruffin opinion (72–77). Paraphrases and direct quotations from Ruffin's opinion appear elsewhere in antislavery fiction: *Clotel* begins with a stark account of the master's legal rights over the slave, ending with Ruffin's assertion that "the slave, to remain a slave, must be sensible that there is no appeal from his master" (Brown 82). And Delany ascribes Ruffin's general philosophy to his fictional character Colonel Franks, who believes that "the will of the master being absolute, his commands should be enforced, let them be what they may, and the consequences what they would. If slavery be right, the master is justifiable in enforcing obedience to his will; deny him this, and you at once deprive him of the right to hold a slave—the one is a necessary sequence of the other" (13–14).

33. See also my reading of the figure of the courtroom in *American Slavery as It Is*, in "Slavery and Civic Recovery."

34. I am referring here to Adorno—in particular to Jameson's reading of Adorno's *Negative Dialectics* in *Late Marxism*—and Gates, *The Signifying Monkey*.

35. Messerli calls this speech "his most intransigent and scathing denunciation of slavery to date" (510).

36. Selections from the speech are also included in Lowance 266–72, erroneously dated 15 February 1852.

37. Booth applies the hermeneutic distinction between "meaning" and "significance" to his discussion of irony (19).

38. For a discussion of Garrison's paternalistic stance toward Douglass, see Baker, *The Journey Back* 147–49.

39. There has been substantial critical attention to Douglass's use of irony, both in his speeches and in his publications, much of which focuses on this problem of his presence in a civic realm that was structured in a way that could not acknowledge him, that "explicitly denied slaves the grounds of being," as Baker has written ("Autobiographical Acts" 96). Referring to the 1845 *Narrative,* Gates calls Douglass "truly the ironic subject, drawing upon an ironic rhetorical strategy, as Kierkegaard says, to feel free, because the subject's 'appearance is the opposite of what he himself subscribes to'" (*Figures in Black* 111). Several critics have suggested that Douglass's use of ironic doubling anticipates W. E. B. Du Bois's concept of "double-consciousness," "two souls, two thoughts, two unreconciled strivings; two warring ideals in one dark body" (*Souls* 3). Bernard Bell argues that Douglass expresses this double consciousness by creating an "ironic tension between himself and his audience," emphasizing not only his exclusion from the vision of liberty articulated by the founders and celebrated on the Fourth of July, but also the disjunction between his own sense of self and his appearance to his mostly white audience, what Du Bois calls "this sense of always looking at one's self through the eyes of others" (149, 141). John Louis Lucaites traces what he calls the "ironic construction of equality" in Douglass's Fourth of July speech. In shifting his focus from the disjunction between past and present to the disjunction between present and future, Lucaites argues, Douglass is able to shift from seeing equality as ironically exclusive to seeing it as ironically inclusive. To render equality ironic, in other words, is to highlight America's history of racial inequality, but also to imagine equality as "a potentially flexible and regulative principle that both accommodates and thrives on difference" (63). For Lucaites, Douglass's irony is not static, but dynamic and "dialogic." Similarly, Robert Terrill identifies what he calls an "ironic dialectic [that] plays throughout the text" of "What to the Slave is the Fourth of July?" "Slavery has made [Douglass] mute," Terrill explains, "yet has authorized him to speak. . . . Both slave and speaker are fully present, set against the need 'to deliver a fourth [of] July oration,' and it is with this unresolved juxtaposition that we enter the realm of irony" (220). For evidence of "double consciousness" elsewhere in Douglass's writing, including his 1876 speech memorializing Abraham Lincoln, see Sundquist, "Frederick Douglass: Literacy and Paternalism," and Lucaites.

40. For readings of the fraught parent-child relationship in midcentury American culture more generally, see Jehlen, *American Incarnation,* chapter 6, and Cavitch chapter 4.

41. Paul Giles points out that Douglass's tour of Britain from 1845 to 1847 traces a similar path. He argues that Douglass developed a "transnational, comparative consciousness" during that period; for Douglass, Giles writes, "*nationalism* and *transnationalism*" relate "paradoxically rather than dialectically to each other. . . . [O]nly by moving outside the charmed circle of the nation can Douglass put himself in a position to redescribe its circumference" (787). Giles draws on Sundquist's reading of the paradoxical

relation of bondage and freedom in *My Bondage and My Freedom* in *To Wake the Nations.*

42. See also Poirier, *Poetry and Pragmatism.*

CHAPTER 2

1. From "An Oration on the Powers of Eloquence, Written for an Exhibition of a School in Boston, 1794": "When the compassionate lawyer, without hope of reward, advocates the cause of the suffering widow, or injured orphan, he *must* be eloquent" (247, emphasis in original).

2. For a classic narration of "the historic unhappiness of women," see chapter 2 of Mill's *The Subjection of Women, On Liberty* 146–65.

3. Scholars who have addressed this problematic tendency include Saidiya Hartman and Ellison. Hartman examines such strategies as tools of domination, resulting in "the obliteration of the other through the slipping on of blackness or an empathic identification in which one substitutes the self for the other" (7). Ellison examines the process by which racial and gender difference are, as she writes, "absorb[ed] . . . into subjectivity." She reads several early eighteenth-century British republican dramas in which "representations of race are also representations of sentiment. If racial discourse signifies traumas of personal identification and political loyalty, then race is already internalized, already subjective in British culture" (49).

4. The biographical information in this chapter is primarily from Lerner and Lumpkin.

5. The epigraph to Jacobs's *Incidents in the Life of a Slave Girl,* attributed to "a woman of North Carolina," succinctly illustrates the means by which antislavery activists wished to accomplish political reform: "Northerners know nothing at all about Slavery. They think it is perpetual bondage only. They have no conception of the depth of *degradation* involved in that word, SLAVERY; if they had, they would never cease their efforts until so horrible a system was overthrown" (333, emphasis in original). Such "knowledge" is not attained through a critical discussion of the abstract principles involved in slavery, but rather through a deeply personal and sympathetic comprehension of the slaves' experience. For a discussion of the "theory of power" at work in nineteenth-century sentimental novels see Tompkins, "Sentimental Power," and for a discussion of the connection between such "power" and the politics of abolitionism (in, for example, what Elizabeth Margaret Chandler called "mental metempsychosis"), see Yellin, esp. 12–13 and, on Grimké, 29–52.

6. Section III of the Pastoral Letter is quoted in its entirety in Ceplair 211–12: "although it did not mention their names," argues Ceplair, "[it] was clearly aimed at the Grimké sisters" (139). Sarah Grimké responded specifically to the Pastoral Letter in the third of her *Letters on the Equality of the Sexes and the Condition of Women.*

7. A phrase from the 1837 Pastoral letter quoted above, cited by Sarah Grimké in the third of her *Letters on the Equality of the Sexes* (212).

8. Scholars have identified various connections between feminism and abolitionism, noting, for example, that it was the antislavery movement that drew women to the lecture platform in unprecedented numbers: not only Sarah and Angelina Grimké, but also Sojourner Truth, Abby Kelley, Lucretia Mott, Lucy Stone, and Frances E. W. Harper, among others. Most of the work that has been done on this relation has tended to assess the concept of emancipation as it was applied to both women and slaves, and as it associated (or conflated) models of gender and racial oppression. See, for example, Yellin and Sánchez-Eppler, "Bodily Bonds." By suggesting that the discourse of abolitionism refigured publicity and public influence in ways that were more conducive to women's participation in public life, I am proposing another way of formulating that link.

9. For an excellent discussion of the "theory of female influence," see Douglas esp. 45–48.

10. The passage from Beecher's *Letters on the Difficulty of Religion* is quoted in Ceplair 138.

11. For discussions of the gendering of the "interior life," see Jehlen, "Archimedes and the Paradox of Feminist Criticism," and Armstrong.

12. Grimké's own speaking career is evidence that the private and public spheres—in Beecher's sense—exist not in opposition but on a continuum: what for Grimké began as "parlor meetings" moved into churches as her audiences grew too large and, eventually, to such venues as the Massachusetts Hall of Representatives and Boston's Odeon Theater. See also Halttunen, *Confidence Men and Painted Women,* in particular her discussion of the parlor as a site of "genteel performance" (101–13).

13. For a discussion of Beecher's ideal of domesticity see Sklar, esp. 155–67.

14. The significant exception is Grimké's frequent reference to her own domestic life after her engagement to fellow abolitionist Theodore Dwight Weld. In February of 1838, for example, she wrote to Weld, "I trust I may be able to see *when* to leave this quiet, lovely place & be willing to work again when the command is given to break up my encampment & enter again upon public duty" (313).

15. See my reading of McKeon and Dillon in the introduction to this book.

16. Beecher herself had touted "purity" as a peculiarly feminine virtue, which distinguished the "truly moral" from the "hypocritically moral" (Sklar 86). See also Cott 64–67.

17. Trilling, and Jehlen, "Imitate Jesus and Socrates," have noted that sincerity is itself paradoxical, becoming a truly social and operable virtue only as it becomes theatrical—inasmuch, that is, as one *appears* sincere to others. It is exactly this tension that interests me in Grimké's rhetoric: its truly radical potential is not in any claim to a "pure" or "truly moral" ground for itself, but rather in the doubts it casts on the very existence of such a ground. "Exposure" works for Grimké when it is understood not as a peeling away of false masks to reveal an underlying truth, but as itself spectacle—as public performance aimed at attracting an audience and influencing public opinion.

18. Nineteenth-century American women who spoke in public often drew on the biblical story of Queen Esther. Lauren Berlant associates the story with what she calls

"diva citizenship," reading Frances E. W. Harper's use of it in *Iola Leroy* (*Queen of America* 224–25).

19. The phrase is Fliegelman's to describe the paradox of converting the theory that public speech was to be "natural expression" rather than "artful representation" into practice (*Declaring Independence* 20). Citing manuals of public speaking that taught students which facial expression, which hand position, which tone of voice to assume in order to convey a wide variety of emotions, Fliegelman contends that the "natural style" was itself made into an art (30–31). "The quest for a natural language," he argues, "led paradoxically to a greater theatricalization of public speaking, to a new social dramaturgy, and to a performative understanding of selfhood" (2). Fliegelman does not, however, address in any detail the ways in which gender is at work in the developments he discusses. He cites, for example, a popular song of the Revolutionary period that mocks certain Patriot orators by referring to them as "Whorators," but he does not comment on the sexual implications of the metaphor (75).

20. As Paine declared in *Common Sense,* "the Object for Attention is the *Doctrine Itself,* not the *Man*" (74, emphasis in original). For a discussion of Paine's claims of "disinterestedness" and the tendency of his publications to invite personal attack, see Larkin, esp. chapter 2.

21. That is, Thomas Grimké who, though a slaveholder, had opposed nullification and maintained dialogue with Sarah and Angelina even after they had begun to associate themselves with abolition (Lumpkin 72).

22. In connection with this examination of Grimké's rhetoric of personal presence, it is useful to consider Warner's discussion of the rhetoric of anonymity in "The Mass Public and the Mass Subject." Warner cites a passage from the final issue of the *Spectator* in which Richard Steele reflects on the disjunction between "himself" and his textual persona. Like Steele, Grimké sees her public self—her "character," her self as it appears to others—as a kind of body that can "suffer" and sustain "injury." But while Steele's figure emphasizes the body's protective qualities, Grimké's emphasizes the body's vulnerability; and while the Spectator remains impenetrable and Steele retains a separate identity, Grimké's text works in the metaphor precisely for its penetrability, for its identification with and therefore exposure of the "person" behind. Warner characterizes the tension in Steele's figure as a "dialectic of embodiment and negativity" (384); we might see that in Grimké's as a dialectic of personal presence and *dis*embodiment.

23. This can usefully be contrasted with Arendt's argument that free public participation requires "a proper establishment and protection of privacy." "The four walls of one's private property," Arendt continues, "offer the only reliable hiding place from the common public world, not only from everything that goes on in it but also from its very publicity, from being seen and heard. A life spent entirely in public, in the presence of others, becomes, as we would say, shallow. While it retains its visibility, it loses the quality of rising into sight from some darker ground which must remain hidden if it is not to lose its depth in a very real, non-subjective sense. The only efficient way to guarantee the

darkness of what needs to be hidden against the light of publicity is private property, a privately owned place to hide in" (*Human Condition* 71).

24. In his *In Memory of Angelina Grimké Weld,* Weld hinted at a mysterious "injury," which Lerner and Lumpkin both identify as a prolapsed uterus. Oliver writes simply that "her voice gave out" (440). Lerner points to her overwhelming domestic responsibilities after marriage: "Angelina and Sarah, for the first time in their lives, began to understand what the 'woman question' was all about. They were no longer sheltered by wealth, privilege or spinsterhood from the basic problem that was to haunt the average woman for the next century: how to have enough energy left over after a day of cooking, housework, and childcare to concern herself with issues outside of the home or to do anything about them, even if she cared" (292–93). See also Ellen DuBois.

25. Douglas writes, "sentimentalism is a cluster of ostensibly private feelings which always attains public and conspicuous expression. Privacy functions in the rituals of sentimentalism only for the sake of titillation, as a convention to be violated. Involved as it is with the exhibition and commercialization of the self, sentimentalism cannot exist without an audience. It has no content but its own exposure, and it invests exposure with a kind of final significance" (254).

CHAPTER 3

1. Leslie Fiedler traces the sentimentalization of the idea of the Old South in the period after Reconstruction—a development made possible, I would argue, by the alignment of the Southern cause with the cause of self-protection.

2. See my reading of the poem below.

3. This specifically Christian image is from *Iola Leroy:* "He was spit upon by the mob, smitten and mocked by the rabble, and died as died Rome's meanest criminal slave. Today that cross of shame is a throne of power" (256).

4. Kenneth Warren cites such arguments to claim that segregation laws are grounded in the premise that the civil and the social realms are inseparable, and therefore it is not possible to permit interracial contact in civil society without also permitting social intermingling. He argues that literary realism is implicated in the promotion of such a premise, and therefore implicated in the rise of Jim Crow and the post-Reconstruction erosion of black civil rights. I would argue, on the contrary, that it is an oversimplification to see literary realism as invested only in the breakdown of such boundaries, and not also in the fantasy of a separation. More specifically, I disagree with Warren's reading of Cable as representative of an enlightened stance on racial issues by virtue of his defense of the boundary between civil and social. Cable did not promote integration, as Warren claims he did (50), but rather envisioned a broad social realm in which racial segregation reproduced itself by choice.

5. Saidiya Hartman offers a similar reading of the effect of an ostensibly antisegregationist argument like Cable's: his "construction of the private and [his] privileging of

sentiment and natural affinity," she argues, "facilitate subjugation as well as the violation of rights and liberties" (168).

6. There is a large body of scholarship on the volatile matrix of the commitment to
racial purity, fears of black sexual aggression, and racial violence and terrorism in the Jim
Crow South, dating back to Ida B. Wells's antilynching pamphlets. Gunnar Myrdal's *An
American Dilemma* is a landmark of white scholarship on the question. See also Wiegman and Gunning.

7. It is illuminating to read this passage in light of the larger liberal project of boundary drawing that I discuss in the introduction. Indeed, it bears a remarkable resemblance
to Jedediah Purdy's description of Frederick Douglass: "In defiance, a slave's dignity
ceases being the master's plaything and becomes the boundary where the master's abuse
must stop" (40).

8. One of the most frequently cited passages in the novel is Tom Anderson's description of Iola—"My! but she's putty. Beautiful long hair comes way down her back; putty
blue eyes, an' jis' ez white ez anybody's in dis place"—which has been interpreted as Harper's attempt to create a heroine with whom a white readership could identify (38). Such
images, it is argued, perpetuate a white standard of beauty along with its implicit deni-
gration of black womanhood. See, for example, Vashti Lewis. For a dissenting view, see
Elkins.

9. Lovalerie King has identified an African American literary tradition that exposes
the racism inherent in property law, its role in enforcing white dominance; the primary
strategy of the literature, she argues, is not so much to assume the position of property
owner as radically to undermine property ownership itself. Inasmuch as property has
functioned as a primary figure for a logic of protection, King's reading of Washington
offers an interesting parallel to my reading of Harper.

10. The same story is told about Uncle Caldwell in "Learning to Read," a poem from
Sketches of Southern Life. Harper, *Brighter Coming Day* 205.

11. The notable exception is Uncle Daniel's unwillingness to tell Robert Johnson and
Tom about the bag of money. The same issue comes up, interestingly, when a nameless
young slave asks Uncle Daniel if he won't tell the authorities about their plans to leave.
Uncle Daniel's response is, again, that he is a man who keeps his word (this time, his
word to the other slaves), and that he is "de same Uncle Daniel [he] eber war," a gesture
to his integrity of character. Nevertheless, we can see that the institution of slavery *itself*
puts slaves like Uncle Daniel in a position of being duplicitous.

12. For a concise account of the problems entailed in establishing representative government, see Wood, *The Creation of the American Republic* 363–72.

13. Samira Kawash uses the term "specularity" to refer to a similar reliance on the dynamics of seeing to portray a transition into a different configuration of selfhood.

14. The disciplinary aspect of Harper's ideal of "home" is clear in a comment Dr.
Latimer makes at Mr. Stillman's *conversazione:* "In civilized society . . . there must be
restraint either within or without. If parents fail to teach restraint within, society has
her check-reins without in the form of chain-gangs, prisons, and the gallows" (254).

Elizabeth Young also reads *Iola Leroy* as both challenging racist and patriarchal systems of exclusion and oppression, and in establishing its own regime of self-discipline.

15. For Habermas's discussion of society's "refeudalization, see 157–59, 194–95. See also Claude Lefort's account of monarchical representation and the body of the king in *Democracy and Political Theory.*

16. This same conflict, I would suggest, can account for the anxiety surrounding the representative relationship in the early years of the republic. Because the fidelity of representation cannot be guaranteed structurally—because, in other words, representative government must be structured so as to admit a possibility of misrepresentation—the representative's authority depends upon the people's confidence in his integrity. And so, although American republicanism defines itself in opposition to the pomp and pageantry of monarchy, it is in the final analysis no less theatrical, no less a matter of display before an audience. Indeed, it could be argued that representative republicanism *must* define itself in opposition to the theatricality of monarchy—must, that is, deny its own theatricality—because to admit that political authority is "staged" is to suggest that the people's confidence might not be warranted, that what they take for reality might after all be illusory. It is precisely such doubt—the doubt that is epitomized in the figure of theater—that representative politics must always generate, and therefore must always strive to eliminate through its "aura" of authenticity. It is significant, in this respect, that Hamilton begins his consideration of the presidency by answering the charge that the office as established by the Constitutional Convention is "not merely . . . the embryo, but . . . the full-grown progeny" of monarchy. It is precisely because the presidency as Hamilton conceives it has clear elements of what Habermas calls "personally represented authority" that Hamilton must distinguish it from monarchy. Madison, Hamilton, and Jay, *Federalist Papers* 389. See also Marshall.

17. The phrase is Alexander Hamilton's, from *The Federalist* No. 49, Madison, Hamilton, and Jay, *Federalist Papers* 401.

18. Although the soldiers whose lives Tom saves are not explicitly identified as white, it can be inferred, I would suggest, from their speech patterns and from the fact that their report of the incident is addressed to Captain Sybil—not Robert Johnson—who is identified as their "superior officer" (52). Moreover, in Harper's account of the same incident in her poem "A Story of the Rebellion," the man who sacrifices his life is distinguished from the rest as "*one* . . . upon whose brow / The ardent sun had left his trace" (*Brighter Coming Day* 365, emphasis added).

19. The narrator explains, "Tom Anderson was a man of herculean strength and remarkable courage. But, on account of physical defects, instead of enlisting as a soldier, he was forced to remain a servant, although he felt as if every nerve in his right arm was tingling to strike a blow for freedom" (40).

20. See, for example, Lott.

21. For a discussion of "strategic essentialism" see Spivak.

22. "The Contrast" was first published in 1857, and "A Double Standard" was first published circa 1894. *Brighter Coming Day* 73–74, 344–46.

23. At the *conversazione* in *Iola Leroy* that I discuss below, for example, Iola's eloquent account of the "negro's" contribution to world civilization compares racial discrimination to the condemnation of Christ, adding, "to-day that cross of shame is a throne of power" (256).

24. For a reading of *Iola Leroy* as a critique of a privatized ideal of domesticity, see Peterson, "Further Liftings of the Veil." Peterson argues, "in refusing Dr. Gresham's marriage proposal, Iola chooses not only loyalty to race but to family and, most especially, to her mother. Beyond that, however, she also rejects the romance of the tragic mulatta plot and its concordant dangers of privatization. Finally, and perhaps most importantly, she resists a world view that is based on a separation of public and private spheres" (101). See also Peterson's *Doers of the Word*.

25. I am also suggesting here that the version of freedom-as-abstraction that Harper associates with passing is gendered male. This suggestion runs counter to the arguments of Phillip Brian Harper and Gayle Wald, both of whom read passing as specifically feminine. I would argue that Frances Harper uses passing in a fundamentally different way than the primarily twentieth-century writers Harper and Wald address. Moreover, in his reading of *Iola Leroy*, Phillip Brian Harper draws on Lorraine's attempt to dissuade his cousin Leroy from marrying a "quadroon girl"—in which Lorraine refers to "these beautiful girls" as "the curse of our homes"—arguing that the tragic mulatta's "feminine identity . . . is deeply implicated in the danger she poses" (104–5). But Frances Harper's novel clearly presents Lorraine's position critically, endorsing instead a sentimentalized vision of feminine virtue, and attributing the "curse" not to the "beautiful girl," but rather to the racist and misogynistic public opinion that Lorraine represents. That does not, of course, mean that the specific configuration of race and gender Phillip Brian Harper identifies—that is, the "illicit sexuality" that is the "mulatto's primary referent"—does not exist; on the contrary, it is powerfully present in Harper's fiction as the position against which she is writing (108). But she refutes it, I would argue, by positing a different configuration of race and gender.

26. See chapter XXX of *Iola Leroy*, "Friends in Council" 246–61. The character of Mr. Stillman is generally thought to be based on William Still.

27. It is worth emphasizing again the difference between this eloquence and the classical conception of speech, which is understood in opposition to the violence of bodily life. Iola's eloquence achieves its peculiar power through its dual nature: it is both a matter of the intellect and at the same time fundamentally implicated in bodily life. That dualism is expressed in the trope of "voice," the bodily medium of speech whose power can be considered apart from the words it utters. As the narrator explains, Iola has a "strangely sympathetic [voice], as if some great sorrow had bound her heart in loving compassion to every sufferer who needed her gentle ministrations" (40).

28. Preface to the New York edition of *Portrait of a Lady*, in *The Art of the Novel* 46.

29. P. Gabrielle Foreman asks, "Why do [Harper and Fauset] drape questions of power with, and place them *under*, a sentimental discourse?" (655, emphasis in original).

Harper titles chapter XXII of *Iola Leroy*—the chapter in which Iola is finally and tearfully reunited with her mother and brother—"Further Lifting of the Veil" (191).

30. Elizabeth Young also reads *Iola Leroy* in the context of Jim Crow segregation and racial violence, noting that "Iola" was a pen name for Ida B. Wells. Young argues that, just as Wells exposed the myth that black men lusted after white women as the fiction justifying lynching, Harper rewrote the Civil War "rape of the South" narrative as the literal attempted rape of her black heroine (218). In other words, Harper "inverts the Southern strategy of using rape plots for racist and misogynist ends" (219). Harper also spoke out frequently and forcefully against lynching. Speaking at the first triennial meeting of the National Council of Women of the United States in February 1891, for example, Harper said, "Our first claim upon the nation and government is the claim for protection to human life. That claim should lie at the basis of our civilization, not simply in theory but in fact. Outside of America, I know of no other civilized country, Catholic, Protestant, or even Muhammadan, where men are still lynched, murdered, and even burned for real or supposed crimes" (qtd. in Boyd 208).

31. As Hazel Carby and others have noted, Harper herself was variously accused of being a man masquerading as a woman, or being painted to look black. See Carby's introduction to the Beacon Press edition of *Iola Leroy*, ix.

Chapter 4

1. Verena's glass box bears a notable resemblance to the transparent plastic cage that Wendy Brown uses as a figure for liberal subjectivity:

> When contemporary anxieties about the difficult imperatives of freedom are installed in the regulatory forces of the state in the form of increasingly specified codes of injury and protection, do we unwittingly increase the power of the state and its various regulatory discourses at the expense of political freedom? Are we fabricating something like a plastic cage that reproduces and further regulates the injured subjects it would protect? Unlike the "iron cage" of Weber's ascetics under capitalism, this cage would be quite transparent to the ordinary eye. Yet it would be distressingly durable on the face of the earth: law and other state institutions are not known for their capacity to historicize themselves nor for their adaptation to cultural particulars. (28)

2. Amitai Etzioni makes a similar observation: in his analysis of the development of the constitutional right of privacy, he writes that "continual efforts by groups such as the ACLU to extend the sphere of privacy paradoxically force increases in governmental interventions." As an example, he points to the arguments over the constitutionality of the government's authority to decipher encrypted messages. "As the ACLU and other individualistic groups have blocked the introduction of public key recovery, which would

have enabled the government, with proper court authorization, to decode encrypted messages," Etzioni writes, "the government has been pushed to use more invasive procedures for the same kind of criminal investigations—for instance, planting microphones in the homes of suspects" (213–14). Etzioni proposes making a distinction between two concepts that he argues have too often been conflated in legal discourse: "privacy," meaning the capacity to shield oneself from public scrutiny or surveillance, and "privateness," meaning autonomy or the capacity to control one's own actions or decisions.

3. See Fraser.

4. In "Sex in Public," Berlant and Warner write, "Intimate life is the endlessly cited *elsewhere* of political public discourse, a promised haven that distracts citizens from the unequal conditions of their political and economic lives, consoles them for the damaged humanity of mass society, and shames them for any divergence between their lives and the intimate sphere that is alleged to be simple personhood" (553). In her introduction to the issue of *Critical Inquiry,* Berlant is even more explicit about the persuasive power of the idea of intimacy: "at its root intimacy has the quality of eloquence and brevity" (281).

5. Verena's home life, significantly, is the antithesis of the safe and private domestic ideal: her father, once "a member of the celebrated Cayuga community, where there were no wives, or no husbands, or something of that sort," is utterly incompetent as a protector and provider, his "temporary lair" fronted by "a little naked piazza, which seemed rather to expose than to protect" (62, 101). And Olive attributes Verena's occasional indiscretions to the absence in her upbringing of what she calls "home-culture," which for Olive has much to do with a richly textured interior, a refuge from the assaults of life on the outside (78).

6. Jürgen Habermas and Ann Douglas tell the familiar story of a public that produces culture gradually supplanted by a public that consumes it in strikingly similar terms. For Douglas, the "death of the critical instinct" is linked to the rise of sentimentalism and "the preparation of the individual for the role of consumer . . . , by definition the man with no interest in theorizing, the person possessed of only the haziest powers of discernment" (189). As Habermas puts it, the mass media "transmogrif[y the public sphere] into a sphere of culture consumption"; discussion itself "assumes the form of a consumer item," and the "capacity for rational criticism of public authority" is "curtail[ed]" (162, 164, 172). Both authors comment on the role of advertising: for Douglas sentimental influence "had a good deal less to do with the faith of the past and a good deal more to do with the advertising industry of the future than its proponents would have liked to believe" (9); for Habermas, quite simply, "the public sphere assumes advertising functions" (175). And both authors attribute the efficiency of these new consumerist versions of publicity to their ability to infiltrate and manufacture private experience, a process that entails what Habermas describes as a "hollowing out" of liberal privacy and subjectivity (157, 162). Douglas contends that the sentimental novel imagines privacy opportunistically, both as a space into which a reader can be absorbed and as a space within the reader that the novel can fill: she writes, "privacy functions in the

rituals of sentimentalism only for the sake of titillation, as a convention to be violated" (254). Habermas writes that "the more the original relationship between the intimate sphere and the public sphere in the world of letters is reversed and permits an undermining of the private sphere through publicity, the more decisions within this latitude can be influenced" (177).

7. For a study of the figurative language of wealth in James's fiction, see Mull.

8. Several critics have commented on Olive's disturbing purchase of Verena for an unnamed sum—in light of which such metaphors take on a certain irony. See, for example, Yellin.

9. Elizabeth Dillon describes women's "voice" in the literary public sphere in similar terms: "The model of the feminine literary public sphere indicates that women have a voice, albeit not the voice of the liberal subject: rather, we might describe such a voice as that of liberal subjectification, a voice that bespeaks the public and literary construction of private subjectivity" (48).

10. The rich critical literature on *The Bostonians'* treatment of privacy and publicity includes Fisher; Ian Bell, "Language, Setting, and Self in *The Bostonians,*" "The Personal, the Private, and the Public in *The Bostonians,*" and *Henry James and the Past;* Thomas; Salmon; Rowe; and Gooder. The problem I discuss here is exemplified by Rowe, who clings to a notion of an authentic privacy that is being (or has been) eroded, and subscribes to the concomitant narrative of decline without examining that narrative critically. Thomas's reading of the legal construction of privacy in the marriage contract is much closer to my understanding of the problematic nature of liberal privacy: Thomas shows that privacy does not preexist legal efforts to protect it, but is on the contrary constructed by those efforts. Salmon's critical analysis of what he calls "the culture of publicity" is by far the fullest and most nuanced.

11. In "Language, Setting, and Self," Ian Bell makes precisely this point about Olive and Ransom, who, he writes, "separates an assumption of a 'real' Verena from the attributes of her performances" (214). I would add that for some critics, too, Verena's seemingly pure performativity has been a source of anxiety. Jean Fagin Yellin, for example, deplores James's creation of a character with no chance for autonomous selfhood, while Philip Fisher seems bent on reading a private selfhood into Verena.

12. Habegger includes, as the title of his essay suggests, a reading of Henry James Sr.'s defense of marriage—a reading that is equally illuminating of the conflicted nature of liberal privacy. Habegger writes, "the only person who sought to efface Henry Sr.'s privacy was Henry Sr. himself, and perhaps the reason he courted exposure and humiliation was that he really did believe, as he so often proclaimed, that his selfhood was damnable. . . . It was to suppress this beast within that he preached, again and again, that man must be confined in marriage in order to be free" (334).

13. See also Thomas.

14. See Warner's analysis of sexual shame in *The Trouble with Normal,* esp. 1–40.

15. Charles Taylor, for one, associates dignity with "a sense of self-responsible autonomy, a freedom from the demands of authority" (*Sources of the Self* 245). Taylor ar-

gues that, with the Cartesian understanding of disengaged reason, the self turns inward for its moral and ethical resources. "If rational control is a matter of mind dominating a disenchanted world of matter," writes Taylor, "then the sense of the superiority of the good life, and the inspiration to attain it, must come from the agent's sense of his own dignity as a rational being. I believe that this modern theme of the dignity of the human person, which has such a considerable place in modern ethical and political thought, arises out of the internalization I have been describing" (152).

16. Emerson represents that moment as the moment of the crowd's disappearance—a trope that in Grimké's account seems almost a technique for coping with shame. At one meeting, Grimké tells Jane Smith, a man came in to hear her speak and refused to leave, thus creating the particularly disgraceful situation that nineteenth-century reporters referred to as a "promiscuous audience." "So there he sat," recounts Grimké, "& somehow I did not feel his presence at all embarrassing & went on *just as tho' he was not there*" (Ceplair 116, emphasis added). Verena, too, seems to treat the crowd at Miss Birdseye's "as if it had been a single person" (*The Bostonians* 56). On the idea of the "promiscuous audience," see Zaeske.

The real shame, for Emerson, is not in speaking but in allowing oneself to be spoken for, in submitting to the tyranny of popular opinion, to a conventional wisdom that uses shame to unnerve and undermine self-reliance; he in effect turns shame against itself, finding true dignity in flouting rather than avoiding shame. "I am ashamed to think how easily we capitulate to badges and names," he writes in "Self-Reliance," to large societies and dead institutions," thereby redefining shame as the wages of "capitulation" rather than of impropriety (*Essays and Lectures* 262). Grimké envisions just such a force for conformity in the "dead institution" of slavery: when she writes in her *Appeal to the Christian Women of the South* of Southerners who "were too *ashamed of slavery* even to speak of it," she, too, turns shame into a force that would silence the voices of reform, a force complicit with the institution of slavery itself (Ceplair 74, emphasis in original). The heroic course of action, clearly, is to overcome the oppressive feelings of shame—an achievement that Grimké figures both as speech and as the public exposure of the South's disgrace. In place of a "decorous and prudent" ideal of modesty, and its attendant regime of shame, Grimké substitutes a distinctly Emersonian ideal of self-exposure, using it to turn the ever-present forces of shame against themselves, and validating not only the tactics of antislavery reformers, but also the public speech of women (265).

17. Richard Salmon associates Ransom explicitly with the Habermasian model of "a public sphere of private persons" (35).

18. Fisher has argued that in *The Bostonians* "the act of disappearing" is essential to "the full possession of an individual self." In charting Verena's growth toward this selfhood, Fisher cites her decision to keep her meeting with Ransom in Cambridge secret from Olive, a decision that necessitates "acts of not speaking, not letting the facts appear, not being entirely visible to another person." "By this strategy of negation," Fisher concludes, "a private self is born and sheltered in the novel" (179). This is a fine description of Ransom's rhetoric of female selfhood—or, at least, the rhetoric Ransom uses to win

Verena away from Olive—but I disagree with Fisher that it is the novel's vision. Lynn Wardley writes, "as Fisher's language confirms, we may only imagine an escape [from the life of performance], for when Basil promises Verena that 'the dining-table . . . be our platform, and you shall mount on top of that,' we see that she will never not be performing (660).

19. Significantly, Hannah Arendt refers to the appeal of such things as their "charm": "what the public realm considers irrelevant can have such an enormous and infectious charm," she writes, "that a whole people may adopt it as their way of life, without for that reason changing its essentially private character." For Arendt, the simple fact that something attracts attention and admiration does not make it public; on the contrary, one of the signs that "the public realm has almost completely receded," she contends, is that "greatness has given way to charm everywhere" (*Human Condition* 52).

20. The significance of shame for Henry James is discussed in Carol Holly's psychobiography of the James family and in Joseph Litvak's reading of what he calls James's "theater of embarrassment" (195–234).

21. Boats have a sexually charged significance elsewhere in James's fiction, like the boat in which Strether sees Chad Newsome and Madame de Vionnet in *The Ambassadors,* or the elaborate, extended image of Adam Verver's burning ships in *The Golden Bowl* when he proposes marriage to Charlotte Stant.

22. The nature of the Jamesean "self" has been of major concern in the criticism; significant contributions include Ross Posnock's chapter on what he calls "mimetic selfhood," and Sharon Cameron's astute reading of the narrative consciousness.

23. For an especially cogent discussion of Ransom's embattled masculinity, see Tanner, esp. 162–64.

24. See my reading of Mill's principle of "self-protection" in the epilogue.

25. "Her battered, unremunerated, unpensioned old age," we are told, "brought angry tears, springing from depths of outraged theory, into Miss Chancellor's eyes" (156). Ann Douglas describes this pleasure brilliantly in her reading of the death of Little Eva (3–13).

26. Olive's shame has a sexual dimension as well, and is therefore fraught with issues of bodily pleasure. According to Tomkins, shame is an "inhibitor of continuing interest and enjoyment," an interruption in the pleasure one takes in some object—in Olive's case, in her intimacy with Verena (134). Recent studies of *The Bostonians* that address Olive's lesbianism include Dimock, Van Leer, and Rohy.

Tomkins offers a particularly useful framework for thinking about Olive, because it is echoed in so many of Olive's principles and convictions, her fantasy of martyrdom, her theory of renunciation, her intense focus on the suffering of women, all of which envision women's bodies as sites of anguish rather than pleasure. As Tomkins points out, shame "operates ordinarily only after interest or enjoyment has been activated," and so the denial or renunciation of pleasure is one way to guard against shame (134). We can see this volatile matrix of sexual pleasure, shame, and infirmity in Verena's profession of fidelity to Olive, so clearly a reflection of Olive's own worldview: she affirms her "deep . . . belie[f] that should she forswear these holy things [namely, their union and their work] she should simply waste away, in the end, with remorse and shame" (352). But the way for Verena to avoid "wasting away" in shame, in this construction, is to dis-avow her sexual attraction to Ransom and devote her life to moving audiences with the historic injuries done to women. It is yet another instance of self-protection through self-exposure, finding relief from a life of private shame in public lectures on suffering. That concept, of course, has more resonance for Olive than it does for Verena.

Epilogue

In universities, this book has been a popular assignment as common reading for incoming freshmen, and P. M. Forni is cofounder of the Johns Hopkins Civility Project.

    1. The lecture was first published in 1899 in *Talks to Teachers on Psychology: And to Students on Some of Life's Ideals*. A description of the Chautauqua visit is in R. W. B. Lewis 554–55.

Works Cited

Alden, Henry Mills. "Editor's Easy Chair." *Harper's New Monthly Magazine* 71.421 (1885): 150–51. Print.

Arendt, Hannah. *The Human Condition.* Chicago: U of Chicago P, 1958. Print.

———. *On Revolution.* New York: Viking, 1965. Print.

Aristotle. *The Politics.* Trans. T. A. Sinclair. Ed. Trevor J. Saunders. London and New York: Penguin, 1981. Print.

Armitage, David. *The Declaration of Independence: A Global History.* Cambridge: Harvard UP, 2007. Print.

Armstrong, Nancy. *Desire and Domestic Fiction: A Political History of the Novel.* New York: Oxford UP, 1987. Print.

Bailyn, Bernard. *The Ideological Origins of the American Revolution.* Cambridge: Harvard UP, 1967. Print.

Baker, Houston A., Jr. "Autobiographical Acts and the Voice of the Southern Slave." *Critical Essays on Frederick Douglass.* Ed. William L. Andrews. Boston: G. K. Hall, 1991. Print.

———. *The Journey Back: Issues in Black Literature and Criticism.* Chicago: U of Chicago P, 1980. Print.

———. *Workings of the Spirit: The Poetics of Afro-American Women's Writing.* Chicago: U of Chicago P, 1991. Print.

Beecher, Catharine E. *An Essay on Slavery and Abolitionism, with Reference to the Duty of American Females.* 1837. Freeport, NY: Books for Libraries P, 1970. Print.

Bell, Bernard W. "The African-American Jeremiad and Frederick Douglass' Fourth of July 1853 Speech." *The Fourth of July: Political Oratory and Literary Reactions, 1776–1876.* Eds. Paul Goetsch and Gerd Hurm. Tübingen: Gunter Narr Verlag, 1992. 139–53. Print.

Bell, Howard Holman. *A Survey of the Negro Convention Movement, 1830–1861.* New York: Arno P and the New York Times, 1969. Print.

Bell, Ian F. A. *Henry James and the Past: Readings into Time.* London: Macmillan, 1991. Print.

———. "Language, Setting, and Self in *The Bostonians*." *MLQ* 49.3 (1988): 211–38. Print.

———. "The Personal, the Private, and the Public in *The Bostonians*." *Texas Studies in Language and Literature* 32.2 (1990): 240–56. Print.

Bercovitch, Sacvan, and Myra Jehlen, eds. *Ideology and Classic American Literature.* Cambridge: Cambridge UP, 1986. Print.

Berlant, Lauren. *The Female Complaint: The Unfinished Business of Sentimentality in American Culture.* Durham: Duke UP, 2008. Print.

———. *The Queen of America Goes to Washington City: Essays on Sex and Citizenship.* Durham: Duke UP, 1997. Print.

Berlant, Lauren, and Michael Warner. "Sex in Public." *Critical Inquiry* 24.2 (1998): 547–66. Print.

Berlin, Isaiah. "Two Concepts of Liberty." *The Proper Study of Mankind, an Anthology of Essays.* Eds. Henry Hardy and Roger Hausheer. New York: Farrar, 1997. 191–242. Print.

Bhabha, Homi K. *The Location of Culture.* London: Routledge, 1994. Print.

Bingham, Caleb. *The Columbian Orator.* Ed. David W. Blight. New York: New York UP, 1998. Print.

Booth, Wayne C. *A Rhetoric of Irony.* Chicago: U of Chicago P, 1974. Print.

Boyd, Melba Joyce. *Discarded Legacy: Politics and Poetics in the Life of Frances E. W. Harper, 1825–1911.* Detroit: Wayne State UP, 1994. Print.

Brown, Gillian. *Domestic Individualism: Imagining Self in Nineteenth-Century America.* Berkeley: U of California P, 1990. Print.

Brown, Wendy. *States of Injury: Power and Freedom in Late Modernity.* Princeton: Princeton UP, 1995. Print.

Brown, William Wells. *Clotel; or, the President's Daughter.* Ed. Robert S. Levine. Boston: Bedford/St. Martin's, 2000. Bedford Cultural Editions. Print.

Burgett, Bruce. *Sentimental Bodies: Sex, Gender, and Citizenship in the Early Republic.* Princeton: Princeton UP, 1998. Print.

Burstein, Andrew. *Sentimental Democracy: The Evolution of America's Romantic Self-Image.* New York: Farrar, 1999. Print.

Butler, Judith. *Excitable Speech: A Politics of the Performative.* New York: Routledge, 1997. Print.

Cable, George W. "The Freedman's Case in Equity." *Century Illustrated Magazine* 29.3 (1885): 409–18. *American Periodicals Series Online.* Web. 9 June 2009.

———. "The Silent South." *Century Illustrated Magazine* 30.5 (1885): 409–18. *American Periodicals Series Online.* Web. 9 June 2009.

Calhoun, Craig, ed. *Habermas and the Public Sphere.* Cambridge: MIT P, 1992. Print.

Cameron, Sharon. *Thinking in Henry James.* Chicago: U of Chicago P, 1989. Print.

Carby, Hazel. *Reconstructing Womanhood: The Emergence of the Afro-American Woman Novelist.* New York: Oxford UP, 1987. Print.

Castiglia, Christopher. *Interior States: Institutional Consciousness and the Inner Life of Democracy in the Antebellum United States.* Durham: Duke UP, 2008. Print.

Cavitch, Max. *American Elegy: The Poetry of Mourning from the Puritans to Whitman.* Minneapolis: U of Minnesota P, 2007. Print.

Ceplair, Larry, ed. *The Public Years of Sarah and Angelina Grimké: Selected Writings, 1835–1838.* New York: Columbia UP, 1989. Print.

Cott, Nancy F. *The Bonds of Womanhood: "Woman's Sphere" in New England, 1780–1835.* New Haven: Yale UP, 1977. Print.

Cover, Robert M. *Justice Accused: Antislavery and the Judicial Process.* New Haven: Yale UP, 1975. Print.

Crane, Gregg D. *Race, Citizenship, and Law in American Literature.* Cambridge: Cambridge UP, 2002. Print.

Davidson, Cathy. *Revolution and the Word: The Rise of the Novel in America.* New York: Oxford UP, 1986. Print.

"Declaration of the Immediate Causes Which Induce and Justify the Secession of South Carolina from the Federal Union." *Lillian Goldman Law Library of the Yale Law School.* Web. 27 April 2009.

Delany, Martin R. *Blake; or, the Huts of America.* Ed. Floyd J. Miller. Boston: Beacon P, 1970. Print.

Derrida, Jacques. *Of Grammatology.* Trans. Gayatri Chakravorty Spivak. Baltimore: Johns Hopkins UP, 1976. Print.

———. "Signature, Event, Context." *Margins—of Philosophy.* Trans. Alan Bass. Chicago: U of Chicago P, 1982. Print.

———. *Writing and Difference.* Trans. Alan Bass. Chicago: U of Chicago P, 1978. Print.

Dillon, Elizabeth Maddock. *The Gender of Freedom: Fictions of Liberalism and the Literary Public Sphere.* Stanford: Stanford UP, 2004. Print.

Dimock, Wai Chee. "Gender, the Market, and the Non-Trivial in James." *The Henry James Review* 15 (1994): 24–30. Print.

Douglas, Ann. *The Feminization of American Culture.* New York: Anchor Books, 1988. Print.

Douglass, Frederick. *Douglass: Autobiographies.* Ed. Henry Louis Gates Jr. New York: Library of America, 1996. Print.

———. *The Heroic Slave.* in *Three Classic African-American Novels.* Ed. William L. Andrews. New York: Penguin Putnam, 2003. Print.

———. "The Meaning of July Fourth for the Negro, Speech at Rochester, New York, July 5, 1852." *Frederick Douglass: Selected Speeches and Writings.* Ed. Philip S. Foner. Chicago: Lawrence Hill, 1999. 188–206. Print.

Du Bois, W. E. B. *John Brown, A Biography.* Ed. John David Smith. Armonk: M. E. Sharp, 1997. Print.

———. *The Souls of Black Folk.* New York: Bantam, 1989. Print.

DuBois, Ellen. "Struggling into Existence—The Feminism of Sarah and Angelina Grimké." *Women: A Journal of Liberation* 1 (Spring 1970): 4–11. Print.

duBois, Page. *Torture and Truth.* New York and London: Routledge, 1991. Print.

Dworkin, Ronald. "Two Concepts of Liberty." *Isaiah Berlin: A Celebration.* Eds. Edna Ulmann-Margalit and Avishai Margalit. Chicago: U of Chicago P, 1991. 100–109. Print.

Elkins, Marilyn. "Reading beyond the Conventions: A Look at Frances E. W. Harper's

Iola Leroy; or, Shadows Uplifted." *American Literary Realism* 22.2 (1990): 44–52. Print.

Ellison, Julie. *Cato's Tears and the Making of Anglo-American Emotion.* Chicago: U of Chicago P, 1999. Print.

Emerson, Ralph Waldo. *Emerson: Essays and Lectures.* Ed. Joel Porte. New York: Library of America, 1983. Print.

Etzioni, Amitai. *The Limits of Privacy.* New York: Basic, 1999. Print.

Fanuzzi, Robert. *Abolition's Public Sphere.* Minneapolis: U of Minnesota P, 2003. Print.

Fiedler, Leslie. *The Inadvertent Epic: From "Uncle Tom's Cabin" to "Roots."* New York: Simon, 1979. Print.

Fisher, Philip. "Appearing and Disappearing in Public: Social Space in Late-Nineteenth-Century Literature and Culture." *Reconstructing American Literary History.* Ed. Sacvan Bercovitch. Cambridge: Harvard UP, 1986. 155–88. Print.

Fitzhugh, George. *Cannibals All! or, Slaves without Masters.* Ed. C. Vann Woodward. Cambridge: Harvard UP, 1960, 1988. Print.

Fliegelman, Jay. *Declaring Independence: Jefferson, Natural Language, and the Culture of Performance.* Stanford: Stanford UP, 1993. Print.

——. *Prodigals and Pilgrims: The American Revolution against Patriarchal Authority, 1750–1800.* Cambridge: Cambridge UP, 1982. Print.

Foner, Philip S. *Frederick Douglass: Selected Speeches and Writings.* Abridged and adapted by Yuval Taylor. Chicago: Lawrence Hill, 1999. Print.

Foreman, P. Gabrielle. "Looking Back from Zora; or, Talking Out Both Sides My Mouth for Those Who Have Two Ears." *Black American Literature Forum* 24.4 (1990): 649–66. Print.

Forni, P. M. *Choosing Civility: The Twenty-Five Rules of Considerate Conduct.* New York: St. Martin's Griffin, 2002. Print.

Foster, Frances Smith. *Witnessing Slavery: The Development of Ante-Bellum Slave Narratives.* 2nd ed. Madison: U of Wisconsin P, 1994. Print.

Fraser, Nancy. "Rethinking the Public Sphere: A Contribution to the Critique of Actually Existing Democracy." *Habermas and the Public Sphere.* Ed. Craig Calhoun. Cambridge: MIT P, 1992. 109–42. Print.

Fruchtman, Jack, Jr. "Classical Republicanism, Whig Political Science, Tory History: The State of Eighteenth-Century Political Thought." *Eighteenth-Century Life* 20.2 (1996): 94–103. Print.

Fuller, Margaret. *Woman in the Nineteenth Century.* In *The Essential Margaret Fuller.* Ed. Jeffrey Steele. New Brunswick: Rutgers UP, 1992. Print.

Gardner, Jared. *Master Plots: Race and the Founding of an American Literature, 1787–1845.* Baltimore: Johns Hopkins UP, 1998. Print.

Gates, Henry Louis, Jr. *Figures in Black: Words, Signs, and the "Racial" Self.* New York: Oxford UP, 1987. Print.

——. *The Signifying Monkey: A Theory of Afro-American Literary Criticism.* New York: Oxford UP, 1988. Print.

Giles, Paul. "Narrative Reversals and Power Exchanges: Frederick Douglass and British Culture." *American Literature* 73.4 (2001): 779–810. Print.

Gillis, Christina Marsden. *The Paradox of Privacy: Epistolary Form in* Clarissa. Gainesville: UP of Florida, 1984. Print.

Ginsberg, Elaine K. *Passing and the Fictions of Identity.* Durham: Duke UP, 1996. Print.

Gooder, Jean. "Henry James's Bostonians: The Voices of Democracy." *Cambridge Quarterly* 30.2 (2001): 97–115. Print.

Grady, Henry W. "In Plain Black and White: A Reply to Mr. Cable." *Century Illustrated Magazine* 29.6 (1885): 909–17. *American Periodicals Series Online.* Web. 9 June 2009.

Gunning, Sandra. *Race, Rape, and Lynching: The Red Record of American Literature, 1890–1912.* Oxford: Oxford UP, 1996. Print.

Gustafson, Thomas. *Representative Words: Politics, Literature, and the American Language, 1776–1875.* Cambridge: Cambridge UP, 1992. Print.

Habegger, Alfred. "*The Bostonians* and Henry James Sr.'s Crusade against Feminism and Free Love." *Women's Studies: An Interdisciplinary Journal* 15.4 (1988): 323–42. Print.

———. "The Disunity of *The Bostonians*." *Nineteenth-Century Fiction* 24.2 (1969): 193–209. Print.

Habermas, Jürgen. *The Structural Transformation of the Public Sphere: An Inquiry into a Category of Bourgeois Society.* Trans. Thomas Burger. Cambridge: MIT P, 1989. Print.

Halttunen, Karen. *Confidence Men and Painted Women: A Study of Middle-Class Culture in America, 1830–1870.* New Haven: Yale UP, 1982. Print.

———. "Humanitarianism and the Pornography of Pain in Anglo-American Culture." *American Historical Review* 100 (April 1995): 303–34. Print.

Harper, Frances E. W. *A Brighter Coming Day: A Frances Ellen Watkins Harper Reader.* Ed. Frances Smith Foster. New York: Feminist P, 1990. Print.

———. *Iola Leroy; or, Shadows Uplifted.* Ed. Hazel V. Carby. Boston: Beacon P, 1987. Print.

Harper, Phillip Brian. *Are We Not Men? Masculine Anxiety and the Problem of African-American Identity.* New York and Oxford: Oxford UP, 1996. Print.

Hartman, Geoffrey H. *Minor Prophecies: The Literary Essay in Culture Wars.* Cambridge: Harvard UP, 1991. Print.

Hartman, Saidiya V. *Scenes of Subjection: Terror, Slavery, and Self-Making in Nineteenth-Century America.* New York and Oxford: Oxford UP, 1997. Print.

Hawthorne, Nathaniel. *The Scarlet Letter.* Ed. Ross C. Murfin. New York: Bedford, 1991. Print.

Hendler, Glenn. *Public Sentiments: Structures of Feeling in Nineteenth-Century American Literature.* Chapel Hill: U of North Carolina P, 2001. Print.

Henry, Katherine. "Slavery and Civic Recovery: Gothic Interventions in Whitman and Weld." *The Gothic Other: Racial and Social Constructions in the Literary Imagi-*

nation. Eds. Ruth Bienstock Anolik and Douglas L. Howard. Jefferson: McFarland, 2004. 32–53. Print.

Hentz, Caroline Lee. *The Planter's Northern Bride*. Philadelphia: T. B. Peterson, 1854. Kessinger Publishing's Rare Reprints. Print.

Hersh, Blanche Glassman. "'Am I Not a Woman and a Sister?': Abolitionist Beginnings of Nineteenth-Century Feminism." *Antislavery Reconsidered: New Perspectives on the Abolitionists*. Eds. Lewis Perry and Michael Fellman. Baton Rouge: Louisiana State UP, 1979. Print.

Holly, Carol. *Intensely Family: The Inheritance of Family Shame and the Autobiographies of Henry James*. Madison: U of Wisconsin P, 1995. Print.

Isenberg, Nancy. *Sex and Citizenship in Antebellum America*. Chapel Hill: U of North Carolina P, 1998. Print.

Jacobs, Harriet. *Incidents in the Life of a Slave Girl, Written by Herself*. In *The Classic Slave Narratives*. Ed. Henry Louis Gates Jr. New York: Penguin, 1987. Print.

James, Henry. *The Art of the Novel*. New York: Scribner's, 1934. Print.

———. *The Bostonians*. New York: Penguin, 1966. Print.

———. "Nathaniel Hawthorne." *Henry James: Literary Criticism*. Ed. Leon Edel. New York: Library of America, 1984. Print.

James, William. "What Makes a Life Significant." *The Writings of William James: A Comprehensive Edition*. Ed. John J. McDermott. Chicago: U of Chicago P, 1977. 645–60. Print.

Jameson, Frederic. *Late Marxism: Adorno; or, the Persistence of the Dialectic*. London and New York: Verso, 1990. Print.

Jefferson, Thomas. *Thomas Jefferson: Writings*. Ed. Merrill D. Peterson. New York: Library of America, 1984. Print.

Jehlen, Myra. *American Incarnation*. Cambridge: Cambridge UP, 1986. Print.

———. "Archimedes and the Paradox of Feminist Criticism." *Readings at the Edge of Literature*. Chicago: U of Chicago P, 2002. 122–48. Print.

———. "The Family Militant: Domesticity versus Slavery in *Uncle Tom's Cabin*." *Criticism* 31.4 (1989): 383–400. Print.

———. "'Imitate Jesus and Socrates': The Making of a Good American." *South Atlantic Quarterly* 89 (Summer 1990): 501–24. Print.

Kahane, Claire. *Passions of the Voice: Hysteria, Narrative, and the Figure of the Speaking Woman*. Baltimore: Johns Hopkins UP, 1995. Print.

Kawash, Samira. "*The Autobiography of an Ex-Coloured Man*: (Passing for) Black Passing for White." *Passing and the Fictions of Identity*. Ed. Elaine K. Ginsberg. Durham: Duke UP, 1996. 59–74. Print.

Kearns, Michael. "Narrative Discourse and the Imperative of Sympathy in *The Bostonians*." *Henry James Review* 17.2 (1996): 162–81. Print.

Kekes, John. *Against Liberalism*. Ithaca: Cornell UP, 1997. Print.

Kelly, Paul. *Liberalism*. Cambridge: Polity P, 2005. Print.

King, Lovalerie. *Race, Theft, and Ethics: Property Matters in African American Literature*. Baton Rouge: Louisiana State UP, 2007. Print.

Kors, Alan Charles, and Harvey A. Silverglate. *The Shadow University: The Betrayal of Liberty on America's Campuses*. New York: Free P, 1998. Print.

Lakoff, George. *Moral Politics: How Liberals and Conservatives Think*. 2nd ed. Chicago: U of Chicago P, 2002. Print.

Lampe, Gregory P. *Frederick Douglass: Freedom's Voice, 1818–1845*. East Lansing: Michigan State UP, 1998. Print.

Landes, Joan B. *Women and the Public Sphere in the Age of the French Revolution*. Ithaca: Cornell UP, 1988. Print.

Larkin, Edward. *Thomas Paine and the Literature of Revolution*. New York: Cambridge UP, 2005. Print.

Lefort, Claude. *Democracy and Political Theory*. Trans. D. Macey. Cambridge: Polity P, 1988. Print.

Lerner, Gerda. *The Grimké Sisters from South Carolina: Pioneers for Women's Rights and Abolition*. New York: Schocken, 1967. Print.

Levander, Caroline Field. *Voices of the Nation: Women and Public Speech in Nineteenth-Century American Literature and Culture*. Cambridge: Cambridge UP, 1998. Print.

Leverenz, David. *Paternalism Incorporated: Fables of American Fatherhood, 1865–1940*. Ithaca: Cornell UP, 2003. Print.

Lewis, R. W. B. *The Jameses: A Family Narrative*. New York: Farrar, 1991. Print.

Lewis, Vashti. "The Near-White Female in Frances Ellen Harper's *Iola Leroy*." *Phylon* 45.4 (1984): 314–22. Print.

Litvak, Joseph. *Caught in the Act: Theatricality in the Nineteenth-Century English Novel*. Berkeley: U of California P, 1992. Print.

Locke, John. *Two Treatises of Government*. Ed. Mark Goldie. London: Everyman, 1993. Print.

Lott, Eric. *Love and Theft: Blackface Minstrelsy and the American Working Class*. New York and Oxford: Oxford UP, 1993. Print.

Lowance, Mason, ed. *Against Slavery: An Abolitionist Reader*. New York: Penguin, 2000. Print.

Lucaites, John Louis. "The Irony of 'Equality' in Black Abolitionist Discourse: The Case of Frederick Douglass's 'What to the Slave is the Fourth of July?'" *Rhetoric and Political Culture in Nineteenth-Century America*. Ed. Thomas W. Benson. East Lansing: Michigan State UP, 1997. 47–69. Print.

Lumpkin, Katharine Du Pre. *The Emancipation of Angelina Grimké*. Chapel Hill: U of North Carolina P, 1974. Print.

Madison, James, Alexander Hamilton, and John Jay. *The Federalist Papers*. Ed. Isaac Kramnick. New York: Penguin, 1987. Print.

Maier, Pauline. *American Scripture: Making the Declaration of Independence*. New York: Knopf, 1997. Print.

Mann, Horace. "Speech Delivered in the United States House of Representatives, February 15, 1850, on the Subject of Slavery in the Territories, and the Consequences of a Dissolution of the Union." 1851. *Slavery: Letters and Speeches*. New York: Negro UP, 1969. Print.

Margolis, Stacey. *The Public Life of Privacy in Nineteenth-Century American Literature.* Durham: Duke UP, 2005. Print.

Marshall, David. *The Figure of Theater: Shaftesbury, Defoe, Adam Smith, and George Eliot.* New York: Columbia UP, 1986. Print.

McDermott, John J., ed. *The Writing of William James: A Comprehensive Edition.* Chicago: U of Chicago P, 1977. Print.

McDowell, Deborah E. "'The Changing Same': Generational Connections and Black Women Novelists." *New Literary History* 18.2 (1987): 281–302. Print.

McKeon, Michael. *The Secret History of Domesticity: Public, Private, and the Division of Knowledge.* Baltimore: Johns Hopkins UP, 2005. Print.

Messerli, Jonathan. *Horace Mann: A Biography.* New York: Knopf, 1972. Print.

Mill, John Stuart. *On Liberty and Other Writings.* Ed. Stefan Collini. Cambridge: Cambridge UP, 1989. Print.

Miller, Perry, and Thomas H. Johnson, eds. *The Puritans: A Sourcebook of Their Writings.* Vol. 1. New York: Harper, 1963. Print.

Morgan, Edmund S. *American Slavery, American Freedom: The Ordeal of Colonial Virginia.* New York: Norton, 1975. Print.

Morrison, Toni. *Playing in the Dark: Whiteness and the Literary Imagination.* Cambridge: Harvard UP, 1992. Print.

Mull, Donald L. *Henry James's "Sublime Economy": Money as Symbolic Center in the Fiction.* Middletown: Wesleyan UP, 1973. Print.

Myrdal, Gunnar. *An American Dilemma: The Negro Problem and Modern Democracy.* New York: Harper, 1944. Print.

Nerad, Julie Cary. "Slippery Language and False Dilemmas: The Passing Novels of Child, Howells, and Harper." *American Literature* 75.4 (2003): 813–41. Print.

Noble, Marianne. "An Ecstasy of Apprehension: The Gothic Pleasures of Sentimental Fiction." *American Gothic: New Interventions in a National Narrative.* Eds. Robert K. Martin and Eric Savoy. Iowa City: U of Iowa P, 1998. 163–82. Print.

Oliver, Robert T. *History of Public Speaking in America.* Boston: Allyn and Bacon, 1965. Print.

Paine, Thomas. *Common Sense and Related Writings.* Ed. Thomas P. Slaughter. Boston: Bedford/St. Martin's, 2001. Print.

Patterson, Orlando. *Freedom, Volume One: Freedom in the Making of Western Culture.* New York: Basic, 1991. Print.

———. *Slavery and Social Death: A Comparative Study.* Cambridge: Harvard UP, 1982. Print.

Pease, Donald E., ed. *National Identities and Post-Americanist Narratives.* Durham: Duke UP, 1994. Print.

Peterson, Carla L. *"Doers of the Word": African-American Women Speakers and Writers in the North, 1830–1880.* New York: Oxford UP, 1995. Print.

———. "'Further Liftings of the Veil': Gender, Class, and Labor in Frances E. W. Harper's *Iola Leroy.*" *Listening to Silences: New Essays in Feminist Criticism.* Eds. Elaine

Hedges and Shelley Fisher Fishkin. New York and Oxford: Oxford UP, 1994. 97–112. Print.

Plessy v. Ferguson. 163 US 537–64. No. 210. Supreme Ct. of the US. 18 May 1896. *FindLaw.* Web. 25 Jan. 2009.

Pocock, J. G. A. *The Machiavellian Moment: Florentine Political Thought and the Atlantic Republican Tradition.* Princeton: Princeton UP, 1975. Print.

Poirier, Richard. *Poetry and Pragmatism.* Cambridge: Harvard UP, 1992. Print.

———. *The Renewal of Literature: Emersonian Reflections.* New York: Random, 1987. Print.

Posnock, Ross. *The Trial of Curiosity: Henry James, William James, and the Challenge of Modernity.* New York and Oxford: Oxford UP, 1991. Print.

Purdy, Jedediah. *A Tolerable Anarchy: Rebels, Reactionaries, and the Making of American Freedom.* New York: Knopf, 2009. Print.

Quarles, Benjamin. *Black Abolitionists.* London: Oxford UP, 1969. Print.

Riss, Arthur. *Race, Slavery, and Liberalism in Nineteenth-Century American Literature.* Cambridge: Cambridge UP, 2006. Print.

Rodin, Judith, and Stephen P. Steinberg, eds. *Public Discourse in America: Conversation and Community in the Twenty-First Century.* Philadelphia: U of Pennsylvania P, 2003. Print.

Rohy, Valery. *Impossible Women: Lesbian Figures and American Literature.* Ithaca: Cornell UP, 2000. Print.

Rossi, Alice S., ed. *The Feminist Papers: From Adams to De Beauvoir.* New York: Columbia UP, 1973. Print.

Rowe, Joyce A. "'Murder, What a Lovely Voice!': Sex, Speech, and the Public/Private Problem in *The Bostonians.*" *Texas Studies in Language and Literature* 40.2 (1998): 158–83. Print.

Ryan, Mary P. *Women in Public: Between Banners and Ballots, 1825–1880.* Baltimore: Johns Hopkins UP, 1990. Print.

Salmon, Richard. *Henry James and the Culture of Publicity.* Cambridge: Cambridge UP, 1997. Print.

Samuels, Shirley, ed. *The Culture of Sentiment: Race, Gender, and Sentimentality in Nineteenth-Century America.* New York: Oxford UP, 1992. Print.

Sánchez-Eppler, Karen. "Bodily Bonds." *Representations* 24 (Fall 1988): 28–59. Print.

———. *Dependent States: The Child's Part in Nineteenth-Century American Culture.* Chicago: U of Chicago P, 2005. Print.

———. *Touching Liberty: Abolition, Feminism, and the Politics of the Body.* Berkeley: U of California P, 1993. Print.

Scarry, Elaine. *The Body in Pain: The Making and Unmaking of the World.* New York: Oxford UP, 1985. Print.

Seltzer, Mark. *Serial Killers: Death and Life in America's Wound Culture.* New York and London: Routledge, 1998. Print.

Sennett, Richard. *Authority.* New York: Knopf, 1980. Print.

Shaffer, Jason. *Performing Patriotism: National Identity in the Colonial and Revolutionary American Theater.* Philadelphia: U of Pennsylvania P, 2007. Print.

Shamir, Milette. *Inexpressible Privacy: The Interior Life of Antebellum American Literature.* Philadelphia: U of Pennsylvania P, 2006. Print.

Shklar, Judith. *Ordinary Vices.* Cambridge: Belknap-Harvard UP, 1984. Print.

Sklar, Kathryn Kish. *Catharine Beecher: A Study in American Domesticity.* New Haven: Yale UP, 1973. Print.

Spivak, Gayatri Chakravorty, and Ellen Rooney. "'In a Word': Interview." *The Second Wave: A Reader in Feminist Theory.* Ed. Linda Nicholson. New York and London: Routledge, 1997. 356–78. Print.

Stepto, Robert B. "Distrust of the Reader in Afro-American Narratives." *Reconstructing American Literary History.* Ed. Sacvan Bercovitch. Cambridge: Harvard UP, 1986. 300–322. Print.

———. "Storytelling in Early Afro-American Fiction: Frederick Douglass's 'The Heroic Slave.'" *Black Literature and Literary Theory.* Ed. Henry Louis Gates Jr. New York: Routledge, 1984. 175–86. Print.

Stern, Julia A. *The Plight of Feeling: Sympathy and Dissent in the Early American Novel.* Chicago: U of Chicago P, 1997. Print.

Stowe, Harriet Beecher. *Dred: A Tale of the Great Dismal Swamp.* Ed. Judie Newman. Krumlin, England: Edinburgh UP, 1999. Print.

———. *A Key to Uncle Tom's Cabin.* Bedford: Applewood, 1998. Print.

———. *Uncle Tom's Cabin; or, Life among the Lowly.* New York: Macmillan, 1962. Print.

Sundquist, Eric J. "Frederick Douglass: Literacy and Paternalism." *Critical Essays on Frederick Douglass.* Ed. William L. Andrews. Boston: G. K. Hall, 1991. 120–32. Print.

———. *To Wake the Nations: Race in the Making of American Literature.* Cambridge: Harvard UP, 1993. Print.

Tanner, Tony. *Scenes of Nature, Signs of Men.* Cambridge: Cambridge UP, 1987. Print.

Taylor, Charles. *Sources of the Self: The Making of Modern Identity.* Cambridge: Harvard UP, 1989. Print.

———. "What's Wrong with Negative Liberty." *Philosophical Papers: Volume 2, Philosophy and the Human Sciences.* Cambridge: Cambridge UP, 1985. 211–29. Print.

Terrill, Robert E. "Irony, Silence, and Time: Frederick Douglass on the Fifth of July." *Quarterly Journal of Speech* 89.3 (2003): 216–34. Print.

Thomas, Brook. "The Construction of Privacy in and around *The Bostonians.*" *American Literature* 64.4 (1992): 719–47. Print.

Tomkins, Sylvan. *Shame and Its Sisters: A Sylvan Tomkins Reader.* Eds. Eve Kosofsky Sedgwick and Adam Frank. Durham: Duke UP, 1995. Print.

Tompkins, Jane. *Sensational Designs: The Cultural Work of American Fiction, 1790–1860.* New York: Oxford UP, 1985. Print.

———. "Sentimental Power: *Uncle Tom's Cabin* and the Politics of Literary History." *Ideology and Classic American Literature.* Eds. Sacvan Bercovitch and Myra Jehlen. Cambridge: Cambridge UP, 1986. Print.

Trilling, Lionel. *Sincerity and Authenticity.* Cambridge: Harvard UP, 1972. Print.

Van Leer, David. "A World of Female Friendship: *The Bostonians.*" *Henry James and Homo-Erotic Desire.* Ed. John R. Bradley. London: Macmillan, 1999. 93–109. Print.

Wald, Gayle. *Crossing the Color Line: Racial Passing in Twentieth-Century U.S. Literature and Culture.* Durham: Duke UP, 2000. Print.

Waldstreicher, David. *Runaway America: Benjamin Franklin, Slavery, and the American Revolution.* New York: Hill and Wang, 2004. Print.

Wardley, Lynn. "Woman's Voice, Democracy's Body, and *The Bostonians.*" *ELH* 56.3 (1989): 639–64. Print.

Warner, Michael. *The Letters of the Republic: Publication and the Public Sphere in Eighteenth-Century America.* Cambridge: Harvard UP, 1990. Print.

———. "The Mass Public and the Mass Subject." *Habermas and the Public Sphere.* Ed. Craig Calhoun. Cambridge: MIT P, 1992. 377–401. Print.

———. *Publics and Counterpublics.* New York: Zone, 2005. Print.

———. *The Trouble with Normal: Sex, Politics, and the Ethics of Queer Life.* Cambridge: Harvard UP, 1999. Print.

Warren, Kenneth W. *Black and White Strangers: Race and American Literary Realism.* Chicago: U of Chicago P, 1994. Print.

Weld, Theodore Dwight. *In Memory of Angelina Grimké Weld.* Boston: P of George H. Ellis, 1880. Print.

Wells-Barnett, Ida B. *Southern Horrors and Other Writings: The Anti-Lynching Campaign of Ida B. Wells, 1892–1900.* Ed. Jacqueline Jones Royster. Boston: Bedford, 1997. Print.

Welter, Barbara. *Dimity Convictions: The American Woman in the Nineteenth Century.* Athens: Ohio UP, 1976. Print.

Wiegman, Robyn. *American Antinomies: Theorizing Race and Gender.* Durham: Duke UP, 1995. Print.

Williams, Juliet A. *Liberalism and the Limits of Power.* New York: Palgrave Macmillan, 2005. Print.

Wilt, Judith. "Desperately Seeking Verena: A Resistant Reading of *The Bostonians.*" *Feminist Studies* 13.2 (1987): 293–316. Print.

Wood, Gordon S. *The Creation of the American Republic, 1776–1787.* New York: Norton, 1969. Print.

———. *The Radicalism of the American Revolution.* New York: Knopf, 1992. Print.

Yellin, Jean Fagan. *Women and Sisters: The Anti-Slavery Feminists in American Culture.* New Haven: Yale UP, 1989. Print.

Young, Elizabeth. *Disarming the Nation: Women's Writing and the American Civil War.* Chicago: U of Chicago P, 1999. Print.

Zaeske, Susan. "The 'Promiscuous Audience': Controversy and the Emergence of the Early Women's Rights Movement." *Quarterly Journal of Speech* 84.2 (1995): 191–207. Print.

Index